BREAD FOR THE DAY

DAILY BIBLE READINGS AND PRAYERS

2023

 AUGSBURG FORTRESS

Minneapolis

BREAD FOR THE DAY 2023
Daily Bible Readings and Prayers

Editors: Dennis Bushkofsky, Laurie J. Hanson
Cover design: Laurie Ingram
Cover and interior art: Mary Button

Contributors to the weekday prayers:
Erica Gibson-Even, Valparaiso, Indiana (January); Kurt Lammi, Dayton, Ohio (February); Deb Grant, Nassau Bay, Texas (March); Ole Schenk, Oak Park, Illinois (April); Phil Ruge-Jones, Eau Claire, Wisconsin (May); Wilbert "Wilk" Miller, Essex, Connecticut (June); Wendy J. Wirth-Brock, Sheboygan, Wisconsin (July); Yolanda Kali Denson-Byers, Becker, Minnesota (August); Stacey Nalean-Carlson, Decorah, Iowa (September); Elise Seyfried, Oreland, Pennsylvania (October); Edward G. Horstmann, Greenwich, Connecticut (November); Laurie Stumme-Diers, Bainbridge Island, Washington (December).

ACKNOWLEDGMENTS
Scripture quotations are from the New Revised Standard Version Bible © 1989 Division of Christian Education of the National Council of the Churches of Christ in the United States of America. Used by permission.

Hymn suggestions and prayers of the day for Sundays and festivals are from *Evangelical Lutheran Worship*, copyright © 2006 Evangelical Lutheran Church in America and *All Creation Sings*, copyright © 2020 Augsburg Fortress.

Materials prepared by the Consultation on Common Texts (CCT), published in *Revised Common Lectionary* © 1992 and *Revised Common Lectionary Daily Readings* © 2005. Used by permission.

"Table prayer for the season of Lent, "Table prayer for summer," "A prayer to begin the work day," "A prayer to begin the school day," "Morning blessing," and "Evening blessing" are from *Reformation 500 Sourcebook: Anniversary Resources for Congregations*, © 2016 Augsburg Fortress.

Materials prepared by the English Language Liturgical Consultation (ELLC), published in *Praying Together* © 1988: "Blessed are you, Lord" and "My soul proclaims the greatness of the Lord." Used by permission.

pISBN 978-1-5064-8099-2
eISBN 978-1-5064-8103-6

Manufactured in the USA

Contents

August

September

October

November

December

Additional Resources

Foreword

Beloved of God,

For generations, the living word has sustained God's people. In times of prosperity and turmoil, joy and sorrow, the church has found hope and consolation in scripture.

In 2007 the Evangelical Lutheran Church in America embraced the initiative called Book of Faith and the commitment to deepening our fluency in the first language of faith, holy scripture. *Bread for the Day* is a wonderful resource for your daily encounter with the word. You will be nourished, encouraged, and sustained, as have the saints before you.

As the Conference of Bishops, we invite you to join us and this whole church in persistent attentiveness to the word. Your faith will be deepened, your witness empowered, and your church enriched. God bless your journey in faith.

Conference of Bishops
Evangelical Lutheran Church in America

Introduction

Daily prayer is an essential practice for those who seek to hear God's voice and cultivate an inner life. Whether you pray alone or with others, with brevity or in sustained meditation, the rhythm of daily prayer reveals the life-sustaining communion to which God invites all human beings. Such prayer is a serene power silently at work, drawing us into the ancient yet vital sources of faith, hope, and love.

The guiding principle of the selection of daily readings in *Bread for the Day* is their relationship to the Sunday readings as presented in the Revised Common Lectionary (a system of readings in widespread use across denominations). The readings are chosen so that the days leading up to Sunday (Thursday through Saturday) prepare for the Sunday readings. The days flowing out from Sunday (Monday through Wednesday) reflect on the Sunday readings.

How this book is organized

- Each day's page is dated and named in relationship to the church's year. Lesser festivals are listed along with the date as part of the day heading. Commemorations are listed just below in smaller type. Notes on those commemorated can be found on pages 407–416.
- Several verses of one of the appointed scripture texts are printed. The full text citation is provided for those who would like to reflect on the entire text. In addition, two or three additional reading citations with short descriptions are provided.
- Two psalms are appointed for each week: one psalm for Monday through Wednesday and a second psalm for Thursday through Saturday. In this way the days leading up to Sunday or flowing

out from Sunday have a distinct relationship with one another in addition to their relationship with the Sunday readings.

- Following the scripture text is a hymn suggestion from *Evangelical Lutheran Worship* (ELW) or *All Creation Sings* (ACS) and a prayer that incorporates a theme from one or more readings.
- Household prayers and blessings appropriate to the changing seasons are placed throughout the book. Simplified forms of morning and evening prayer, morning and evening blessings, and prayers with children can be found on pages 424–431.

How to use this book

- Use the weekday readings to prepare for and reflect on the Sunday readings.
- Use the questions printed on page 432 to guide your reflection on the scripture texts.
- Use the resources for household prayer placed throughout the book. See the Contents on pages 3–4 for a complete list.
- Record prayer requests on the first page for each month.
- In addition to being used to guide individual prayer, this book may be used to guide family prayer, prayer in congregational or other settings during the week, prayer with those who are sick or homebound, or prayer with other groups.

Even though Christians gather on the Lord's day, Sunday, for public worship, much of our time is spent in the home. We first learn the words, gestures, and songs of faith in the home. We discover our essential identity as a community of faith and mark significant transitions of life in the home. To surround and infuse the daily rhythm of sleeping and waking, working, resting, and eating with the words and gestures of Christian prayer is to discover the ancient truth of the gospel: the ordinary and the human can reveal the mystery of God and divine grace. Like planets around the sun, our daily prayer draws us to the Sunday assembly where we gather for the word and the breaking of the bread in the changing seasons of the year. From the Sunday assembly, our daily prayer flows into the week.

Prayer List for January

_____

_____

_____

_____

_____

_____

_____

_____

_____

Sunday, January 1, 2023
Name of Jesus

Philippians 2:5-11

God takes on human form

Therefore God also highly exalted him
>and gave him the name
>that is above every name,
so that at the name of Jesus
>every knee should bend,
>in heaven and on earth and under the earth,
and every tongue should confess
>that Jesus Christ is Lord,
>to the glory of God the Father. (Phil. 2:9-11)

Psalm

Psalm 8
How exalted is your name

Additional Readings

Numbers 6:22-27
The Aaronic blessing

Luke 2:15-21
The child is named Jesus

Hymn: All Hail the Power of Jesus' Name! ELW 634

Eternal Father, you gave your incarnate Son the holy name of Jesus to be a sign of our salvation. Plant in every heart the love of the Savior of the world, Jesus Christ our Lord, who lives and reigns with you and the Holy Spirit, one God, now and forever.

Monday, January 2, 2023
Week of Christmas 2

Johann Konrad Wilhelm Loehe, renewer of the church, died 1872

Psalm 72
Prayers for the king

Give the king your justice, O God,
    and your righteousness to a king's son.
May he judge your people with righteousness,
    and your poor with justice.
May the mountains yield prosperity for the people,
    and the hills, in righteousness.
May he defend the cause of the poor of the people,
    give deliverance to the needy,
    and crush the oppressor. (Ps. 72:1-4)

Additional Readings
Genesis 12:1-7
Abram and Sarai

Hebrews 11:1-12
Abraham's faith

Hymn: The God of Abraham Praise, ELW 831

God, you reign over all the earth and call us to righteousness. Give us discernment, that we may choose leaders who will pursue justice. Grant all leaders the will and wisdom to defend the poor and needy.

Tuesday, January 3, 2023
Week of Christmas 2

Genesis 28:10-22
Jacob's ladder

Jacob left Beer-sheba and went toward Haran. He came to a certain place and stayed there for the night, because the sun had set. Taking one of the stones of the place, he put it under his head and lay down in that place. And he dreamed that there was a ladder set up on the earth, the top of it reaching to heaven; and the angels of God were ascending and descending on it. . . . Then Jacob woke from his sleep and said, "Surely the LORD is in this place—and I did not know it!" And he was afraid, and said, "How awesome is this place! This is none other than the house of God, and this is the gate of heaven."

So Jacob rose early in the morning, and he took the stone that he had put under his head and set it up for a pillar and poured oil on the top of it. (Gen. 28:10-12, 16-18)

Psalm
Psalm 72
Prayers for the king

Additional Reading
Hebrews 11:13-22
Abraham, Isaac, and Jacob act on faith

Hymn: The First Noel, ELW 300

God, your faithful presence surprises us again and again. Open our eyes and our hearts, that we may see and celebrate your presence in our lives. Teach us to trust you, that all our ways will honor you.

Wednesday, January 4, 2023
Week of Christmas 2

Exodus 3:1-5
The burning bush

Moses was keeping the flock of his father-in-law Jethro, the priest of Midian; he led his flock beyond the wilderness, and came to Horeb, the mountain of God. There the angel of the LORD appeared to him in a flame of fire out of a bush; he looked, and the bush was blazing, yet it was not consumed. Then Moses said, "I must turn aside and look at this great sight, and see why the bush is not burned up." When the LORD saw that he had turned aside to see, God called to him out of the bush, "Moses, Moses!" And he said, "Here I am." Then he said, "Come no closer! Remove the sandals from your feet, for the place on which you are standing is holy ground." (Exod. 3:1-5)

Psalm
Psalm 72
Prayers for the king

Additional Reading
Hebrews 11:23-31
Moses acts on faith

Hymn: Your Little Ones, Dear Lord, ELW 286

God, your presence makes ordinary soil into holy ground. Teach us to turn aside and look for you in all our days. Teach us reverence and give us courage to follow your call.

Thursday, January 5, 2023
Week of Christmas 2

Hebrews 11:32—12:2

Surrounded by a cloud of witnesses

Therefore, since we are surrounded by so great a cloud of witnesses, let us also lay aside every weight and the sin that clings so closely, and let us run with perseverance the race that is set before us, looking to Jesus the pioneer and perfecter of our faith, who for the sake of the joy that was set before him endured the cross, disregarding its shame, and has taken his seat at the right hand of the throne of God. (Heb. 12:1-2)

Psalm

Psalm 72
Prayers for the king

Additional Reading

Joshua 1:1-9
Be strong

Hymn: It Came upon the Midnight Clear, ELW 282

In Christ you set us free and laid a new course for us, O God. Equip us now for this day's leg of the race. Set Jesus before our eyes and encourage us through all people who journey with us.

Blessing for a Home at Epiphany

Matthew writes that when the magi saw the shining star stop overhead, they were filled with joy. "On entering the house, they saw the child with Mary his mother" (Matt. 2:10-11). In the home, Christ is met in family and friends, in visitors and strangers. In the home, faith is shared, nurtured, and put into action. In the home, Christ is welcome.

Twelfth Night (January 5), Epiphany of Our Lord (January 6), or another day during the time after Epiphany offers an occasion for gathering with friends and family members for a blessing for the home. Someone may lead the greeting and blessing, while another person may read the scripture passage. Following an eastern European tradition, a visual blessing may be inscribed with white chalk above the main door; for example, 20 + CMB + 23. The numbers change with each new year. The three letters stand for either the ancient Latin blessing *Christe mansionem benedicat*, which means "Christ, bless this house," or the legendary names of the magi (Caspar, Melchior, and Balthasar).

Greeting

Peace to this house and to all who enter here.
By wisdom a house is built,
and through understanding it is established;
through knowledge its rooms are filled
with rare and beautiful treasures. *(Prov. 24:3-4)*

Reading

As we prepare to ask God's blessing on this household,
let us listen to the words of scripture:
In the beginning was the Word,
and the Word was with God, and the Word was God.
He was in the beginning with God.
All things came into being through him,
and without him not one thing came into being.
What has come into being in him was life,
and the life was the light of all people . . .

The Word became flesh and lived among us, and we have seen his glory, the glory as of a father's only son, full of grace and truth . . .
From his fullness we have all received, grace upon grace.
(John 1:1-4, 14, 16)

Inscription

This inscription may be made with chalk above the entrance:

20 + C M B + 23

Write the appropriate character (left) while speaking the text (right).

The magi of old, known as

C   Caspar,

M   Melchior, and

B   Balthasar,

followed the star of God's Son who came to dwell among us

20   two thousand

23   and twenty-three years ago.

+   Christ, bless this house,

+   and remain with us throughout the new year.

Prayer of Blessing

O God,
you revealed your Son to all people by the shining light of a star.
We pray that you bless this home and all who live here
with your gracious presence.
May your love be our inspiration, your wisdom our guide,
your truth our light, and your peace our benediction;
through Christ our Lord. Amen.

Then everyone may walk from room to room, blessing the house with incense or by sprinkling with water, perhaps using a branch from the Christmas tree.

Friday, January 6, 2023
Epiphany of Our Lord

Matthew 2:1-12
Christ revealed to the nations

Then Herod secretly called for the wise men and learned from them the exact time when the star had appeared. Then he sent them to Bethlehem, saying, "Go and search diligently for the child; and when you have found him, bring me word so that I may also go and pay him homage." When they had heard the king, they set out; and there, ahead of them, went the star that they had seen at its rising, until it stopped over the place where the child was. When they saw that the star had stopped, they were overwhelmed with joy. On entering the house, they saw the child with Mary his mother; and they knelt down and paid him homage. Then, opening their treasure chests, they offered him gifts of gold, frankincense, and myrrh. (Matt. 2:7-11)

Psalm
Psalm 72:1-7, 10-14
All shall bow down

Additional Readings
Isaiah 60:1-6
Nations come to the light

Ephesians 3:1-12
The gospel's promise for all

Hymn: Bright and Glorious Is the Sky, ELW 301

O God, on this day you revealed your Son to the nations by the leading of a star. Lead us now by faith to know your presence in our lives, and bring us at last to the full vision of your glory, through your Son, Jesus Christ our Lord, who lives and reigns with you and the Holy Spirit, one God, now and forever.

Time after Epiphany

On the Epiphany of Our Lord (January 6), the household joins the church throughout the world in celebrating the manifestation, the "epiphany," of Christ to the world. The festival of Christmas is thus set within the context of outreach to the larger community; it possesses an outward movement. The festival of the Epiphany asks the Christian household: How might our faith in Christ the Light be shared with friends and family, with our neighbors, with the poor and needy in our land, with those who live in other nations?

Table Prayer for Epiphany and the Time after Epiphany (January 6–February 21)

Generous God,
you have made yourself known in Jesus, the light of the world.
As this food and drink give us refreshment,
so strengthen us by your Spirit,
that as your baptized sons and daughters
we may share your light with all the world.
Grant this through Christ our Lord.
Amen.

Saturday, January 7, 2023
Time after Epiphany

1 Kings 10:1-13
Gifts to Solomon from Sheba

When the queen of Sheba heard of the fame of Solomon (fame due to the name of the LORD), she came to test him with hard questions. She came to Jerusalem with a very great retinue, with camels bearing spices, and very much gold, and precious stones; and when she came to Solomon, she told him all that was on her mind. Solomon answered all her questions; there was nothing hidden from the king that he could not explain to her. When the queen of Sheba had observed all the wisdom of Solomon, the house that he had built, the food of his table, the seating of his officials, and the attendance of his servants, their clothing, his valets, and his burnt offerings that he offered at the house of the LORD, there was no more spirit in her. (1 Kings 10:1-5)

Psalm
Psalm 72
Prayers for the king

Additional Reading
Ephesians 3:14-21
Knowing the love of Christ

Hymn: Brightest and Best of the Stars, ELW 303

Source of all wisdom, you welcome our hard questions. Embolden us to bring our struggles and confusion before you in prayer. Guide us and inspire us to respond in faithfulness and generosity.

Matthew 3:13-17

Christ revealed as God's Son

Then Jesus came from Galilee to John at the Jordan, to be baptized by him. John would have prevented him, saying, "I need to be baptized by you, and do you come to me?" But Jesus answered him, "Let it be so now; for it is proper for us in this way to fulfill all righteousness." Then he consented. And when Jesus had been baptized, just as he came up from the water, suddenly the heavens were opened to him and he saw the Spirit of God descending like a dove and alighting on him. And a voice from heaven said, "This is my Son, the Beloved, with whom I am well pleased." (Matt. 3:13-17)

Psalm

Psalm 29
The voice of God upon the waters

Additional Readings

Isaiah 42:1-9
The servant of God brings justice

Acts 10:34-43
Jesus' ministry after his baptism

Hymn: Down Galilee's Slow Roadways, ACS 916

O God our Father, at the baptism of Jesus you proclaimed him your beloved Son and anointed him with the Holy Spirit. Make all who are baptized into Christ faithful to their calling to be your daughters and sons, and empower us all with your Spirit, through Jesus Christ, our Savior and Lord, who lives and reigns with you and the Holy Spirit, one God, now and forever.

Monday, January 9, 2023
Time after Epiphany

Psalm 89:5-37
God anoints David to be a son

Then you spoke in a vision to your faithful one, and said:
>"I have set the crown on one who is mighty,
>I have exalted one chosen from the people.
I have found my servant David;
>with my holy oil I have anointed him;
my hand shall always remain with him;
>my arm also shall strengthen him.
The enemy shall not outwit him,
>the wicked shall not humble him.
I will crush his foes before him
>and strike down those who hate him." (Ps. 89:19-23)

Additional Readings

Genesis 35:1-15
God calls and blesses Jacob

Acts 10:44-48
Through Peter, God calls Gentiles to be baptized

Hymn: Blessed Be the God of Israel, ELW 250

Faithful God, you are the source of all safety and strength. Help us look to you in our need and honor your provision in any abundance. Called through baptism, make us into signs of your blessing in this world.

Tuesday, January 10, 2023
Time after Epiphany

Jeremiah 1:4-10
God calls Jeremiah

Now the word of the LORD came to me saying,
"Before I formed you in the womb I knew you,

and before you were born I consecrated you;

I appointed you a prophet to the nations."
Then I said, "Ah, Lord GOD! Truly I do not know how to speak, for I am
only a boy." But the LORD said to me,

"Do not say, 'I am only a boy';

for you shall go to all to whom I send you,

and you shall speak whatever I command you,

Do not be afraid of them,
for I am with you to deliver you,

says the LORD." (Jer. 1:4-8)

Psalm
Psalm 89:5-37
God anoints David to be a son

Additional Reading
Acts 8:4-13
Philip preaches and baptizes

Hymn: Lord, Speak to Us, That We May Speak, ELW 676

Your call reorients our lives, O God. Calm our fears with the promise of your accompaniment. Go with us and open our mouths, that we may bear your creative and redeeming word to all the world.

Wednesday, January 11, 2023
Time after Epiphany

Isaiah 51:1-16
Through water God's people cross over

Awake, awake, put on strength,
    O arm of the LORD!
Awake, as in days of old,
    the generations of long ago!
Was it not you who cut Rahab in pieces,
    who pierced the dragon?
Was it not you who dried up the sea,
    the waters of the great deep;
who made the depths of the sea a way
    for the redeemed to cross over?
So the ransomed of the LORD shall return,
    and come to Zion with singing;
everlasting joy shall be upon their heads;
    they shall obtain joy and gladness,
    and sorrow and sighing shall flee away. (Isa. 51:9-11)

Psalm
Psalm 89:5-37
God anoints David to be a son

Additional Reading
Matthew 12:15-21
The words of Isaiah applied to Jesus

Hymn: Come, We That Love the Lord, ELW 625

Make a way for your people, saving God. In times of trouble, remind us about your deliverance of people in generations past, as well as your deliverance in our own lives. Teach us to live in hope and trust.

Thursday, January 12, 2023
Time after Epiphany

Psalm 40:1-11
Doing the will of God

I waited patiently for the LORD;
    he inclined to me and heard my cry.
He drew me up from the desolate pit,
    out of the miry bog,
and set my feet upon a rock,
    making my steps secure.
He put a new song in my mouth,
    a song of praise to our God.
Many will see and fear,
    and put their trust in the LORD. (Ps. 40:1-3)

Additional Readings
Isaiah 22:15-25
God replaces disobedient leaders

Galatians 1:6-12
Paul's calling through a revelation of Christ

Hymn: Out of the Depths I Cry to You, ELW 600

You are the God who hears. No pit is deep enough to separate us from you. With your rescue, train us in trust. Make us ready to cry to you, ready to sing your love for all to hear.

Friday, January 13, 2023
Time after Epiphany

Acts 1:1-5

The promise of the Holy Spirit

In the first book, Theophilus, I wrote about all that Jesus did and taught from the beginning until the day when he was taken up to heaven, after giving instructions through the Holy Spirit to the apostles whom he had chosen. After his suffering he presented himself alive to them by many convincing proofs, appearing to them during forty days and speaking about the kingdom of God. While staying with them, he ordered them not to leave Jerusalem, but to wait there for the promise of the Father. "This," he said, "is what you have heard from me; for John baptized with water, but you will be baptized with the Holy Spirit not many days from now." (Acts 1:1-5)

Psalm
Psalm 40:1-11
Doing the will of God

Additional Reading
Genesis 27:30-38
Isaac and Esau discover Jacob's deceit

Hymn: This Is the Spirit's Entry Now, ELW 448

O God, you keep your promise, sending your Spirit on all the baptized. By the Spirit empower us with wisdom and understanding, counsel and might, knowledge and the fear of the Lord. Give us joy in your presence.

Saturday, January 14, 2023
Time after Epiphany

1 Kings 19:19-21
Elijah calls Elisha to follow him

So [Elijah] set out from there, and found Elisha son of Shaphat, who was plowing. There were twelve yoke of oxen ahead of him, and he was with the twelfth. Elijah passed by him and threw his mantle over him. He left the oxen, ran after Elijah, and said, "Let me kiss my father and my mother, and then I will follow you." Then Elijah said to him, "Go back again; for what have I done to you?" He returned from following him, took the yoke of oxen, and slaughtered them; using the equipment from the oxen, he boiled their flesh, and gave it to the people, and they ate. Then he set out and followed Elijah, and became his servant. (1 Kings 19:19-21)

Psalm
Psalm 40:1-11
Doing the will of God

Additional Reading
Luke 5:1-11
Jesus calls the first disciples

Hymn: How Clear Is Our Vocation, Lord, ELW 580

Insistent God, you interrupt our lives with your call, but you always provide what we need to follow. As you gave Elisha courage to follow, strengthen us. As you gave Elijah a companion in the work, bless us with faithful community.

Sunday, January 15, 2023
Second Sunday after Epiphany

Martin Luther King Jr., renewer of society, martyr, died 1968

John 1:29-42

Christ revealed as the Lamb of God

The next day [John] saw Jesus coming toward him and declared, "Here is the Lamb of God who takes away the sin of the world! This is he of whom I said, 'After me comes a man who ranks ahead of me because he was before me.' I myself did not know him; but I came baptizing with water for this reason, that he might be revealed to Israel." And John testified, "I saw the Spirit descending from heaven like a dove, and it remained on him. I myself did not know him, but the one who sent me to baptize with water said to me, 'He on whom you see the Spirit descend and remain is the one who baptizes with the Holy Spirit.' And I myself have seen and have testified that this is the Son of God." (John 1:29-34)

Psalm

Psalm 40:1-11
Doing the will of God

Additional Readings

Isaiah 49:1-7
The servant brings light to the nations

1 Corinthians 1:1-9
Paul's greeting to the church at Corinth

Hymn: Lamb of God, ELW 336

Holy God, our strength and our redeemer, by your Spirit hold us forever, that through your grace we may worship you and faithfully serve you, follow you and joyfully find you, through Jesus Christ, our Savior and Lord.

Monday, January 16, 2023
Time after Epiphany

Psalm 40:6-17
Not sacrifice, but divine mercy

Sacrifice and offering you do not desire,
>   but you have given me an open ear.
Burnt offering and sin offering
>   you have not required.
Then I said, "Here I am;
>   in the scroll of the book it is written of me.
I delight to do your will, O my God;
>   your law is within my heart." (Ps. 40:6-8)

Additional Readings
Exodus 12:1-13, 21-28
The passover lamb

Acts 8:26-40
Philip teaches about the lamb

Hymn: Lord of Glory, You Have Bought Us, ELW 707

God of grace, open our ears to the promise that you are the one who saves. Free us from trying to earn your mercy. Write your law in our hearts and give us gratitude that overflows in grace for others.

Tuesday, January 17, 2023
Time after Epiphany

Antony of Egypt, renewer of the church, died around 356
Pachomius, renewer of the church, died 346

Hebrews 10:1-4

Animal sacrifices cannot take away sins

Since the law has only a shadow of the good things to come and not the true form of these realities, it can never, by the same sacrifices that are continually offered year after year, make perfect those who approach. Otherwise, would they not have ceased being offered, since the worshipers, cleansed once for all, would no longer have any consciousness of sin? But in these sacrifices there is a reminder of sin year after year. For it is impossible for the blood of bulls and goats to take away sins. (Heb. 10:1-4)

Psalm
Psalm 40:6-17
Not sacrifice, but divine mercy

Additional Reading
Isaiah 53:1-12
The one like a lamb

Hymn: Search Me, O God, ACS 1076

Forgiving God, Christ your Son gave himself for us. Remind us to cling to Jesus, whose cross and resurrection have given redemption and new life, once for all.

Wednesday, January 18, 2023
Confession of Peter

Week of Prayer for Christian Unity begins

Matthew 16:13-19

Peter confesses: You are the Messiah

[Jesus] said to [his disciples], "But who do you say that I am?" Simon Peter answered, "You are the Messiah, the Son of the living God." And Jesus answered him, "Blessed are you, Simon son of Jonah! For flesh and blood has not revealed this to you, but my Father in heaven. And I tell you, you are Peter, and on this rock I will build my church, and the gates of Hades will not prevail against it. I will give you the keys of the kingdom of heaven, and whatever you bind on earth will be bound in heaven, and whatever you loose on earth will be loosed in heaven." (Matt. 16:15-19)

Psalm

Psalm 18:1-6, 16-19
My God, my rock, worthy of praise

Additional Readings

Acts 4:8-13
Salvation is in no one other than Jesus

1 Corinthians 10:1-5
Drinking from the spiritual rock of Christ

Hymn: Built on a Rock, ELW 652

Almighty God, you inspired Simon Peter to confess Jesus as the Messiah and Son of the living God. Keep your church firm on the rock of this faith, that in unity and peace it may proclaim one truth and follow one Lord, your Son, Jesus Christ our Savior, who lives and reigns with you and the Holy Spirit, one God, now and forever.

Thursday, January 19, 2023
Time after Epiphany

Henry, Bishop of Uppsala, martyr, died 1156

Psalm 27:1-6
God is light and salvation

The LORD is my light and my salvation;
>   whom shall I fear?
The LORD is the stronghold of my life;
>   of whom shall I be afraid?

When evildoers assail me
>   to devour my flesh—
my adversaries and foes—
>   they shall stumble and fall.

Though an army encamp against me,
>   my heart shall not fear;
though war rise up against me,
>   yet I will be confident. (Ps. 27:1-3)

Additional Readings

1 Samuel 1:1-20
The birth of Samuel

Galatians 1:11-24
The divine origin of Paul's gospel

Hymn: If God My Lord Be for Me, ELW 788

God our stronghold, you shelter all in time of need. Give us confidence that your presence will not fail us. Use us to protect and accompany vulnerable people with signs of your presence and provision.

Friday, January 20, 2023
Time after Epiphany

Galatians 2:1-10
Paul's authority in the growing church

Then after fourteen years I went up again to Jerusalem with Barnabas, taking Titus along with me. I went up in response to a revelation. Then I laid before them (though only in a private meeting with the acknowledged leaders) the gospel that I proclaim among the Gentiles, in order to make sure that I was not running, or had not run, in vain. But even Titus, who was with me, was not compelled to be circumcised, though he was a Greek. But because of false believers secretly brought in, who slipped in to spy on the freedom we have in Christ Jesus, so that they might enslave us—we did not submit to them even for a moment, so that the truth of the gospel might always remain with you. (Gal. 2:1-5)

Psalm
Psalm 27:1-6
God is light and salvation

Additional Reading
1 Samuel 9:27—10:8
Saul anointed by Samuel as king

Hymn: God, Whose Almighty Word, ELW 673

God of all people, you call us into a community that includes people we do not understand. Grant us wisdom and discernment to hear your freeing gospel clearly. Give us the patience and love needed to live as one body.

Saturday, January 21, 2023
Time after Epiphany

Agnes, martyr, died around 304

1 Samuel 15:34—16:13

David anointed as king to replace King Saul

Samuel said to Jesse, "Are all your sons here?" And he said, "There remains yet the youngest, but he is keeping the sheep." And Samuel said to Jesse, "Send and bring him; for we will not sit down until he comes here." He sent and brought him in. Now he was ruddy, and had beautiful eyes, and was handsome. The LORD said, "Rise and anoint him; for this is the one." Then Samuel took the horn of oil, and anointed him in the presence of his brothers; and the spirit of the LORD came mightily upon David from that day forward. Samuel then set out and went to Ramah. (1 Sam. 16:11-13)

Psalm
Psalm 27:1-6
God is light and salvation

Additional Reading
Luke 5:27-32
The call of Levi

Hymn: In Christ Called to Baptize, ELW 575

God, your call comes to the unlikely and overlooked. It challenges our values and sense of order. Prepare your people to receive those whom you have called. Bless their leadership and give us openness to your work in and through them.

Sunday, January 22, 2023
Third Sunday after Epiphany

Matthew 4:12-23

Christ revealed as a prophet

Now when Jesus heard that John had been arrested, he withdrew to Galilee. He left Nazareth and made his home in Capernaum by the sea, in the territory of Zebulun and Naphtali, so that what had been spoken through the prophet Isaiah might be fulfilled:

"Land of Zebulun, land of Naphtali,

on the road by the sea, across the Jordan, Galilee of the Gentiles—

the people who sat in darkness

have seen a great light,

and for those who sat in the region and shadow of death

light has dawned." (Matt. 4:12-16)

Psalm

Psalm 27:1, 4-9
God is light and salvation

Additional Readings

Isaiah 9:1-4
Light shines for those in darkness

1 Corinthians 1:10-18
An appeal for unity in the gospel

Hymn: Light Shone in Darkness, ELW 307

Lord God, your lovingkindness always goes before us and follows after us. Summon us into your light, and direct our steps in the ways of goodness that come through the cross of your Son, Jesus Christ, our Savior and Lord.

Monday, January 23, 2023
Time after Epiphany

Psalm 27:7-14
Take courage in God

Teach me your way, O LORD,
>> and lead me on a level path
>> because of my enemies.
Do not give me up to the will of my adversaries,
>> for false witnesses have risen against me,
>> and they are breathing out violence.

I believe that I shall see the goodness of the LORD
>> in the land of the living.
Wait for the LORD;
>> be strong, and let your heart take courage;
>> wait for the LORD! (Ps. 27:11-14)

Additional Readings
Judges 6:11-24
God calls Gideon to lead the people

Ephesians 5:6-14
Live as children of the light

Hymn: Lead Me, Guide Me, ELW 768

You are the God who keeps promises. Hold before us the vision of your reign of justice, mercy, and peace, that we will wait with courage, not relying on or accepting anything less than the fullness of your goodness.

Tuesday, January 24, 2023
Time after Epiphany

Philippians 2:12-18
The call to shine like stars

Do all things without murmuring and arguing, so that you may be
blameless and innocent, children of God without blemish in the midst
of a crooked and perverse generation, in which you shine like stars in
the world. It is by your holding fast to the word of life that I can boast
on the day of Christ that I did not run in vain or labor in vain. But even
if I am being poured out as a libation over the sacrifice and the offering
of your faith, I am glad and rejoice with all of you—and in the same way
you also must be glad and rejoice with me. (Phil. 2:14-18)

Psalm
Psalm 27:7-14
Take courage in God

Additional Reading
Judges 7:12-22
God leads Gideon to victory

Hymn: Rejoice in God's Saints, ELW 418

*Anchor us in your word of life, O God, so we can persist through trials and
rejoice despite suffering. And when we cannot envision a way forward, illumine our paths with the shining witness of your saints.*

Wednesday, January 25, 2023
Conversion of Paul

Week of Prayer for Christian Unity ends

Galatians 1:11-24

Paul receives a revelation of Christ

You have heard, no doubt, of my earlier life in Judaism. I was violently persecuting the church of God and was trying to destroy it. I advanced in Judaism beyond many among my people of the same age, for I was far more zealous for the traditions of my ancestors. But when God, who had set me apart before I was born and called me through his grace, was pleased to reveal his Son to me, so that I might proclaim him among the Gentiles, I did not confer with any human being, nor did I go up to Jerusalem to those who were already apostles before me, but I went away at once into Arabia, and afterwards I returned to Damascus. (Gal. 1:13-17)

Psalm

Psalm 67
Let all the peoples praise you, O God

Additional Readings

Acts 9:1-22
Saul is converted to Christ

Luke 21:10-19
The end times will require endurance

Hymn: By All Your Saints, ELW 420, st. 8

O God, by the preaching of your apostle Paul you have caused the light of the gospel to shine throughout the world. Grant that we may follow his example and be witnesses to the truth of your Son, Jesus Christ, our Savior and Lord, who lives and reigns with you and the Holy Spirit, one God, now and forever.

Thursday, January 26, 2023
Time after Epiphany

Timothy, Titus, and Silas, missionaries

Psalm 15
Abiding on God's holy hill

O LORD, who may abide in your tent?
Who may dwell on your holy hill?

Those who walk blamelessly, and do what is right,
and speak the truth from their heart;
who do not slander with their tongue,
and do no evil to their friends,
nor take up a reproach against their neighbors;
in whose eyes the wicked are despised,
but who honor those who fear the LORD;
who stand by their oath even to their hurt;
who do not lend money at interest,
and do not take a bribe against the innocent.

Those who do these things shall never be moved. (Ps. 15:1-5)

Additional Readings
Deuteronomy 16:18-20
Pursue only justice

1 Peter 3:8-12
Repay evil with a blessing

Hymn: God of Grace and God of Glory, ELW 705

Holy God, your mercy and forgiveness invite us into your presence. As you have made us new, so also make us into signs of your righteousness for others. Fill us with kindness, integrity, and mercy for the sake of our neighbors.

Friday, January 27, 2023
Time after Epiphany

Lydia, Dorcas, and Phoebe, witnesses to the faith

1 Timothy 5:17-24

Good works are conspicuous

In the presence of God and of Christ Jesus and of the elect angels, I warn you to keep these instructions without prejudice, doing nothing on the basis of partiality. Do not ordain anyone hastily, and do not participate in the sins of others; keep yourself pure.

No longer drink only water, but take a little wine for the sake of your stomach and your frequent ailments.

The sins of some people are conspicuous and precede them to judgment, while the sins of others follow them there. (1 Tim. 5:21-24)

Psalm
Psalm 15
Abiding on God's holy hill

Additional Reading
Deuteronomy 24:17—25:4
Do not deprive others of justice

Hymn: To Be Your Presence, ELW 546

God, your holiness calls us to account for our deeds. Give us such confidence in your love that we may live with integrity, acting with justice and prudence, and caring for the needs of others.

Saturday, January 28, 2023
Time after Epiphany

Thomas Aquinas, teacher, died 1274

Micah 3:1-4

Should you not know justice?

And I said:
Listen, you heads of Jacob
        and rulers of the house of Israel!
Should you not know justice?—
        you who hate the good and love the evil,
who tear the skin off my people,
        and the flesh off their bones;
who eat the flesh of my people,
        flay their skin off them,
break their bones in pieces,
        and chop them up like meat in a kettle,
        like flesh in a caldron.

Then they will cry to the LORD,
        but he will not answer them;
he will hide his face from them at that time,
        because they have acted wickedly. (Micah 3:1-4)

Psalm
Psalm 15
Abiding on God's holy hill

Additional Reading
John 13:31-35
The new commandment

Hymn: God Bless to Us Our Bread, ACS 1056

God of justice, you appoint leaders to seek the welfare of all, and send prophets to call us back to you. Open us to repentance, to the needs of our neighbors, and to join in calling leaders toward justice.

Sunday, January 29, 2023
Fourth Sunday after Epiphany

Matthew 5:1-12

The teaching of Christ: Beatitudes

When Jesus saw the crowds, he went up the mountain; and after he sat down, his disciples came to him. Then he began to speak, and taught them, saying: . . .

"Blessed are those who are persecuted for righteousness' sake, for theirs is the kingdom of heaven.

"Blessed are you when people revile you and persecute you and utter all kinds of evil against you falsely on my account. Rejoice and be glad, for your reward is great in heaven, for in the same way they persecuted the prophets who were before you." (Matt. 5:1-2, 10-12)

Psalm
Psalm 15
Abiding on God's holy hill

Additional Readings
Micah 6:1-8
The offering of justice, kindness, humility

1 Corinthians 1:18-31
Christ crucified, the wisdom and power of God

Hymn: When the Poor Ones, ELW 725

Holy God, you confound the world's wisdom in giving your kingdom to the lowly and the pure in heart. Give us such a hunger and thirst for justice, and perseverance in striving for peace, that in our words and deeds the world may see the life of your Son, Jesus Christ, our Savior and Lord.

Monday, January 30, 2023
Time after Epiphany

Psalm 37:1-17

God will bless the righteous

The wicked draw the sword and bend their bows
>   to bring down the poor and needy,
>   to kill those who walk uprightly;
their sword shall enter their own heart,
>   and their bows shall be broken.

Better is a little that the righteous person has
>   than the abundance of many wicked.
For the arms of the wicked shall be broken,
>   but the LORD upholds the righteous. (Ps. 37:14-17)

Additional Readings

Ruth 1:1-18
Ruth, one of the poor

Philemon 1-25
Concerning the slave Onesimus

Hymn: The People Walk, ELW 706

Lord, you uphold the righteous. Free us from the greed that tempts us to acquire constantly, to the detriment of our neighbors. Strengthen us in our desire to walk uprightly and give us gratitude for what you have given.

Tuesday, January 31, 2023
Time after Epiphany

James 5:1-6

A warning to the ungenerous

Come now, you rich people, weep and wail for the miseries that are coming to you. Your riches have rotted, and your clothes are moth-eaten. Your gold and silver have rusted, and their rust will be evidence against you, and it will eat your flesh like fire. You have laid up treasure for the last days. Listen! The wages of the laborers who mowed your fields, which you kept back by fraud, cry out, and the cries of the harvesters have reached the ears of the Lord of hosts. You have lived on the earth in luxury and in pleasure; you have fattened your hearts in a day of slaughter. You have condemned and murdered the righteous one, who does not resist you. (James 5:1-6)

Psalm
Psalm 37:1-17
God will bless the righteous

Additional Reading
Ruth 2:1-16
Ruth, one of the hungry

Hymn: Where Charity and Love Prevail, ELW 359

Generous God, you provide for those who are needy and defend the vulnerable. Free us from the rot and rust of our riches and teach us to treasure your ways. Open our hearts and our hands in justice and generosity.

Prayer List for February

_____

_____

_____

_____

_____

_____

_____

_____

_____

_____

Wednesday, February 1, 2023
Time after Epiphany

Ruth 3:1-13; 4:13-22
Ruth, one of the blessed

So Boaz took Ruth and she became his wife. When they came together, the LORD made her conceive, and she bore a son. Then the women said to Naomi, "Blessed be the LORD, who has not left you this day without next-of-kin; and may his name be renowned in Israel! He shall be to you a restorer of life and a nourisher of your old age; for your daughter-in-law who loves you, who is more to you than seven sons, has borne him." Then Naomi took the child and laid him in her bosom, and became his nurse. The women of the neighborhood gave him a name, saying, "A son has been born to Naomi." They named him Obed; he became the father of Jesse, the father of David. (Ruth 4:13-17)

Psalm
Psalm 37:1-17
God will bless the righteous

Additional Reading
Luke 6:17-26
The beatitudes in Luke's gospel

Hymn: Borning Cry, ELW 732

God of all people, you created us to live in families of love. Bless expectant mothers and those who support them. Bring comfort to those who wish to be parents but are not.

Thursday, February 2, 2023
Presentation of Our Lord

Luke 2:22-40

The child is brought to the temple

Simeon took [the child Jesus] in his arms and praised God, saying,
> "Master, now you are dismissing your servant in peace,
>> according to your word;
> for my eyes have seen your salvation,
>> which you have prepared in the presence of all peoples,
> a light for revelation to the Gentiles
>> and for glory to your people Israel." (Luke 2:28-32)

Psalm

Psalm 84
How dear to me is your dwelling, O Lord

Additional Readings

Malachi 3:1-4
My messenger, a refiner and purifier

Hebrews 2:14-18
Jesus shares human flesh and sufferings

Hymn: In Peace and Joy I Now Depart, ELW 440

Almighty and ever-living God, your only-begotten Son was presented this day in the temple. May we be presented to you with clean and pure hearts by the same Jesus Christ our great high priest, who lives and reigns with you and the Holy Spirit, one God, now and forever.

Friday, February 3, 2023
Time after Epiphany

Ansgar, Bishop of Hamburg, missionary to Denmark and Sweden, died 865

James 3:13-18
A gentle life born of wisdom

Who is wise and understanding among you? Show by your good life that your works are done with gentleness born of wisdom. But if you have bitter envy and selfish ambition in your hearts, do not be boastful and false to the truth. Such wisdom does not come down from above, but is earthly, unspiritual, devilish. For where there is envy and selfish ambition, there will also be disorder and wickedness of every kind. But the wisdom from above is first pure, then peaceable, gentle, willing to yield, full of mercy and good fruits, without a trace of partiality or hypocrisy. And a harvest of righteousness is sown in peace for those who make peace. (James 3:13-18)

Psalm
Psalm 112:1-9 [10]
Light shines in the darkness

Additional Reading
Isaiah 29:1-12
Hunger that goes unsatisfied

Hymn: Salvation unto Us Has Come, ELW 590

God of all wisdom, you provide us with all good things, including wise teachers and leaders. Be with those in positions of leadership. Help them avoid envy and selfish ambition, leading instead with humility, gentleness, and love.

Saturday, February 4, 2023
Time after Epiphany

Isaiah 29:13-16
Hearts far from God

The Lord said:
Because these people draw near with their mouths
    and honor me with their lips,
    while their hearts are far from me,
and their worship of me is a human commandment
    learned by rote;
so I will again do
    amazing things with this people,
    shocking and amazing.
The wisdom of their wise shall perish,
    and the discernment of the discerning shall be hidden.
(Isa. 29:13-14)

Psalm
Psalm 112:1-9 [10]
Light shines in the darkness

Additional Reading
Mark 7:1-8
The hypocrisy of lip service

Hymn: Glorious Things of You Are Spoken, ELW 647

God of all creation, you are the one whom we worship and adore. Forgive us when our worship is rote or repetitive and not from the heart. Open our hearts and minds and help us commit ourselves to you.

Sunday, February 5, 2023
Fifth Sunday after Epiphany

The Martyrs of Japan, died 1597

Luke 5:1-11

The teaching of Christ: salt and light

[Jesus said:] "You are the salt of the earth; but if salt has lost its taste, how can its saltiness be restored? It is no longer good for anything, but is thrown out and trampled under foot.

"You are the light of the world. A city built on a hill cannot be hid. No one after lighting a lamp puts it under the bushel basket, but on the lampstand, and it gives light to all in the house. In the same way, let your light shine before others, so that they may see your good works and give glory to your Father in heaven." (Matt. 5:13-16)

Psalm

Psalm 112:1-9 [10]
Light shines in the darkness

Additional Readings

Isaiah 58:1-9a [9b-12]
The fast that God chooses

1 Corinthians 2:1-12 [13-16]
God's wisdom revealed through the Spirit

Hymn: Gather Us In, ELW 532

Lord God, with endless mercy you receive the prayers of all who call upon you. By your Spirit show us the things we ought to do, and give us the grace and power to do them, through Jesus Christ, our Savior and Lord.

Monday, February 6, 2023
Time after Epiphany

Psalm 119:105-112
The law is light

Accept my offerings of praise, O LORD,
   and teach me your ordinances.
I hold my life in my hand continually,
   but I do not forget your law.
The wicked have laid a snare for me,
   but I do not stray from your precepts.
Your decrees are my heritage forever;
   they are the joy of my heart.
I incline my heart to perform your statutes
   forever, to the end. (Ps. 119:108-112)

Additional Readings
2 Kings 22:3-20
Huldah urges Josiah to keep the law

Romans 11:2-10
A remnant remains faithful

Hymn: Oh, That the Lord Would Guide My Ways, ELW 772

God of majesty, your holy scripture is a gift to us. Fill us with a deep longing for your word. No matter what troubles may come, keep us rooted in your promises so we find our delight in you.

Tuesday, February 7, 2023
Time after Epiphany

2 Corinthians 4:1-12
Christ, the light

Therefore, since it is by God's mercy that we are engaged in this ministry, we do not lose heart. We have renounced the shameful things that one hides; we refuse to practice cunning or to falsify God's word; but by the open statement of the truth we commend ourselves to the conscience of everyone in the sight of God. And even if our gospel is veiled, it is veiled to those who are perishing. In their case the god of this world has blinded the minds of the unbelievers, to keep them from seeing the light of the gospel of the glory of Christ, who is the image of God. For we do not proclaim ourselves; we proclaim Jesus Christ as Lord and ourselves as your slaves for Jesus' sake. For it is the God who said, "Let light shine out of darkness," who has shone in our hearts to give the light of the knowledge of the glory of God in the face of Jesus Christ. (2 Cor. 4:1-6)

Psalm
Psalm 119:105-112
The law is light

Additional Reading
2 Kings 23:1-8, 21-25
King Josiah keeps the law

Hymn: Christ, Be Our Light, ELW 715

God of light, you shine your promises into our darkest days. Bless the work of pastors, preachers, missionaries, and all others who share your word with others. Let their words reflect your light and bring hope to others.

Wednesday, February 8, 2023
Time after Epiphany

John 8:12-30
Christ the light of the world

Again Jesus spoke to [the scribes and Pharisees], saying, "I am the light of the world. Whoever follows me will never walk in darkness but will have the light of life." Then the Pharisees said to him, "You are testifying on your own behalf; your testimony is not valid." Jesus answered, "Even if I testify on my own behalf, my testimony is valid because I know where I have come from and where I am going." (John 8:12-14)

Psalm
Psalm 119:105-112
The law is light

Additional Reading
Proverbs 6:6-23
The law is a lamp

Hymn: Jesus, the Light of the World, ACS 914

God of all goodness, in great love for us you revealed your light in the person of Jesus Christ. Stir up faith in us, that we may share his light with others in all we say and do.

Thursday, February 9, 2023
Time after Epiphany

Psalm 119:1-8
Happy are those who walk in the law

Happy are those whose way is blameless,
    who walk in the law of the LORD.
Happy are those who keep his decrees,
    who seek him with their whole heart,
who also do no wrong,
    but walk in his ways. (Ps. 119:1-3)

Additional Readings
Genesis 26:1-5
God blesses Isaac

James 1:12-16
God tempts no one

Hymn: O God beyond All Praising, ELW 880

God of joy and happiness, you are the source of all true delight. Help us to find our delight in you and not in the things of this world. Keep us rooted in your laws and your decrees.

Friday, February 10, 2023
Time after Epiphany

1 John 2:7-17
Old and new commandments

Beloved, I am writing you no new commandment, but an old commandment that you have had from the beginning; the old commandment is
the word that you have heard. Yet I am writing you a new commandment
that is true in him and in you, because the darkness is passing away
and the true light is already shining. Whoever says, "I am in the light,"
while hating a brother or sister, is still in the darkness. Whoever loves a
brother or sister lives in the light, and in such a person there is no cause
for stumbling. But whoever hates another believer is in the darkness,
walks in the darkness, and does not know the way to go, because the
darkness has brought on blindness. (1 John 2:7-11)

Psalm
Psalm 119:1-8
Happy are those who walk in the law

Additional Reading
Leviticus 26:34-46
God's covenant remembered

Hymn: The Right Hand of God, ELW 889

*God of healing and wholeness, you make all things new and bring us to new
life. Restore broken relationships in the church. Heal divisions. Unite the
body of Christ. Help us show your love to all people.*

Saturday, February 11, 2023
Time after Epiphany

Deuteronomy 30:1-9a
God's fidelity assured

When all these things have happened to you, the blessings and the curses that I have set before you, if you call them to mind among all the nations where the LORD your God has driven you, and return to the LORD your God, and you and your children obey him with all your heart and with all your soul, just as I am commanding you today, then the LORD your God will restore your fortunes and have compassion on you, gathering you again from all the peoples among whom the LORD your God has scattered you. Even if you are exiled to the ends of the world, from there the LORD your God will gather you, and from there he will bring you back. The LORD your God will bring you into the land that your ancestors possessed, and you will possess it; he will make you more prosperous and numerous than your ancestors. (Deut. 30:1-5)

Psalm
Psalm 119:1-8
Happy are those who walk in the law

Additional Reading
Matthew 15:1-9
God's commandments and religious tradition

Hymn: Day by Day, ELW 790

God of steadfast love, you remain faithful to us even when we are not faithful to you. Forgive our sin and help us to stay focused on you. Guide us in teaching our children about your love.

Sunday, February 12, 2023
Sixth Sunday after Epiphany

Matthew 5:21-37

The teaching of Christ: forgiveness

[Jesus said:] "You have heard that it was said to those of ancient times, 'You shall not murder'; and 'whoever murders shall be liable to judgment.' But I say to you that if you are angry with a brother or sister, you will be liable to judgment; and if you insult a brother or sister, you will be liable to the council; and if you say, 'You fool,' you will be liable to the hell of fire. So when you are offering your gift at the altar, if you remember that your brother or sister has something against you, leave your gift there before the altar and go; first be reconciled to your brother or sister, and then come and offer your gift. Come to terms quickly with your accuser while you are on the way to court with him, or your accuser may hand you over to the judge, and the judge to the guard, and you will be thrown into prison. Truly I tell you, you will never get out until you have paid the last penny." (Matt. 5:21-26)

Psalm

Psalm 119:1-8
Happy are those who walk in the law

Additional Readings

Deuteronomy 30: 15-20
Choose life

1 Corinthians 3:1-9
God gives the growth

Hymn: God, When Human Bonds Are Broken, ELW 603

O God, the strength of all who hope in you, because we are weak mortals we accomplish nothing good without you. Help us to see and understand the things we ought to do, and give us grace and power to do them; through Jesus Christ, our Savior and Lord.

Monday, February 13, 2023
Time after Epiphany

Psalm 119:9-16
I delight in the law

Blessed are you, O Lord;
    teach me your statutes.
With my lips I declare
    all the ordinances of your mouth.
I delight in the way of your decrees
    as much as in all riches.
I will meditate on your precepts,
    and fix my eyes on your ways.
I will delight in your statutes;
    I will not forget your word. (Ps. 119:12-16)

Additional Readings
Exodus 20:1-21
The ten commandments

James 1:2-8
Facing trials

Hymn: All Depends on Our Possessing, ELW 589

God of all knowledge, you make your promises for all people. Bless all teachers, professors, administrators, and all people who are responsible for teaching your word to others in educational settings. Give open minds to the students who will learn from them.

Tuesday, February 14, 2023
Time after Epiphany

Cyril, monk, died 869; Methodius, bishop, died 885; missionaries to the Slavs

James 2:1-13
The law, judgment, and mercy

You do well if you really fulfill the royal law according to the scripture, "You shall love your neighbor as yourself." But if you show partiality, you commit sin and are convicted by the law as transgressors. For whoever keeps the whole law but fails in one point has become accountable for all of it. For the one who said, "You shall not commit adultery," also said, "You shall not murder." Now if you do not commit adultery but if you murder, you have become a transgressor of the law. So speak and so act as those who are to be judged by the law of liberty. For judgment will be without mercy to anyone who has shown no mercy; mercy triumphs over judgment. (James 2:8-13)

Psalm
Psalm 119:9-16
I delight in the law

Additional Reading
Deuteronomy 23:21—24:4, 10-15
Israel's communal laws

Hymn: Our Father, God in Heaven Above, ELW 747

God of mercy, you are rich toward us even when we are stingy to our neighbors. Help us think outside of ourselves. Open us to showing your abundant love to all. Keep us centered on your law and your grace.

Wednesday, February 15, 2023
Time after Epiphany

Proverbs 2:1-15
The way of wisdom

My child, if you accept my words
　　and treasure up my commandments within you,
making your ear attentive to wisdom
　　and inclining your heart to understanding;
if you indeed cry out for insight,
　　and raise your voice for understanding;
if you seek it like silver,
　　and search for it as for hidden treasures—
then you will understand the fear of the LORD
　　and find the knowledge of God. (Prov. 2:1-5)

Psalm
Psalm 119:9-16
I delight in the law

Additional Reading
Matthew 19:1-12
Jesus teaches about divorce

Hymn: Be Thou My Vision, ELW 793

God of insight and wisdom, you enlighten the minds and open the hearts of people of all ages. Stir up a hunger for learning in students and give courage and strength to those who teach them.

Thursday, February 16, 2023
Time after Epiphany

Psalm 2
The one begotten of God

I will tell of the decree of the LORD:
He said to me, "You are my son;
>   today I have begotten you.
Ask of me, and I will make the nations your heritage,
>   and the ends of the earth your possession.
You shall break them with a rod of iron,
>   and dash them in pieces like a potter's vessel."

Now therefore, O kings, be wise;
>   be warned, O rulers of the earth.
Serve the LORD with fear,
>   with trembling kiss his feet,
or he will be angry, and you will perish in the way;
>   for his wrath is quickly kindled. (Ps. 2:7-12b)

Additional Readings
Exodus 6:2-9   **Hebrews 8:1-7**
God promises deliverance through Moses   *Christ, the mediator*

Hymn: O God of Love, O King of Peace, ELW 749

God of the universe, you are the one with all authority and power in this world. Guide people in leadership positions so they focus on you and not themselves. Help them serve you in all they do.

Friday, February 17, 2023
Time after Epiphany

Hebrews 11:23-28
The faith of Moses

By faith Moses was hidden by his parents for three months after his birth, because they saw that the child was beautiful; and they were not afraid of the king's edict. By faith Moses, when he was grown up, refused to be called a son of Pharaoh's daughter, choosing rather to share ill-treatment with the people of God than to enjoy the fleeting pleasures of sin. He considered abuse suffered for the Christ to be greater wealth than the treasures of Egypt, for he was looking ahead to the reward. By faith he left Egypt, unafraid of the king's anger; for he persevered as though he saw him who is invisible. By faith he kept the Passover and the sprinkling of blood, so that the destroyer of the firstborn would not touch the firstborn of Israel. (Heb. 11:23-28)

Psalm
Psalm 2
The one begotten of God

Additional Reading
Exodus 19:9b-25
Israel consecrated at Sinai

Hymn: We've Come This Far by Faith, ELW 633

God of promises, you worked in the life of your servant Moses. Work in our lives today. Stir up our faith in you as you stirred up faith in Moses. Help us to obey you even when we are uncertain.

Saturday, February 18, 2023
Time after Epiphany

Martin Luther, renewer of the church, died 1546

Mark 9:9-13

The coming of Elijah

As [Jesus, Peter, James, and John] were coming down the mountain, Jesus ordered them to tell no one about what they had seen, until after the Son of Man had risen from the dead. So they kept the matter to themselves, questioning what this rising from the dead could mean. Then they asked him, "Why do the scribes say that Elijah must come first?" He said to them, "Elijah is indeed coming first to restore all things. How then is it written about the Son of Man, that he is to go through many sufferings and be treated with contempt? But I tell you that Elijah has come, and they did to him whatever they pleased, as it is written about him." (Mark 9:9-13)

Psalm

Psalm 2
The one begotten of God

Additional Reading

1 Kings 21:20-29
Elijah pronounces God's sentence

Hymn: How Good, Lord, to Be Here! ELW 315

God of light, you revealed the glory of your Son in the transfiguration. Reveal yourself to us today. Help us to treasure what you show us, even when we don't understand what it means right away.

Sunday, February 19, 2023
Transfiguration of Our Lord

Matthew 17:1-9

Christ revealed as God's beloved Son

Six days later, Jesus took with him Peter and James and his brother John and led them up a high mountain, by themselves. And he was transfigured before them, and his face shone like the sun, and his clothes became dazzling white. Suddenly there appeared to them Moses and Elijah, talking with him. Then Peter said to Jesus, "Lord, it is good for us to be here; if you wish, I will make three dwellings here, one for you, one for Moses, and one for Elijah." While he was still speaking, suddenly a bright cloud overshadowed them, and from the cloud a voice said, "This is my Son, the Beloved; with him I am well pleased; listen to him!" (Matt. 17:1-5)

Psalm

Psalm 2
The one begotten of God

Additional Readings

Exodus 24:12-18
Moses enters the cloud of God's glory

2 Peter 1:16-21
Shining with the glory of God

Hymn: Dazzling Presence on the Mountain, ACS 917

O God, in the transfiguration of your Son you confirmed the mysteries of the faith by the witness of Moses and Elijah, and in the voice from the bright cloud declaring Jesus your beloved Son, you foreshadowed our adoption as your children. Make us heirs with Christ of your glory, and bring us to enjoy its fullness, through Jesus Christ, our Savior and Lord, who lives and reigns with you and the Holy Spirit, one God, now and forever.

Monday, February 20, 2023
Time after Epiphany

Psalm 78:17-20, 52-55
Israel led to God's holy mountain

Then he led out his people like sheep,
>and guided them in the wilderness like a flock.
He led them in safety, so that they were not afraid;
>but the sea overwhelmed their enemies.
And he brought them to his holy hill,
>to the mountain that his right hand had won.
He drove out nations before them;
>he apportioned them for a possession
>and settled the tribes of Israel in their tents. (Ps. 78:52-55)

Additional Readings
Exodus 33:7-23
Moses asks to see God's glory

Acts 7:30-34
Moses on holy ground

Hymn: All People That on Earth Do Dwell, ELW 883

God of mercy and protection, you shelter us like a shepherd protecting sheep. Thank you for giving us comfort when we are scared and for giving us direction when we are lost. Help us stay close to you always.

Tuesday, February 21, 2023
Time after Epiphany

Romans 11:1-6

A remnant chosen by grace

I ask, then, has God rejected his people? By no means! I myself am an Israelite, a descendant of Abraham, a member of the tribe of Benjamin. God has not rejected his people whom he foreknew. Do you not know what the scripture says of Elijah, how he pleads with God against Israel? "Lord, they have killed your prophets, they have demolished your altars; I alone am left, and they are seeking my life." But what is the divine reply to him? "I have kept for myself seven thousand who have not bowed the knee to Baal." So too at the present time there is a remnant, chosen by grace. (Rom. 11:1-5)

Psalm
Psalm 78:17-20, 52-55
Israel led to God's holy mountain

Additional Reading
1 Kings 19:9-18
Elijah hears God

Hymn: Through the Night of Doubt and Sorrow, ELW 327

God of all, you provide community for your people. In those times when we feel alone and scared, remind us of the support of your holy people. Help us to care for others when they feel lost and alone too.

Lent

Lent is a forty-day journey to Easter. Christians keep company with Noah and his family, who were in the ark for forty days; with the Hebrews, who journeyed through the desert for forty years; and with Moses, Elijah, and Jesus, who fasted for forty days before they embarked on the tasks God had prepared for them.

During Lent Christians journey with those who are making final preparations for baptism at Easter. Together, Christians struggle with the meaning of their baptismal promises: Do you reject evil? Do you believe in God the Father, the Son, and the Holy Spirit? Do you believe in the church, the forgiveness of sins, the resurrection of the dead?

The disciples of the Lord Jesus are called to contend against everything that leads them away from love of God and neighbor. Fasting, prayer, and works of love—the disciplines of Lent—help the household rejoice in the gifts of baptism: God's forgiveness and mercy.

Table Prayer for the Season of Lent

Blessed are you, O God, giver of all.
You adorn our tables with food
and give companionship for our journeys.
Be present with us as we are fed in body and spirit
that our sharing this meal is a sign of your life
broken and shared for the world.
In Jesus' name we pray.
Amen.

Wednesday, February 22, 2023
Ash Wednesday

Matthew 6:1-6, 16-21
The practice of faith

[Jesus said,] "Do not store up for yourselves treasures on earth, where moth and rust consume and where thieves break in and steal; but store up for yourselves treasures in heaven, where neither moth nor rust consumes and where thieves do not break in and steal. For where your treasure is, there your heart will be also." (Matt. 6:19-21)

Psalm
Psalm 51:1-17
Plea for mercy

Additional Readings
Joel 2:1-2, 12-17
Return to God

2 Corinthians 5:20b—6:10
Now is the day of salvation

Hymn: All Things of Dust to Dust Return, ACS 920

Gracious God, out of your love and mercy you breathed into dust the breath of life, creating us to serve you and our neighbors. Call forth our prayers and acts of kindness, and strengthen us to face our mortality with confidence in the mercy of your Son, Jesus Christ, our Savior and Lord, who lives and reigns with you and the Holy Spirit, one God, now and forever.

Thursday, February 23, 2023
Week before Lent 1

Polycarp, Bishop of Smyrna, martyr, died 156

Psalm 51
Create in me a clean heart

Have mercy on me, O God,
>according to your steadfast love;
according to your abundant mercy
>blot out my transgressions.
Wash me thoroughly from my iniquity,
>and cleanse me from my sin.

For I know my transgressions,
>and my sin is ever before me.
Against you, you alone, have I sinned,
>and done what is evil in your sight,
so that you are justified in your sentence
>and blameless when you pass judgment.
Indeed, I was born guilty,
>a sinner when my mother conceived me. (Ps. 51:1-5)

Additional Readings

Jonah 3:1-10
Nineveh hears Jonah's preaching and repents

Romans 1:1-7
Appointed to preach the good news of Christ

Hymn: Lord, Teach Us How to Pray Aright, ELW 745

God of forgiveness, you are our source of mercy and grace. Open us to see the danger of our sin and bring us to repentance. Guide us to be your people who share your mercy and grace with others.

Friday, February 24, 2023
Week before Lent 1

Jonah 4:1-11

God mercifully reproves Jonah

But [God's change of mind] was very displeasing to Jonah, and he became angry. He prayed to the LORD and said, "O LORD! Is not this what I said while I was still in my own country? That is why I fled to Tarshish at the beginning; for I knew that you are a gracious God and merciful, slow to anger, and abounding in steadfast love, and ready to relent from punishing. And now, O LORD, please take my life from me, for it is better for me to die than to live." And the LORD said, "Is it right for you to be angry?" Then Jonah went out of the city and sat down east of the city, and made a booth for himself there. He sat under it in the shade, waiting to see what would become of the city. (Jonah 4:1-5)

Psalm

Psalm 51
Create in me a clean heart

Additional Reading

Romans 1:8-17
Live by faith

Hymn: God, Whose Giving Knows No Ending, ELW 678

God of patience, your faithfulness is far beyond our imagination. Forgive us for those times when we think we know better than you. Humble us and use us to share your life-changing love with others.

Saturday, February 25, 2023
Week before Lent 1

Elizabeth Fedde, deaconess, died 1921

Isaiah 58:1-12

The fast that God chooses

Is not this the fast that I choose:
> to loose the bonds of injustice,
> to undo the thongs of the yoke,
to let the oppressed go free,
> and to break every yoke?
Is it not to share your bread with the hungry,
> and bring the homeless poor into your house;
when you see the naked, to cover them,
> and not to hide yourself from your own kin?
Then your light shall break forth like the dawn,
> and your healing shall spring up quickly;
your vindicator shall go before you,
> the glory of the LORD shall be your rear guard.
Then you shall call, and the LORD will answer;
> you shall cry for help, and he will say, Here I am. (Isa. 58:6-9a)

Psalm
Psalm 51
Create in me a clean heart

Additional Reading
Matthew 18:1-7
The humble one is the greatest

Hymn: Light Dawns on a Weary World, ELW 726

God of provision and plenty, you bless us and call us your own. Help us share the abundance of your love with people who are oppressed, hungry, homeless, and naked. Open our hearts and hands to the needs of others.

Sunday, February 26, 2023
First Sunday in Lent

Matthew 4:1-11

The temptation of Jesus

Then Jesus was led up by the Spirit into the wilderness to be tempted by the devil. He fasted forty days and forty nights, and afterwards he was famished. The tempter came and said to him, "If you are the Son of God, command these stones to become loaves of bread."
But he answered, "It is written,

'One does not live by bread alone,

but by every word that comes from the mouth of God.'"
(Matt. 4:1-4)

Psalm

Psalm 32
Mercy embraces us

Additional Readings

Genesis 2:15-17; 3:1-7
Eating of the tree of knowledge

Romans 5:12-19
Death came, life comes

Hymn: When We Are Tested, ACS 922

Lord God, our strength, the struggle between good and evil rages within and around us, and the devil and all the forces that defy you tempt us with empty promises. Keep us steadfast in your word, and when we fall, raise us again and restore us through your Son, Jesus Christ, our Savior and Lord, who lives and reigns with you and the Holy Spirit, one God, now and forever.

Monday, February 27, 2023
Week of Lent 1

Psalm 32
Mercy embraces us

Happy are those whose transgression is forgiven,
> whose sin is covered.
Happy are those to whom the LORD imputes no iniquity,
> and in whose spirit there is no deceit.

While I kept silence, my body wasted away
> through my groaning all day long.
For day and night your hand was heavy upon me;
> my strength was dried up as by the heat of summer.

Then I acknowledged my sin to you,
> and I did not hide my iniquity;
I said, "I will confess my transgressions to the LORD,"
> and you forgave the guilt of my sin. (Ps. 32:1-5)

Additional Readings

1 Kings 19:1-8
An angel feeds Elijah in the wilderness

Hebrews 2:10-18
Christ goes before us in suffering

Hymn: God, My Lord, My Strength, ELW 795

God of all, you know us even better than we know ourselves and yet you still stay with us. Forgive us for our sins, both known and unknown. Help us find happiness and joy in you again.

Tuesday, February 28, 2023
Week of Lent 1

Hebrews 4:14—5:10
Christ was tempted as we are

Since, then, we have a great high priest who has passed through the heavens, Jesus, the Son of God, let us hold fast to our confession. For we do not have a high priest who is unable to sympathize with our weaknesses, but we have one who in every respect has been tested as we are, yet without sin. Let us therefore approach the throne of grace with boldness, so that we may receive mercy and find grace to help in time of need. (Heb. 4:14-16)

Psalm
Psalm 32
Mercy embraces us

Additional Reading
Genesis 4:1-16
God protects Cain

Hymn: Lord Jesus, Think on Me, ELW 599

God of mercy and grace, you came to us in the person of Jesus and shared in our humanity. You know our brokenness and our temptations. Forgive us when we sin, encourage us to listen, and strengthen us to follow.

Prayer List for March

_____

_____

_____

_____

_____

_____

_____

_____

_____

_____

Wednesday, March 1, 2023
Week of Lent 1

George Herbert, hymnwriter, died 1633

Matthew 18:10-14

Not one of these little ones should be lost

[Jesus said,] "Take care that you do not despise one of these little ones; for, I tell you, in heaven their angels continually see the face of my Father in heaven. What do you think? If a shepherd has a hundred sheep, and one of them has gone astray, does he not leave the ninety-nine on the mountains and go in search of the one that went astray? And if he finds it, truly I tell you, he rejoices over it more than over the ninety-nine that never went astray. So it is not the will of your Father in heaven that one of these little ones should be lost." (Matt. 18:10-14)

Psalm

Psalm 32
Mercy embraces us

Additional Reading

Exodus 34:1-9, 27-28
God's revelation of mercy

Hymn: Have No Fear, Little Flock, ELW 764

God of every detail, you attend to your creation with an artist's eye, a parent's heart, and a worker's faithful stewardship. May we be as tender to ourselves and one another as we wander on uncharted paths.

Thursday, March 2, 2023
Week of Lent 1

John Wesley, died 1791; Charles Wesley, died 1788; renewers of the church

Psalm 121
The Lord watches over you

The LORD is your keeper;
>   the LORD is your shade at your right hand.
The sun shall not strike you by day,
>   nor the moon by night.

The LORD will keep you from all evil;
>   he will keep your life.
The LORD will keep
>   your going out and your coming in
>   from this time on and forevermore. (Ps. 121:5-8)

Additional Readings

Isaiah 51:1-3
Look to Abraham and Sarah

2 Timothy 1:3-7
Faith handed down from faithful mothers

Hymn: Sing Praise to God, the Highest Good, ELW 871

God, all your creation continues to be surrounded by your daily care. Help us to be mindful of your presence so that we can be less fearful and more grateful from the rising to the setting of the sun.

Friday, March 3, 2023
Week of Lent 1

Micah 7:18-20
God's faithfulness

Who is a God like you, pardoning iniquity
    and passing over the transgression
    of the remnant of your possession?
He does not retain his anger forever,
    because he delights in showing clemency.
He will again have compassion upon us;
    he will tread our iniquities under foot.
You will cast all our sins
    into the depths of the sea.
You will show faithfulness to Jacob
    and unswerving loyalty to Abraham,
as you have sworn to our ancestors
    from the days of old. (Micah 7:18-20)

Psalm
Psalm 121
The Lord watches over you

Additional Reading
Romans 3:21-31
Paul relates law and faith

Hymn: Abide, O Dearest Jesus, ELW 539

God, keeper of promises, your faithfulness through human frailty is carved in our ancestors' names. Forgive our failures and grant us a measure of your resilience to weather our doubts, that we may lean toward you.

Saturday, March 4, 2023
Week of Lent 1

Isaiah 51:4-8

God's word means justice for all

Listen to me, my people,
    and give heed to me, my nation;
for a teaching will go out from me,
    and my justice for a light to the peoples.
I will bring near my deliverance swiftly,
    my salvation has gone out
    and my arms will rule the peoples;
the coastlands wait for me,
    and for my arm they hope.
Lift up your eyes to the heavens,
    and look at the earth beneath;
for the heavens will vanish like smoke,
    the earth will wear out like a garment,
    and those who live on it will die like gnats;
but my salvation will be forever,
    and my deliverance will never be ended. (Isa. 51:4-6)

Psalm

Psalm 121
The Lord watches over you

Additional Reading

Luke 7:1-10
Room at the table of Abraham

Hymn: O God of Light, ELW 507

God of salvation, when the nations fail and the earth trembles, people look for hope. Your voice always sounds the truth. Through the din of injustice and the disintegration of our arrogance, help us to hear and know your deliverance.

Sunday, March 5, 2023
Second Sunday in Lent

John 3:1-17
The mission of Christ: saving the world

[Jesus answered Nicodemus:] "And just as Moses lifted up the serpent in the wilderness, so must the Son of Man be lifted up, that whoever believes in him may have eternal life.

"For God so loved the world that he gave his only Son, so that everyone who believes in him may not perish but may have eternal life.

"Indeed, God did not send the Son into the world to condemn the world, but in order that the world might be saved through him." (John 3:14-17)

Psalm
Psalm 121
The Lord watches over you

Additional Readings
Genesis 12:1-4a
The blessing of God upon Abram

Romans 4:1-5, 13-17
The promise to those of Abraham's faith

Hymn: God Loved the World, ELW 323

O God, our leader and guide, in the waters of baptism you bring us to new birth to live as your children. Strengthen our faith in your promises, that by your Spirit we may lift up your life to all the world through your Son, Jesus Christ, our Savior and Lord, who lives and reigns with you and the Holy Spirit, one God, now and forever.

Monday, March 6, 2023
Week of Lent 2

Psalm 128
God promises life

Happy is everyone who fears the LORD,
　　who walks in his ways.
You shall eat the fruit of the labor of your hands;
　　you shall be happy, and it shall go well with you.

Your wife will be like a fruitful vine
　　within your house;
your children will be like olive shoots
　　around your table.
Thus shall the man be blessed
　　who fears the LORD. (Ps. 128:1-4)

Additional Readings
Numbers 21:4-9
Moses lifts up the serpent

Hebrews 3:1-6
Moses the servant, Christ the son

Hymn: What a Fellowship, What a Joy Divine, ELW 774

Blessed God, in the labor of our daily chores you have given us the seeds for what is needful. May we sow with reverence and humility, that row by row we will encounter the bounty of your gracious hands.

Tuesday, March 7, 2023
Week of Lent 2

Perpetua and Felicity and companions, martyrs at Carthage, died 202

Isaiah 65:17-25

God promises a new creation

For I am about to create new heavens
    and a new earth;
the former things shall not be remembered
    or come to mind.
But be glad and rejoice forever
    in what I am creating;
for I am about to create Jerusalem as a joy,
    and its people as a delight.
I will rejoice in Jerusalem,
    and delight in my people;
no more shall the sound of weeping be heard in it,
    or the cry of distress. (Isa. 65:17-19)

Psalm
Psalm 128
God promises life

Additional Reading
Romans 4:6-13
Abraham saved through faith

Hymn: Jerusalem, My Happy Home, ELW 628

Creator God, you were not content to give up your creative work. As we mourn the past, you create new delights in the present. Spark our imaginations so we can join you in the joy of a new day.

Wednesday, March 8, 2023
Week of Lent 2

John 7:53—8:11
Jesus does not condemn the sinner

The scribes and the Pharisees brought a woman who had been caught in adultery; and making her stand before all of them, they said to Jesus, "Teacher, this woman was caught in the very act of committing adultery. Now in the law Moses commanded us to stone such women. Now what do you say?" They said this to test him, so that they might have some charge to bring against him. Jesus bent down and wrote with his finger on the ground. When they kept on questioning him, he straightened up and said to them, "Let anyone among you who is without sin be the first to throw a stone at her." (John 8:3-7)

Psalm
Psalm 128
God promises life

Additional Reading
Ezekiel 36:22-32
God will renew the people

Hymn: Softly and Tenderly Jesus Is Calling, ELW 608

God, you are the judge of all. We are stones and stone throwers. To all of us, your hefty work of mercy outweighs the hardness of our hearts. May we learn the wisdom of your ways.

Thursday, March 9, 2023
Week of Lent 2

Psalm 95
The rock of our salvation

O come, let us sing to the LORD;
>   let us make a joyful noise to the rock of our salvation!
Let us come into his presence with thanksgiving;
>   let us make a joyful noise to him with songs of praise!
For the LORD is a great God,
>   and a great King above all gods.
In his hand are the depths of the earth;
>   the heights of the mountains are his also.
The sea is his, for he made it,
>   and the dry land, which his hands have formed. (Ps. 95:1-5)

Additional Readings
Exodus 16:1-8
Israel complains of hunger in the wilderness

Colossians 1:15-23
Christ, the reconciliation of all things

Hymn: Let All Things Now Living, ELW 881

Great God, you are the height, depth, width, and strength of the sky and the earth. You wrap us in sunlight and ground us in the potential of the soil. Open our hearts to the wonder of your care.

Friday, March 10, 2023
Week of Lent 2

Harriet Tubman, died 1913; Sojourner Truth, died 1883; renewers of society

Ephesians 2:11-22
Christ, the reconciliation of Jew and Gentile

So then, remember that at one time you Gentiles by birth, called "the uncircumcision" by those who are called "the circumcision"—a physical circumcision made in the flesh by human hands—remember that you were at that time without Christ, being aliens from the commonwealth of Israel, and strangers to the covenants of promise, having no hope and without God in the world. But now in Christ Jesus you who once were far off have been brought near by the blood of Christ. For he is our peace; in his flesh he has made both groups into one and has broken down the dividing wall, that is, the hostility between us. (Eph. 2:11-14)

Psalm
Psalm 95
The rock of our salvation

Additional Reading
Exodus 16:9-21
God gives manna and quail

Hymn: Commonwealth Is God's Commandment, ACS 1036

Holy One, you offer wholeness that we have broken by our divisiveness. You offer us healing daily through your power. May our righteousness be born in the Risen One whose purpose is to make all one with you.

Saturday, March 11, 2023
Week of Lent 2

Exodus 16:27-35
Manna and the sabbath

On the seventh day some of the people went out to gather [manna], and they found none. The LORD said to Moses, "How long will you refuse to keep my commandments and instructions? See! The LORD has given you the sabbath, therefore on the sixth day he gives you food for two days; each of you stay where you are; do not leave your place on the seventh day." So the people rested on the seventh day. (Exod. 16:27-30)

Psalm
Psalm 95
The rock of our salvation

Additional Reading
John 4:1-6
Jesus travels to Jacob's well in Samaria

Hymn: O Day of Rest and Gladness, ELW 521

Compassionate God, by the bounty of your creation you have sustained us with food to eat. Through the wisdom of your heart you have provided us with time to rest. Help us to be careful stewards of your generosity.

Sunday, March 12, 2023
Third Sunday in Lent

Gregory the Great, Bishop of Rome, died 604

John 4:5-42

The woman at the well

Jesus said to [the Samaritan woman], "Everyone who drinks of this water will be thirsty again, but those who drink of the water that I will give them will never be thirsty. The water that I will give will become in them a spring of water gushing up to eternal life." The woman said to him, "Sir, give me this water, so that I may never be thirsty or have to keep coming here to draw water." (John 4:13-15)

Psalm

Psalm 95
The rock of our salvation

Additional Readings

Exodus 17:1-7
Water from the rock

Romans 5:1-11
Reconciled to God by Christ's death

Hymn: Come to Me, All Pilgrims Thirsty, ELW 777

Merciful God, the fountain of living water, you quench our thirst and wash away our sin. Give us this water always. Bring us to drink from the well that flows with the beauty of your truth through Jesus Christ, our Savior and Lord, who lives and reigns with you and the Holy Spirit, one God, now and forever.

Monday, March 13, 2023
Week of Lent 3

Psalm 81
We drink from the rock

"But my people did not listen to my voice;
    Israel would not submit to me.
So I gave them over to their stubborn hearts,
    to follow their own counsels.
O that my people would listen to me,
    that Israel would walk in my ways!
Then I would quickly subdue their enemies,
    and turn my hand against their foes.
Those who hate the LORD would cringe before him,
    and their doom would last forever.
I would feed you with the finest of the wheat,
    and with honey from the rock I would satisfy you." (Ps. 81:11-16)

Additional Readings
Genesis 24:1-27
Rebekah at the well

2 John 1-13
A woman reminded to abide in Christ

Hymn: You Satisfy the Hungry Heart, ELW 484

Holy God, relentlessly you call to your beloveds who stubbornly turn up the volume of other voices. Your voice outlasts the din. When the empty echoes end, we hear your love again. May we listen to you more deeply.

Tuesday, March 14, 2023
Week of Lent 3

1 Corinthians 10:1-4

Drinking from Christ, the spiritual rock

I do not want you to be unaware, brothers and sisters, that our ancestors were all under the cloud, and all passed through the sea, and all were baptized into Moses in the cloud and in the sea, and all ate the same spiritual food, and all drank the same spiritual drink. For they drank from the spiritual rock that followed them, and the rock was Christ. (1 Cor. 10:1-4)

Psalm
Psalm 81
We drink from the rock

Additional Reading
Genesis 29:1-14
Rachel at the well

Hymn: O Jesus, Joy of Loving Hearts, ELW 658

Spirit of life, you surrounded your creation with the breath of life. Out of water we are born and renewed each day. Grow our trust in your presence yesterday, today, and forever.

Wednesday, March 15, 2023
Week of Lent 3

John 7:14-31, 37-39
Drink of Jesus, the Messiah

On the last day of the festival, the great day, while Jesus was standing at the temple, he cried out, "Let anyone who is thirsty come to me, and let the one who believes in me drink. As the scripture has said, 'Out of the believer's heart shall flow rivers of living water.'" Now he said this about the Spirit, which believers in him were to receive; for as yet there was no Spirit, because Jesus was not yet glorified. (John 7:37-39)

Psalm
Psalm 81
We drink from the rock

Additional Reading
Jeremiah 2:4-13
God, the living water

Hymn: Shall We Gather at the River, ELW 423

God, from your generative word came water that sustains our daily life. From the depths of your heart, the living waters spring and sustain our faith. When we are thirsty for hope, we come to the well of your spirit.

Thursday, March 16, 2023
Week of Lent 3

Psalm 23
My head anointed with oil

Even though I walk through the darkest valley,
> I fear no evil;
for you are with me;
> your rod and your staff—
> they comfort me.

You prepare a table before me
> in the presence of my enemies;
you anoint my head with oil;
> my cup overflows.
Surely goodness and mercy shall follow me
> all the days of my life,
and I shall dwell in the house of the LORD
> my whole life long. (Ps. 23:4-6)

Additional Readings
1 Samuel 15:10-21
The prophet Samuel confronts the king

Ephesians 4:25-32
Called to honesty and forbearance

Hymn: My Shepherd, You Supply My Need, ELW 782

Lord of the valley, you choose to walk with us through the shadows. Lord of the table, you welcome us all into your presence. Lord of our lives, you call us every day to find goodness with you always.

Friday, March 17, 2023
Week of Lent 3

Patrick, bishop, missionary to Ireland, died 461

Ephesians 5:1-9
Now in the Lord you are light

Let no one deceive you with empty words, for because of these things the wrath of God comes on those who are disobedient. Therefore do not be associated with them. For once you were darkness, but now in the Lord you are light. Live as children of light—for the fruit of the light is found in all that is good and right and true. (Eph. 5:6-9)

Psalm
Psalm 23
My head anointed with oil

Additional Reading
1 Samuel 15:22-31
The king confesses his sinful disobedience

Hymn: I Want to Walk as a Child of the Light, ELW 815

God of light, you gave us the ability to seek out the truth and to be wary of what is false. When we are confused by empty voices, help us to discern your will clearly and to shine with courage.

Saturday, March 18, 2023
Week of Lent 3

1 Samuel 15:32-34
Samuel grieves over Saul

Then Samuel said, "Bring Agag king of the Amalekites here to me." And Agag came to him haltingly. Agag said, "Surely this is the bitterness of death." But Samuel said,

"As your sword has made women childless,
     so your mother shall be childless among women."
And Samuel hewed Agag in pieces before the LORD in Gilgal.

Then Samuel went to Ramah; and Saul went up to his house in Gibeah of Saul. (1 Sam. 15:32-34)

Psalm
Psalm 23   **John 1:1-9**
My head anointed with oil   *Christ comes with light and life*

Hymn: In All Our Grief, ELW 615

God, you are acquainted with sorrow and grief, beginnings and endings. Relationships shatter with fear, anger, despair, and death. Inside the sorrow, we draw close to you and to your eternal desire for love that learns and lasts.

Sunday, March 19, 2023
Fourth Sunday in Lent

Joseph, Guardian of Jesus transferred to March 20

John 9:1-41
The man born blind

Jesus heard that [the Pharisees] had driven [out the man who had been blind], and when he found him, he said, "Do you believe in the Son of Man?" He answered, "And who is he, sir? Tell me, so that I may believe in him." Jesus said to him, "You have seen him, and the one speaking with you is he." He said, "Lord, I believe." And he worshiped him. Jesus said, "I came into this world for judgment so that those who do not see may see, and those who do see may become blind." (John 9:35-39)

Psalm
Psalm 23
My head anointed with oil

Additional Readings
1 Samuel 16:1-13
David is chosen and anointed

Ephesians 5:8-14
Live as children of light

Hymn: O Christ, Our Light, O Radiance True, ELW 675

Bend your ear to our prayers, Lord Christ, and come among us. By your gracious life and death for us, bring light into the darkness of our hearts, and anoint us with your Spirit, for you live and reign with the Father and the Holy Spirit, one God, now and forever.

Monday, March 20, 2023
Joseph, Guardian of Jesus (transferred)

Matthew 1:16, 18-21, 24a
The Lord appears to Joseph in a dream

Now the birth of Jesus the Messiah took place in this way. When his mother Mary had been engaged to Joseph, but before they lived together, she was found to be with child from the Holy Spirit. Her husband Joseph, being a righteous man and unwilling to expose her to public disgrace, planned to dismiss her quietly. But just when he had resolved to do this, an angel of the Lord appeared to him in a dream and said, "Joseph, son of David, do not be afraid to take Mary as your wife, for the child conceived in her is from the Holy Spirit. She will bear a son, and you are to name him Jesus, for he will save his people from their sins." (Matt. 1:18-21)

Psalm
Psalm 89:1-29
The Lord's steadfast love is established forever

Additional Readings
2 Samuel 7:4, 8-16
God makes a covenant with David

Romans 4:13-18
The promise to those who share Abraham's faith

Hymn: By All Your Saints, ELW 420, st. 9

O God, from the family of your servant David you raised up Joseph to be the guardian of your incarnate Son and the husband of his blessed mother. Give us grace to imitate his uprightness of life and his obedience to your commands, through Jesus Christ, our Savior and Lord, who lives and reigns with you and the Holy Spirit, one God, now and forever.

Tuesday, March 21, 2023
Week of Lent 4

Thomas Cranmer, Bishop of Canterbury, martyr, died 1556

Isaiah 42:14-21
God will heal the blind

For a long time I have held my peace,
    I have kept still and restrained myself;
now I will cry out like a woman in labor,
    I will gasp and pant.
I will lay waste mountains and hills,
    and dry up all their herbage;
I will turn the rivers into islands,
    and dry up the pools.
I will lead the blind
    by a road they do not know,
by paths they have not known
    I will guide them.
I will turn the darkness before them into light,
    the rough places into level ground.
These are the things I will do,
    and I will not forsake them. (Isa. 42:14-16)

Psalm
Psalm 146
God opens the eyes of the blind

Additional Reading
Colossians 1:9-14
The inheritance of the saints in light

Hymn: In Deepest Night, ELW 699

God, at the right time you push through your pain to give birth to a new vision of what it means to be your people. Grant that we might open our eyes to see what we have overlooked and underseen.

Wednesday, March 22, 2023
Week of Lent 4

Jonathan Edwards, teacher, missionary to American Indians, died 1758

Matthew 9:27-34
Jesus heals the blind

As Jesus went on from [the house of a leader of the synagogue], two blind men followed him, crying loudly, "Have mercy on us, Son of David!" When he entered the house, the blind men came to him; and Jesus said to them, "Do you believe that I am able to do this?" They said to him, "Yes, Lord." Then he touched their eyes and said, "According to your faith let it be done to you." And their eyes were opened. Then Jesus sternly ordered them, "See that no one knows of this." But they went away and spread the news about him throughout that district. (Matt. 9:27-31)

Psalm
Psalm 146
God opens the eyes of the blind

Additional Reading
Isaiah 60:17-22
God our light

Hymn: Amazing Grace, How Sweet the Sound, ELW 779

Holy God, you are drawn to those in need of wholeness and relief from suffering. Help us to understand your compassion. May we be bold in our self-awareness to acknowledge our vulnerabilities and to enter your comforting presence.

Thursday, March 23, 2023
Week of Lent 4

Psalm 130
Mercy and redemption

Out of the depths I cry to you, O LORD.
>   Lord, hear my voice!
Let your ears be attentive
>   to the voice of my supplications!

If you, O LORD, should mark iniquities,
>   Lord, who could stand?
But there is forgiveness with you,
>   so that you may be revered. (Ps. 130:1-4)

Additional Readings
Ezekiel 1:1-3; 2:8—3:3
The word of God: lamentation and sweetness

Revelation 10:1-11
The word of God: bitter and sweet

Hymn: Out of the Depths I Cry to You, ELW 600

God, you choose not to keep a record of human foolishness and cruelty and stand at the ready to hear an honest cry for help. Embrace us, that we might grow in offering others the healing hand of grace.

Friday, March 24, 2023
Week of Lent 4

Oscar Arnulfo Romero, Bishop of El Salvador, martyr, died 1980

Revelation 11:15-19

The word of God: thanksgiving and singing

Then the twenty-four elders who sit on their thrones before God fell on their faces and worshiped God, singing,

"We give you thanks, Lord God Almighty,
>who are and who were,
for you have taken your great power
>and begun to reign.
The nations raged,
>but your wrath has come,
>and the time for judging the dead,
for rewarding your servants, the prophets
>and saints and all who fear your name,
>both small and great,
and for destroying those who destroy the earth."
Then God's temple in heaven was opened, and the ark of his covenant was seen within his temple; and there were flashes of lightning, rumblings, peals of thunder, an earthquake, and heavy hail. (Rev. 11:16-19)

Psalm
Psalm 130
Mercy and redemption

Additional Reading
Ezekiel 33:10-16
The word of God: repent and live

Hymn: Blessing and Honor, ELW 854

Almighty God, you have used your creativity and power for the good of all. The sound of our gratitude rising together is the greatest worship we can offer to you. Thanksgiving is the best way to respond to your love.

Saturday, March 25, 2023
Annunciation of Our Lord

Luke 1:26-38

The angel greets Mary

In the sixth month the angel Gabriel was sent by God to a town in Galilee called Nazareth, to a virgin engaged to a man whose name was Joseph, of the house of David. The virgin's name was Mary. And he came to her and said, "Greetings, favored one! The Lord is with you." But she was much perplexed by his words and pondered what sort of greeting this might be. The angel said to her, "Do not be afraid, Mary, for you have found favor with God. And now, you will conceive in your womb and bear a son, and you will name him Jesus." (Luke 1:26-31)

Psalm

Psalm 45
Your name will be remembered

Additional Readings

Isaiah 7:10-14
A young woman will bear a son

Hebrews 10:4-10
The offering of Jesus' body sanctifies us

Hymn: The Only Son from Heaven, ELW 309

Pour your grace into our hearts, O God, that we who have known the incarnation of your Son, Jesus Christ, announced by an angel, may by his cross and passion be brought to the glory of his resurrection; for he lives and reigns with you, in the unity of the Holy Spirit, one God, now and forever.

Sunday, March 26, 2023
Fifth Sunday in Lent

John 11:1-45
The raising of Lazarus

And Jesus looked upward and said, "Father, I thank you for having heard me. I knew that you always hear me, but I have said this for the sake of the crowd standing here, so that they may believe that you sent me." When he had said this, he cried with a loud voice, "Lazarus, come out!" The dead man came out, his hands and feet bound with strips of cloth, and his face wrapped in a cloth. Jesus said to them, "Unbind him, and let him go."

Many of the Jews therefore, who had come with Mary and had seen what Jesus did, believed in him. (John 11:41b-45)

Psalm

Psalm 130
Mercy and redemption

Additional Readings

Ezekiel 37:1-14
The dry bones of Israel

Romans 8:6-11
Life in the Spirit

Hymn: When We Are Living, ELW 639

Almighty God, your Son came into the world to free us all from sin and death. Breathe upon us the power of your Spirit, that we may be raised to new life in Christ and serve you in righteousness all our days, through Jesus Christ, our Savior and Lord, who lives and reigns with you and the Holy Spirit, one God, now and forever.

Monday, March 27, 2023
Week of Lent 5

Psalm 143
Save me from death

Save me, O LORD, from my enemies;
>   I have fled to you for refuge.
Teach me to do your will,
>   for you are my God.
Let your good spirit lead me
>   on a level path.

For your name's sake, O LORD, preserve my life.
>   In your righteousness bring me out of trouble.
In your steadfast love cut off my enemies,
>   and destroy all my adversaries,
>   for I am your servant. (Ps. 143:9-12)

Additional Readings
1 Kings 17:17-24
Elijah raises the widow's son

Acts 20:7-12
Paul raises a young man

Hymn: Lord of Our Life, ELW 766

Steadfast God, when your people are frightened, we fight and flee. You open your heart for our protection, that we may rest in you. Give us the peace of your presence in an anxious time.

Tuesday, March 28, 2023
Week of Lent 5

2 Kings 4:18-37
Elisha raises a child from death

When Elisha came into the house, he saw the child lying dead on his bed. So he went in and closed the door on the two of them, and prayed to the LORD. Then he got up on the bed and lay upon the child, putting his mouth upon his mouth, his eyes upon his eyes, and his hands upon his hands; and while he lay bent over him, the flesh of the child became warm. He got down, walked once to and fro in the room, then got up again and bent over him; the child sneezed seven times, and the child opened his eyes. Elisha summoned Gehazi and said, "Call the Shunammite woman." So he called her. When she came to him, he said, "Take your son." She came and fell at his feet, bowing to the ground; then she took her son and left. (2 Kings 4:32-37)

Psalm
Psalm 143
Save me from death

Additional Reading
Ephesians 2:1-10
Alive in Christ

Hymn: O Christ, the Healer, We Have Come, ELW 610

Living God, in your presence death has no dominion. We struggle with our grief and our powerlessness against suffering and death. Teach us to embrace the joys and sorrows of our lives with faith in your never-ending love.

Wednesday, March 29, 2023
Week of Lent 5

Hans Nielsen Hauge, renewer of the church, died 1824

Jeremiah 32:1-9, 36-41
Jeremiah buys a field

Jeremiah said, The word of the LORD came to me: Hanamel son of your uncle Shallum is going to come to you and say, "Buy my field that is at Anathoth, for the right of redemption by purchase is yours." Then my cousin Hanamel came to me in the court of the guard, in accordance with the word of the LORD, and said to me, "Buy my field that is at Anathoth in the land of Benjamin, for the right of possession and redemption is yours; buy it for yourself." Then I knew that this was the word of the LORD. (Jer. 32:6-8)

Psalm
Psalm 143
Save me from death

Additional Reading
Matthew 22:23-33
God of the living

Hymn: Jesus, Priceless Treasure, ELW 775

Holy God, through the witness of ancient ones we have heard the trustworthiness of your word. The intention of your heart is to nurture and protect your people. Help us look to you always for guidance and trust in your wisdom.

Thursday, March 30, 2023
Week of Lent 5

Psalm 31:9-16
I commend my spirit

Be gracious to me, O LORD, for I am in distress;
    my eye wastes away from grief,
    my soul and body also.
For my life is spent with sorrow,
    and my years with sighing;
my strength fails because of my misery,
    and my bones waste away. . . .

But I trust in you, O LORD;
    I say, "You are my God."
My times are in your hand;
    deliver me from the hand of my enemies and persecutors.
Let your face shine upon your servant;
    save me in your steadfast love. (Ps. 31:9-10, 14-16)

Additional Readings

1 Samuel 16:11-13
Samuel anoints David

Philippians 1:1-11
Encouraged to follow Christ's righteousness

Hymn: Jesus, Still Lead On, ELW 624

Tender God, you protect your creation with the fierceness of a parent's love. When nothing seems to stand between your people and grave harm, you are present with compassion and strength. In our weariness, help us to lean on you.

Friday, March 31, 2023
Week of Lent 5

John Donne, poet, died 1631

Philippians 1:21-30
Seeing Christ in this life

Only, live your life in a manner worthy of the gospel of Christ, so that, whether I come and see you or am absent and hear about you, I will know that you are standing firm in one spirit, striving side by side with one mind for the faith of the gospel, and are in no way intimidated by your opponents. For them this is evidence of their destruction, but of your salvation. And this is God's doing. For he has graciously granted you the privilege not only of believing in Christ, but of suffering for him as well—since you are having the same struggle that you saw I had and now hear that I still have. (Phil. 1:27-30)

Psalm
Psalm 31:9-16
I commend my spirit

Additional Reading
Job 13:13-19
A servant keeps silence

Hymn: Give Thanks for Saints, ELW 428

God, you are the living power of grace. You call us to join the good fights for justice and peace. Give us the wisdom to choose our battles wisely and strengthen us with the witness of all the saints.

Prayer List for April

_____

_____

_____

_____

_____

_____

_____

_____

_____

Saturday, April 1, 2023
Week of Lent 5

Mark 10:32-34
Going up to Jerusalem

[Jesus' disciples] were on the road, going up to Jerusalem, and Jesus was walking ahead of them; they were amazed, and those who followed were afraid. He took the twelve aside again and began to tell them what was to happen to him, saying, "See, we are going up to Jerusalem, and the Son of Man will be handed over to the chief priests and the scribes, and they will condemn him to death; then they will hand him over to the Gentiles; they will mock him, and spit upon him, and flog him, and kill him; and after three days he will rise again." (Mark 10:32-34)

Psalm
Psalm 31:9-16
I commend my spirit

Additional Reading
Lamentations 3:55-66
A cry for help

Hymn: Tree of Life and Awesome Mystery, ELW 334

God beyond our fears, you send Jesus ahead of us. We follow but are afraid. Find us in our fear. Turn us aside to you. Tell us again of your passionate will to save this world and of your resurrection promises.

Holy Week

On the Sunday of the Passion, Christians enter into Holy Week. This day opens before the Christian community the final period of preparation before the celebration of the Three Days of the Lord's passion, death, and resurrection.

In many churches, palm branches will be given to worshipers for the procession into the worship space. Following an ancient custom, many Christians bring their palms home and place them in the household prayer center, behind a cross or sacred image, or above the indoor lintel of the entryway.

At sunset on Maundy Thursday, Lent comes to an end as the church begins the celebration of the events through which Christ has become the life and the resurrection for all who believe.

Prayer for Placing Palms in the Home

Use this blessing when placing palms in the home after the Palm Sunday liturgy.

Blessed is the One who comes in the name of the Lord!
May we who place these palms receive Christ into our midst
with the joy that marked the entrance to Jerusalem.
May we hold no betrayal in our hearts,
but peacefully welcome Christ
who lives and reigns with you and the Holy Spirit,
one God, now and forever. Amen.

Sunday, April 2, 2023
Sunday of the Passion / Psalm Sunday

Matthew 26:14—27:66
The passion and death of Jesus

Then Jesus cried again with a loud voice and breathed his last. At that moment the curtain of the temple was torn in two, from top to bottom. The earth shook, and the rocks were split. The tombs also were opened, and many bodies of the saints who had fallen asleep were raised. After his resurrection they came out of the tombs and entered the holy city and appeared to many. Now when the centurion and those with him, who were keeping watch over Jesus, saw the earthquake and what took place, they were terrified and said, "Truly this man was God's Son!" (Matt. 27:50-54)

Psalm
Psalm 31:9-16
I commend my spirit

Additional Readings
Isaiah 50:4-9a
The servant submits to suffering

Philippians 2:5-11
Death on a cross

Hymn: Pave the Way with Branches, ACS 928

Sovereign God, you have established your rule in the human heart through the servanthood of Jesus Christ. By your Spirit, keep us in the joyful procession of those who with their tongues confess Jesus as Lord and with their lives praise him as Savior, who lives and reigns with you and the Holy Spirit, one God, now and forever.

Monday, April 3, 2023
Monday in Holy Week

Psalm 36:5-11
Refuge under the shadow of your wings

Your steadfast love, O LORD, extends to the heavens,
    your faithfulness to the clouds.
Your righteousness is like the mighty mountains,
    your judgments are like the great deep;
    you save humans and animals alike, O LORD.

How precious is your steadfast love, O God!
    All people may take refuge in the shadow of your wings.
They feast on the abundance of your house,
    and you give them drink from the river of your delights.
For with you is the fountain of life;
    in your light we see light. (Ps. 36:5-9)

Additional Readings

Isaiah 42:1-9
The servant brings forth justice

Hebrews 9:11-15
The blood of Christ redeems for eternal life

John 12:1-11
Mary of Bethany anoints Jesus

Hymn: My Song Is Love Unknown, ELW 343

O God, your Son chose the path that led to pain before joy and the cross before glory. Plant his cross in our hearts, so that in its power and love we may come at last to joy and glory, through Jesus Christ, our Savior and Lord, who lives and reigns with you and the Holy Spirit, one God, now and forever.

Tuesday, April 4, 2023
Tuesday in Holy Week

Benedict the African, confessor, died 1589

1 Corinthians 1:18-31

The cross of Christ reveals God's power and wisdom

Where is the one who is wise? Where is the scribe? Where is the debater of this age? Has not God made foolish the wisdom of the world? For since, in the wisdom of God, the world did not know God through wisdom, God decided, through the foolishness of our proclamation, to save those who believe. For Jews demand signs and Greeks desire wisdom, but we proclaim Christ crucified, a stumbling block to Jews and foolishness to Gentiles, but to those who are the called, both Jews and Greeks, Christ the power of God and the wisdom of God. For God's foolishness is wiser than human wisdom, and God's weakness is stronger than human strength. (1 Cor. 1:20-25)

Psalm

Psalm 71:1-14
From my mother's womb you have been my strength

Additional Readings

Isaiah 49:1-7
The servant brings salvation to earth's ends

John 12:20-36
Jesus speaks of his death

Hymn: Jesus, Keep Me Near the Cross, ELW 335

Lord Jesus, you have called us to follow you. Grant that our love may not grow cold in your service, and that we may not fail or deny you in the time of trial, for you live and reign with the Father and the Holy Spirit, one God, now and forever.

Wednesday, April 5, 2023
Wednesday in Holy Week

Isaiah 50:4-9a
The servant is vindicated by God

The Lord GOD has opened my ear,
 and I was not rebellious,
 I did not turn backward.
I gave my back to those who struck me,
 and my cheeks to those who pulled out the beard;
I did not hide my face
 from insult and spitting.

The Lord GOD helps me;
 therefore I have not been disgraced;
therefore I have set my face like flint,
 and I know that I shall not be put to shame;
 he who vindicates me is near. . . .
It is the Lord GOD who helps me;
 who will declare me guilty? (Isa. 50:5-8a, 9a)

Psalm

Psalm 70
Be pleased, O God, to deliver me

Additional Readings

Hebrews 12:1-3
Look to Jesus, who endured the cross

John 13:21-32
Jesus foretells his betrayal

Hymn: Ah, Holy Jesus, ELW 349

Almighty God, your Son our Savior suffered at human hands and endured the shame of the cross. Grant that we may walk in the way of his cross and find it the way of life and peace, through Jesus Christ, our Savior and Lord, who lives and reigns with you and the Holy Spirit, one God, now and forever.

The Three Days

As the sun sets on Maundy Thursday, so Lent ends and the Three Days begin, ending with sunset on Easter Day. During these central days, Christians prepare to celebrate God's gift of new life given in baptism. Indeed, the readings of the Three Days move toward the baptismal font where new brothers and sisters are born of water and the Spirit, and where the baptized renew their baptismal promises.

In the home and in the church community, special attention is given to these days through prayer and keeping greater silence until the great Vigil of Easter is celebrated. Many Christians keep a fast from food, work, and entertainment on Good Friday and Holy Saturday. In the home, preparations can be made for the celebration of Easter: cleaning, coloring eggs, baking Easter breads, gathering greens or flowers to adorn crosses and sacred images. In those communities where baptisms will be celebrated, prayers may be offered for those to be received into the church.

Table Prayer for the Three Days

Blessed are you, O Lord our God.
With this food strengthen us on our journey from death to life.
We glory in the cross of Christ.
Raise us, with him, to the joy of the resurrection,
through Jesus Christ our Lord. Amen.

Thursday, April 6, 2023
Maundy Thursday

Albrecht Dürer, died 1528; Matthias Grünewald, died 1529; Lucas Cranach, died 1553; artists

John 13:1-17, 31b-35
The service of Christ: footwashing and meal

After [Jesus] had washed [the disciples'] feet, had put on his robe, and had returned to the table, he said to them, "Do you know what I have done to you? You call me Teacher and Lord—and you are right, for that is what I am. So if I, your Lord and Teacher, have washed your feet, you also ought to wash one another's feet. For I have set you an example, that you also should do as I have done to you." (John 13:12-15)

Psalm
Psalm 116:1-2, 12-19
The cup of salvation

Additional Readings
Exodus 12:1-4 [5-10] 11-14
The passover of the LORD

1 Corinthians 11:23-26
Proclaim the Lord's death

Hymn: Three Holy Days Enfold Us Now, ACS 930

Eternal God, in the sharing of a meal your Son established a new covenant for all people, and in the washing of feet he showed us the dignity of service. Grant that by the power of your Holy Spirit these signs of our life in faith may speak again to our hearts, feed our spirits, and refresh our bodies, through Jesus Christ, our Savior and Lord, who lives and reigns with you and the Holy Spirit, one God, now and forever.

Friday, April 7, 2023
Good Friday

John 18:1—19:42
The passion and death of Jesus

When Jesus saw his mother and the disciple whom he loved standing beside her, he said to his mother, "Woman, here is your son." Then he said to the disciple, "Here is your mother." And from that hour the disciple took her into his own home.

After this, when Jesus knew that all was now finished, he said (in order to fulfill the scripture), "I am thirsty." A jar full of sour wine was standing there. So they put a sponge full of the wine on a branch of hyssop and held it to his mouth. When Jesus had received the wine, he said, "It is finished." Then he bowed his head and gave up his spirit. (John 19:26-30)

Psalm
Psalm 22
Why have you forsaken me?

Additional Readings
Isaiah 52:13—53:12
The suffering servant

Hebrews 10:16-25
The way to God is opened

Hymn: There in God's Garden, ELW 342

Merciful God, your Son was lifted up on the cross to draw all people to himself. Grant that we who have been born out of his wounded side may at all times find mercy in him, Jesus Christ, our Savior and Lord, who lives and reigns with you and the Holy Spirit, one God, now and forever.

Saturday, April 8, 2023

Resurrection of Our Lord
Vigil of Easter

Romans 6:3-11

Dying and rising with Christ

Do you not know that all of us who have been baptized into Christ Jesus were baptized into his death? Therefore we have been buried with him by baptism into death, so that, just as Christ was raised from the dead by the glory of the Father, so we too might walk in newness of life.

For if we have been united with him in a death like his, we will certainly be united with him in a resurrection like his. (Rom. 6:3-5)

Psalm

Psalm 46
The God of Jacob is our stronghold

Additional Readings

Genesis 7:1-5, 11-18; 8:6-18; 9:8-13
Flood

John 20:1-18
Seeing the risen Christ

Hymn: Come, You Faithful, Raise the Strain, ELW 363

O God, you are the creator of the world, the liberator of your people, and the wisdom of the earth. By the resurrection of your Son free us from our fears, restore us in your image, and ignite us with your light, through Jesus Christ, our Savior and Lord, who lives and reigns with you and the Holy Spirit, one God, now and forever.

Sunday, April 9, 2023
Resurrection of Our Lord
Easter Day

Dietrich Bonhoeffer, theologian, died 1945

Matthew 28:1-10
Proclaim the resurrection

But the angel said to the women, "Do not be afraid; I know that you are looking for Jesus who was crucified. He is not here; for he has been raised, as he said. Come, see the place where he lay. Then go quickly and tell his disciples, 'He has been raised from the dead, and indeed he is going ahead of you to Galilee; there you will see him.' This is my message for you." So they left the tomb quickly with fear and great joy, and ran to tell his disciples. (Matt. 28:5-8)

Psalm
Psalm 118:1-2, 14-24
On this day God has acted

Additional Readings
Acts 10:34-43
God raised Jesus on the third day

Colossians 3:1-4
Raised with Christ

Hymn: Day of Delight and Beauty Unbounded, ACS 933

God of mercy, we no longer look for Jesus among the dead, for he is alive and has become the Lord of life. Increase in our minds and hearts the risen life we share with Christ, and help us to grow as your people toward the fullness of eternal life with you, through Jesus Christ, our Savior and Lord, who lives and reigns with you and the Holy Spirit, one God, now and forever.

Easter

The Three Days flow into the rejoicing of the fifty days of Easter. During this "week of weeks," Christians explore the meaning of the central actions of baptism for daily life: the renouncing of evil and the professing of faith, washing in water, being marked with the cross, being clothed in the white robe, receiving the light of the paschal/ Easter candle, and eating and drinking the bread of life and the cup of salvation.

The fifty days were once called *Pentecost*, Greek for "fifty." On the fiftieth day of Easter, Christians celebrate the pentecostal mystery of the risen Christ breathing on the church the breath, the wind, and the fire of the Holy Spirit.

Table Prayer for the Season of Easter

O God of our risen Lord, we praise you, we bless you,
we worship you for the gifts of life you give us.
Always you offer us life, and for this we bless your holy name.
And we ask you,
give your life also to all who know only hunger and the pangs of death.
So may the whole world be raised to life,
through Jesus Christ, our Savior and Lord. Amen.

Monday, April 10, 2023
Week of Easter 1

Mikael Agricola, Bishop of Turku, died 1557

Psalm 118:1-2, 14-24
On this day God has acted

The stone that the builders rejected
>   has become the chief cornerstone.
This is the LORD's doing;
>   it is marvelous in our eyes.
This is the day that the LORD has made;
>   let us rejoice and be glad in it. (Ps. 118:22-24)

Additional Readings
Exodus 14:10-31; 15:20-21
Israel crosses over the sea

Colossians 3:5-11
The new life in Christ

Hymn: Now All the Vault of Heaven Resounds, ELW 367

Resurrecting God, the plans we try to live by often end up failing us, yet you are the God who raised Christ when all thought he had failed. Help us receive your saving presence with joy.

Tuesday, April 11, 2023
Week of Easter 1

Colossians 3:12-17

The new life in Christ

As God's chosen ones, holy and beloved, clothe yourselves with compassion, kindness, humility, meekness, and patience. Bear with one another and, if anyone has a complaint against another, forgive each other; just as the Lord has forgiven you, so you also must forgive. Above all, clothe yourselves with love, which binds everything together in perfect harmony. And let the peace of Christ rule in your hearts, to which indeed you were called in the one body. And be thankful. (Col. 3:12-15)

Psalm
Psalm 118:1-2, 14-24
On this day God has acted

Additional Reading
Exodus 15:1-18
Song at the sea

Hymn: Christ Is Risen! Shout Hosanna! ELW 383

God whose rule is peace, how difficult it is to fit patience and compassion into our routines. Clothe us with the love you give, that we may live in peace and harmony with others.

Wednesday, April 12, 2023
Week of Easter 1

Matthew 28:1-10
Proclaim the resurrection

But the angel said to the women, "Do not be afraid; I know that you are looking for Jesus who was crucified. He is not here; for he has been raised, as he said. Come, see the place where he lay. Then go quickly and tell his disciples, 'He has been raised from the dead, and indeed he is going ahead of you to Galilee; there you will see him.' This is my message for you." So they left the tomb quickly with fear and great joy, and ran to tell his disciples. Suddenly Jesus met them and said, "Greetings!" And they came to him, took hold of his feet, and worshiped him. Then Jesus said to them, "Do not be afraid; go and tell my brothers to go to Galilee; there they will see me." (Matt. 28:5-10)

Psalm
Psalm 118:1-2, 14-24
On this day God has acted

Additional Reading
Joshua 3:1-17
Israel crosses into the promised land

Hymn: Christ Has Risen While Earth Slumbers, ACS 938

Holy One of the open tomb, you sent Jesus on ahead of the ones who came to grieve. Open us to the message of your goodness. Free us to follow in our times of fear and joy.

Thursday, April 13, 2023
Week of Easter 1

Psalm 16
Fullness of joy

I bless the LORD who gives me counsel;
>in the night also my heart instructs me.
I keep the LORD always before me;
>because he is at my right hand, I shall not be moved.

Therefore my heart is glad, and my soul rejoices;
>my body also rests secure.
For you do not give me up to Sheol,
>or let your faithful one see the Pit.

You show me the path of life.
>In your presence there is fullness of joy;
>in your right hand are pleasures forevermore. (Ps. 16:7-11)

Additional Readings

Song of Solomon 2:8-15
Arise, for the winter is past

Colossians 4:2-5
The new life in Christ

Hymn: In Thee Is Gladness, ELW 867

*Giver of gladness and good counsel, you bring fullness even amid scarcity.
We lift up to you our communities and all who struggle while working for
the benefit of others in need. Give them encouragement.*

Friday, April 14, 2023
Week of Easter 1

1 Corinthians 15:1-11

Witnesses to the risen Christ

For I handed on to you as of first importance what I in turn had received: that Christ died for our sins in accordance with the scriptures, and that he was buried, and that he was raised on the third day in accordance with the scriptures, and that he appeared to Cephas, then to the twelve. Then he appeared to more than five hundred brothers and sisters at one time, most of whom are still alive, though some have died. Then he appeared to James, then to all the apostles. Last of all, as to one untimely born, he appeared also to me. (1 Cor. 15:3-8)

Psalm
Psalm 16
Fullness of joy

Additional Reading
Song of Solomon 5:9—6:3
The beloved in the garden

Hymn: Now the Green Blade Rises, ELW 379

Saving God, you multiply your words to share with many people. Help us to build each other up through your word and to be witnesses who include and encourage those who feel they are not important.

Saturday, April 15, 2023
Week of Easter 1

Song of Solomon 8:6-7
Love is strong as death

Set me as a seal upon your heart,
    as a seal upon your arm;
for love is strong as death,
    passion fierce as the grave.
Its flashes are flashes of fire,
    a raging flame.
Many waters cannot quench love,
    neither can floods drown it.
If one offered for love
    all the wealth of his house,
    it would be utterly scorned. (Song of Sol. 8:6-7)

Psalm
Psalm 16
Fullness of joy

Additional Reading
John 20:11-20
The witness of Mary Magdalene

Hymn: Come, My Way, My Truth, My Life, ELW 816

You, O God, are the source of all the love we give and receive in this life. Have mercy on all who grieve their beloved dead. Guide and accompany everyone in marriage and in singleness.

Sunday, April 16, 2023
Second Sunday of Easter

John 20:19-31
Beholding the wounds of the risen Christ

A week later [Jesus'] disciples were again in the house, and Thomas was with them. Although the doors were shut, Jesus came and stood among them and said, "Peace be with you." Then he said to Thomas, "Put your finger here and see my hands. Reach out your hand and put it in my side. Do not doubt but believe." Thomas answered him, "My Lord and my God!" Jesus said to him, "Have you believed because you have seen me? Blessed are those who have not seen and yet have come to believe." (John 20:26-29)

Psalm
Psalm 16
Fullness of joy

Additional Readings
Acts 2:14a, 22-32
God fulfills the promise to David

1 Peter 1:3-9
New birth to a living hope

Hymn: The Risen Christ, ELW 390

Almighty and eternal God, the strength of those who believe and the hope of those who doubt, may we, who have not seen, have faith in you and receive the fullness of Christ's blessing, who lives and reigns with you and the Holy Spirit, one God, now and forever.

Monday, April 17, 2023
Week of Easter 2

Psalm 114
God saves through water

Why is it, O sea, that you flee?
    O Jordan, that you turn back?
O mountains, that you skip like rams?
    O hills, like lambs?

Tremble, O earth, at the presence of the LORD,
    at the presence of the God of Jacob,
who turns the rock into a pool of water,
    the flint into a spring of water. (Ps. 114:5-8)

Additional Readings
Judges 6:36-40
Gideon and the fleece

1 Corinthians 15:12-20
Paul teaches the resurrection

Hymn: We Know That Christ Is Raised, ELW 449

God of rescue, generations have called out to you in times of danger. In these times we join our voices to pray for the natural world, for relief to burning lands and raging waters.

Tuesday, April 18, 2023
Week of Easter 2

1 Corinthians 15:19-28
Paul teaches the resurrection

For since death came through a human being, the resurrection of the dead has also come through a human being; for as all die in Adam, so all will be made alive in Christ. But each in his own order: Christ the first fruits, then at his coming those who belong to Christ. Then comes the end, when he hands over the kingdom to God the Father, after he has destroyed every ruler and every authority and power. For he must reign until he has put all his enemies under his feet. (1 Cor. 15:21-25)

Psalm
Psalm 114
God saves through water

Additional Reading
Jonah 1:1-17
Jonah saved from the sea

Hymn: This Joyful Eastertide, ELW 391

Living God, Christ is the first of the multitude whom you will raise from death. As we who are living still fear death, we pray that you would place our fears in your care.

Wednesday, April 19, 2023
Week of Easter 2

Olavus Petri, priest, died 1552; Laurentius Petri, Bishop of Uppsala, died 1573;
renewers of the church

Matthew 12:38-42
Jesus speaks of the sign of Jonah

Then some of the scribes and Pharisees said to [Jesus], "Teacher,
we wish to see a sign from you." But he answered them, "An evil and
adulterous generation asks for a sign, but no sign will be given to it
except the sign of the prophet Jonah. For just as Jonah was three
days and three nights in the belly of the sea monster, so for three days
and three nights the Son of Man will be in the heart of the earth. The
people of Nineveh will rise up at the judgment with this generation and
condemn it, because they repented at the proclamation of Jonah, and
see, something greater than Jonah is here! The queen of the South will
rise up at the judgment with this generation and condemn it, because
she came from the ends of the earth to listen to the wisdom of Solomon,
and see, something greater than Solomon is here!" (Matt. 12:38-42)

Psalm
Psalm 114
God saves through water

Additional Reading
Jonah 2:1-10
Jonah's praise for deliverance

Hymn: The Strife Is O'er, the Battle Done, ELW 366

*God of mercy, as you sent Jonah to Nineveh and Jesus to Jerusalem, so you
even send us. We ask for your mercy on those with whom we are not yet reconciled as well as for ourselves.*

Thursday, April 20, 2023
Week of Easter 2

Psalm 116:1-4, 12-19
I will call upon God

I love the LORD, because he has heard
　　my voice and my supplications.
Because he inclined his ear to me,
　　therefore I will call on him as long as I live.
The snares of death encompassed me;
　　the pangs of Sheol laid hold on me;
　　I suffered distress and anguish.
Then I called on the name of the LORD:
　　"O LORD, I pray, save my life!" (Ps. 116:1-4)

Additional Readings
Isaiah 25:1-5　　　　　　　**1 Peter 1:8b-12**
Praise for deliverance　　　　*The promised salvation comes*

Hymn: Christ, the Life of All the Living, ELW 339

Lord, in your love for the sick and the anguished, we call to you. We remember this day people who are hospitalized, people who seek treatment for mental health, and people who are supporters and caregivers.

Friday, April 21, 2023
Week of Easter 2

Anselm, Bishop of Canterbury, died 1109

Isaiah 26:1-4

God sets up victory like bulwarks

On that day this song will be sung in the land of Judah:
We have a strong city;
    he sets up victory
    like walls and bulwarks.
Open the gates,
    so that the righteous nation that keeps faith
    may enter in.
Those of steadfast mind you keep in peace—
    in peace because they trust in you.
Trust in the LORD forever,
    for in the LORD GOD
    you have an everlasting rock. (Isa. 26:1-4)

Psalm
Psalm 116:1-4, 12-19
I will call upon God

Additional Reading
1 Peter 1:13-16
A holy life

Hymn: Dear Christians, One and All, Rejoice, ELW 594

God of peace, we pray for veterans and their families, those who are injured and those in active service, and all who flee wars and who work for peace. May Christ's victory put an end to all human desire for war.

Saturday, April 22, 2023
Week of Easter 2

Luke 14:12-14

Welcome those in need to your table

[Jesus] said also to the one who had invited him, "When you give a luncheon or a dinner, do not invite your friends or your brothers or your relatives or rich neighbors, in case they may invite you in return, and you would be repaid. But when you give a banquet, invite the poor, the crippled, the lame, and the blind. And you will be blessed, because they cannot repay you, for you will be repaid at the resurrection of the righteous." (Luke 14:12-14)

Psalm
Psalm 116:1-4, 12-19
I will call upon God

Additional Reading
Isaiah 25:6-9
The feast for all peoples

Hymn: Build a Longer Table, ACS 1062

Lord, you prepare a table for us. We cannot repay you for what you have done in Christ. Open our hearts that we may graciously participate in the ways you give to all people who are poor.

Sunday, April 23, 2023
Third Sunday of Easter

Toyohiko Kagawa, renewer of society, died 1960

Luke 24:13-35

Eating with the risen Christ

As [two disciples] came near the village to which they were going, [Jesus] walked ahead as if he were going on. But they urged him strongly, saying, "Stay with us, because it is almost evening and the day is now nearly over." So he went in to stay with them. When he was at the table with them, he took bread, blessed and broke it, and gave it to them. Then their eyes were opened, and they recognized him; and he vanished from their sight. They said to each other, "Were not our hearts burning within us while he was talking to us on the road, while he was opening the scriptures to us?" (Luke 24:28-32)

Psalm

Psalm 116:1-4, 12-19
I will call upon God

Additional Readings

Acts 2:14a, 36-41
Receiving God's promise through baptism

1 Peter 1:17-23
Born anew

Hymn: Day of Arising, ELW 374

O God, your Son makes himself known to all his disciples in the breaking of the bread. Open the eyes of our faith, that we may see him in his redeeming work, who lives and reigns with you and the Holy Spirit, one God, now and forever.

Monday, April 24, 2023
Week of Easter 3

Psalm 134
Praise God day and night

Come, bless the LORD, all you servants of the LORD,
>who stand by night in the house of the LORD!
Lift up your hands to the holy place,
>and bless the LORD.

May the LORD, maker of heaven and earth,
>bless you from Zion. (Ps. 134:1-3)

Additional Readings
Genesis 18:1-14
Abraham and Sarah eat with God

1 Peter 1:23-25
The word of God endures

Hymn: The Trumpets Sound, the Angels Sing, ELW 531

God of blessing, night and day are yours. Protect, sustain, and guide first responders in our communities. We also pray for all people laboring long hours and whose shifts last through the night.

Tuesday, April 25, 2023
Mark, Evangelist

Mark 1:1-15
The beginning of the gospel of Jesus Christ

The beginning of the good news of Jesus Christ, the Son of God. As it is written in the prophet Isaiah,
"See, I am sending my messenger ahead of you,
> who will prepare your way;
the voice of one crying out in the wilderness:
> 'Prepare the way of the Lord,
> make his paths straight,'"
John the baptizer appeared in the wilderness, proclaiming a baptism of repentance for the forgiveness of sins. And people from the whole Judean countryside and all the people of Jerusalem were going out to him, and were baptized by him in the river Jordan, confessing their sins. (Mark 1:1-5)

Psalm

Psalm 57
Be merciful to me, O God

Additional Readings

Isaiah 52:7-10
The messenger announces salvation

2 Timothy 4:6-11, 18
The good fight of faith

Hymn: Open Your Ears, O Faithful People, ELW 519

Almighty God, you have enriched your church with Mark's proclamation of the gospel. Give us grace to believe firmly in the good news of salvation and to walk daily in accord with it, through Jesus Christ, our Savior and Lord, who lives and reigns with you and the Holy Spirit, one God, now and forever.

Wednesday, April 26, 2023
Week of Easter 3

Exodus 24:1-11
Moses and the elders eat with God

Then Moses and Aaron, Nadab, and Abihu, and seventy of the elders of Israel went up, and they saw the God of Israel. Under his feet there was something like a pavement of sapphire stone, like the very heaven for clearness. God did not lay his hand on the chief men of the people of Israel; also they beheld God, and they ate and drank. (Exod. 24:9-11)

Psalm
Psalm 134
Praise God day and night

Additional Reading
John 21:1-14
The risen Christ eats with the disciples

Hymn: At the Lamb's High Feast We Sing, ELW 362

God of liberation, as the prophets were bold to stand in your presence, so we pray that you would strengthen us in our courage to witness to your way of justice and mercy.

Thursday, April 27, 2023
Week of Easter 3

Psalm 23
God our shepherd

Even though I walk through the darkest valley,
    I fear no evil;
for you are with me;
    your rod and your staff—
    they comfort me.

You prepare a table before me
    in the presence of my enemies;
you anoint my head with oil;
    my cup overflows.
Surely goodness and mercy shall follow me
    all the days of my life,
and I shall dwell in the house of the LORD
    my whole life long. (Ps. 23:4-6)

Additional Readings
Exodus 2:15b-25   **1 Peter 2:9-12**
Moses the shepherd   *Living as God's people*

Hymn: Shepherd Me, O God, ELW 780

Our good Shepherd, in the presence of our enemies you are the source of goodness and life. May your encouraging words come to us, especially in times and places where we feel hurt and fear.

Friday, April 28, 2023
Week of Easter 3

1 Peter 2:13-17

Living honorably in the world

For the Lord's sake accept the authority of every human institution, whether of the emperor as supreme, or of governors, as sent by him to punish those who do wrong and to praise those who do right. For it is God's will that by doing right you should silence the ignorance of the foolish. As servants of God, live as free people, yet do not use your freedom as a pretext for evil. Honor everyone. Love the family of believers. Fear God. Honor the emperor. (1 Peter 2:13-17)

Psalm
Psalm 23
God our shepherd

Additional Reading
Exodus 3:16-22; 4:18-20
Moses the shepherd of Israel

Hymn: What God Ordains Is Good Indeed, ELW 776

God of the weak and the powerful, we pray for public servants, officeholders, and institutions entrusted with judgments of law, that they may serve the good and uphold the rights of all.

Saturday, April 29, 2023
Week of Easter 3

Catherine of Siena, theologian, died 1380

Ezekiel 34:1-16
God gathers the scattered flock

For thus says the Lord GOD: I myself will search for my sheep, and will seek them out. As shepherds seek out their flocks when they are among their scattered sheep, so I will seek out my sheep. I will rescue them from all the places to which they have been scattered on a day of clouds and thick darkness. I will bring them out from the peoples and gather them from the countries, and will bring them into their own land; and I will feed them on the mountains of Israel, by the watercourses, and in all the inhabited parts of the land. I will feed them with good pasture, and the mountain heights of Israel shall be their pasture; there they shall lie down in good grazing land, and they shall feed on rich pasture on the mountains of Israel. I myself will be the shepherd of my sheep, and I will make them lie down, says the Lord GOD. (Ezek. 34:11-15)

Psalm
Psalm 23
God our shepherd

Additional Reading
Luke 15:1-7
Parable of the lost sheep

Hymn: Savior, like a Shepherd Lead Us, ELW 789

Saving God, as your people fled from famine and war and as they languished in exile, so you sought them out. We pray now for refugees on dangerous journeys and in crowded encampments, that relief may come soon.

Sunday, April 30, 2023
Fourth Sunday of Easter

John 10:1-10
Christ the shepherd

So again Jesus said to [the Pharisees], "Very truly, I tell you, I am the gate for the sheep. All who came before me are thieves and bandits; but the sheep did not listen to them. I am the gate. Whoever enters by me will be saved, and will come in and go out and find pasture. The thief comes only to steal and kill and destroy. I came that they may have life, and have it abundantly." (John 10:7-10)

Psalm

Psalm 23
God our shepherd

Additional Readings

Acts 2:42-47
The believers' common life

1 Peter 2:19-25
Follow the shepherd, even in suffering

Hymn: The Lord's My Shepherd, ELW 778

O God our shepherd, you know your sheep by name and lead us to safety through the valleys of death. Guide us by your voice, that we may walk in certainty and security to the joyous feast prepared in your house, through Jesus Christ, our Savior and Lord, who lives and reigns with you and the Holy Spirit, one God, now and forever.

Prayer List for May

_____

_____

_____

_____

_____

_____

_____

_____

_____

_____

Monday, May 1, 2023
Philip and James, Apostles

John 14:8-14
The Son and the Father are one

Philip said to [Jesus], "Lord, show us the Father, and we will be satisfied." Jesus said to him, "Have I been with you all this time, Philip, and you still do not know me? Whoever has seen me has seen the Father. How can you say, 'Show us the Father'? Do you not believe that I am in the Father and the Father is in me? The words that I say to you I do not speak on my own; but the Father who dwells in me does his works." (John 14:8-10)

Psalm
Psalm 44:1-3, 20-26
Save us for the sake of your love

Additional Readings
Isaiah 30:18-21
God's mercy and justice

2 Corinthians 4:1-6
Proclaiming Jesus Christ as Lord

Hymn: Thine Is the Glory, ELW 376

Almighty God, you gave to your apostles Philip and James grace and strength to bear witness to your Son. Grant that we, remembering their victory of faith, may glorify in life and death the name of our Lord Jesus Christ, who lives and reigns with you and the Holy Spirit, one God, now and forever.

Tuesday, May 2, 2023
Week of Easter 4

Athanasius, Bishop of Alexandria, died 373

Hebrews 13:20-21

God's blessing through Christ the shepherd

Now may the God of peace, who brought back from the dead our Lord Jesus, the great shepherd of the sheep, by the blood of the eternal covenant, make you complete in everything good so that you may do his will, working among us that which is pleasing in his sight, through Jesus Christ, to whom be the glory forever and ever. Amen. (Heb. 13:20-21)

Psalm

Psalm 100
We are the sheep of God's pasture

Additional Reading

Ezekiel 34:23-31
God provides perfect pasture

Hymn: Go, My Children, with My Blessing, ELW 543

God of peace, with your power you conquer sin and death. Raise us up and shepherd us so that what we do is pleasing in your sight and Christ is glorified in the lives we lead.

Wednesday, May 3, 2023
Week of Easter 4

Jeremiah 23:1-8

God will gather the flock

Woe to the shepherds who destroy and scatter the sheep of my pasture! says the LORD. Therefore thus says the LORD, the God of Israel, concerning the shepherds who shepherd my people: It is you who have scattered my flock, and have driven them away, and you have not attended to them. So I will attend to you for your evil doings, says the LORD. Then I myself will gather the remnant of my flock out of all the lands where I have driven them, and I will bring them back to their fold, and they shall be fruitful and multiply. I will raise up shepherds over them who will shepherd them, and they shall not fear any longer, or be dismayed, nor shall any be missing, says the LORD. (Jer. 23:1-4)

Psalm

Psalm 100
We are the sheep of God's pasture

Additional Reading

Matthew 20:17-28
Jesus came to serve

Hymn: Gather Us In, ELW 532

Holy God, we are a confused and scattered people, fearful and dismayed. Gather us together, that we might know the gift of your embrace. Give us leaders who reflect your fruitful ways of justice and love.

Thursday, May 4, 2023
Week of Easter 4

Monica, mother of Augustine, died 387

Psalm 31:1-5, 15-16
I commend my spirit

In you, O LORD, I seek refuge;
> do not let me ever be put to shame;
> in your righteousness deliver me.
Incline your ear to me;
> rescue me speedily.
Be a rock of refuge for me,
> a strong fortress to save me.

You are indeed my rock and my fortress;
> for your name's sake lead me and guide me,
take me out of the net that is hidden for me,
> for you are my refuge.
Into your hand I commit my spirit;
> you have redeemed me, O LORD, faithful God. (Ps. 31:1-5)

Additional Readings

Genesis 12:1-3
The call of Abram

Acts 6:8-15
Stephen is arrested

Hymn: God Alone Be Praised, ACS 1023

Listening God, be attentive to our voices and responsive to our needs. You alone are our redeemer and our rescuer from all that makes us feel ashamed. Teach us to trust in you alone.

Exodus 3:1-12

Moses at the burning bush

When the Lord saw that [Moses] had turned aside to see, God called to him out of the bush, "Moses, Moses!" And he said, "Here I am." Then he said, "Come no closer! Remove the sandals from your feet, for the place on which you are standing is holy ground." He said further, "I am the God of your father, the God of Abraham, the God of Isaac, and the God of Jacob." And Moses hid his face, for he was afraid to look at God. (Exod. 3:4-6)

Psalm

Psalm 31:1-5, 15-16
I commend my spirit

Additional Reading

Acts 7:1-16
Stephen addresses the council

Hymn: Christ Is Risen! Alleluia! ELW 382

Great I am, flame of our faith that does not destroy, may we know that each place you encounter us is holy ground. Help us to join with our ancestors as each of us responds to you, "Here I am."

Saturday, May 6, 2023
Week of Easter 4

Jeremiah 26:20-24
A prophet of the Lord persecuted

There was another man prophesying in the name of the LORD, Uriah son of Shemaiah from Kiriath-jearim. He prophesied against this city and against this land in words exactly like those of Jeremiah. And when King Jehoiakim, with all his warriors and all the officials, heard his words, the king sought to put him to death; but when Uriah heard of it, he was afraid and fled and escaped to Egypt. Then King Jehoiakim sent Elnathan son of Achbor and men with him to Egypt, and they took Uriah from Egypt and brought him to King Jehoiakim, who struck him down with the sword and threw his dead body into the burial place of the common people.

But the hand of Ahikam son of Shaphan was with Jeremiah so that he was not given over into the hands of the people to be put to death. (Jer. 26:20-24)

Psalm
Psalm 31:1-5, 15-16
I commend my spirit

Additional Reading
John 8:48-59
Jesus the greater prophet

Hymn: Faith of Our Fathers, ELW 812/813

We cry out to you, God of life, because violence, death, and brutality surround us on all sides. Help us to not give ourselves over to the seductive power of cruelty and hatred, but to walk in your ways.

Sunday, May 7, 2023
Fifth Sunday of Easter

John 14:1-14
Christ the way, truth, life

Philip said to [Jesus], "Lord, show us the Father, and we will be satisfied." Jesus said to him, "Have I been with you all this time, Philip, and you still do not know me? Whoever has seen me has seen the Father. How can you say, 'Show us the Father'? Do you not believe that I am in the Father and the Father is in me? The words that I say to you I do not speak on my own; but the Father who dwells in me does his works. Believe me that I am in the Father and the Father is in me; but if you do not, then believe me because of the works themselves. Very truly, I tell you, the one who believes in me will also do the works that I do and, in fact, will do greater works than these, because I am going to the Father." (John 14:8-12)

Psalm
Psalm 31:1-5, 15-16
I commend my spirit

Additional Readings
Acts 7:55-60
Martyrdom of Stephen

1 Peter 2:2-10
God's chosen people

Hymn: You Are the Way, ELW 758

Almighty God, your Son Jesus Christ is the way, the truth, and the life. Give us grace to love one another, to follow in the way of his commandments, and to share his risen life with all the world, for he lives and reigns with you and the Holy Spirit, one God, now and forever.

Monday, May 8, 2023
Week of Easter 5

Julian of Norwich, renewer of the church, died around 1416

Psalm 102:1-17
Prayer for deliverance

But you, O Lord, are enthroned forever;
    your name endures to all generations.
You will rise up and have compassion on Zion,
    for it is time to favor it;
    the appointed time has come.
For your servants hold its stones dear,
    and have pity on its dust.
The nations will fear the name of the Lord,
    and all the kings of the earth your glory.
For the Lord will build up Zion;
    he will appear in his glory. (Ps. 102:12-16)

Additional Readings

Exodus 13:17-22
God leads the way

Acts 7:17-40
Stephen addresses the council

Hymn: O God of Every Nation, ELW 713

Compassionate God, you make yourself known to us in particular times and places. Awaken us, that we might recognize you in our own holy places, loving their dust and their glory because therein you have revealed yourself.

Tuesday, May 9, 2023
Week of Easter 5

Nicolaus Ludwig von Zinzendorf, renewer of the church, hymnwriter, died 1760

Proverbs 3:5-12
God, the truth and life

Trust in the LORD with all your heart,
    and do not rely on your own insight.
In all your ways acknowledge him,
    and he will make straight your paths.
Do not be wise in your own eyes;
    fear the LORD, and turn away from evil.
It will be a healing for your flesh
    and a refreshment for your body. (Prov. 3:5-8)

Psalm
Psalm 102:1-17
Prayer for deliverance

Additional Reading
Acts 7:44-56
Stephen confronts the council

Hymn: All My Hope on God Is Founded, ELW 757

Healing God, when we do not know what to do, we turn to you. Make us a humble and wise people, acknowledging you in all our ways. In you we will be refreshed in body and soul.

Wednesday, May 10, 2023
Week of Easter 5

John 8:31-38
Jesus, the truth of God

Jesus answered [the Jews who had believed in him], "Very truly, I tell you, everyone who commits sin is a slave to sin. The slave does not have a permanent place in the household; the son has a place there forever. So if the Son makes you free, you will be free indeed. I know that you are descendants of Abraham; yet you look for an opportunity to kill me, because there is no place in you for my word. I declare what I have seen in the Father's presence; as for you, you should do what you have heard from the Father." (John 8:34-38)

Psalm
Psalm 102:1-17
Prayer for deliverance

Additional Reading
Proverbs 3:13-18
God, the truth and life

Hymn: Awake, My Heart, with Gladness, ELW 378

God of our ancestors, we are so deep in slavery that we do not see our own chains. Make us free so that we inhabit the dwelling places you have prepared for your people with joy.

Thursday, May 11, 2023
Week of Easter 5

Psalm 66:8-20
Be joyful in God, all you lands

Bless our God, O peoples,
    let the sound of his praise be heard,
who has kept us among the living,
    and has not let our feet slip.
For you, O God, have tested us;
    you have tried us as silver is tried.
You brought us into the net;
    you laid burdens on our backs;
you let people ride over our heads;
    we went through fire and through water;
yet you have brought us out to a spacious place. (Ps. 66:8-12)

Additional Readings
Genesis 6:5-22
God's command to Noah

Acts 27:1-12
Paul sails for Rome

Hymn: Christ Jesus Lay in Death's Strong Bands, ELW 370

Our voices raised to you, blessed God, are proof that we are still among the living. We give you praise when we are burdened and when we know relief, because all our days are in your hands.

Friday, May 12, 2023
Week of Easter 5

Genesis 7:1-24
The great flood

Then the LORD said to Noah, "Go into the ark, you and all your household, for I have seen that you alone are righteous before me in this generation. Take with you seven pairs of all clean animals, the male and its mate; and a pair of the animals that are not clean, the male and its mate; and seven pairs of the birds of the air also, male and female, to keep their kind alive on the face of all the earth. For in seven days I will send rain on the earth for forty days and forty nights; and every living thing that I have made I will blot out from the face of the ground." And Noah did all that the LORD had commanded him. (Gen. 7:1-5)

Psalm
Psalm 66:8-20
Be joyful in God, all you lands

Additional Reading
Acts 27:13-38
Paul survives shipwreck

Hymn: God, Bless the Hands, ACS 1022

May our communities be an ark, Lord, where we live in harmony with all your creation. We know that on our own we can claim no righteousness, but you make all things new.

Saturday, May 13, 2023
Week of Easter 5

John 14:27-29
Peace I leave with you

[Jesus said,] "Peace I leave with you; my peace I give to you. I do not give to you as the world gives. Do not let your hearts be troubled, and do not let them be afraid. You heard me say to you, 'I am going away, and I am coming to you.' If you loved me, you would rejoice that I am going to the Father, because the Father is greater than I. And now I have told you this before it occurs, so that when it does occur, you may believe." (John 14:27-29)

Psalm
Psalm 66:8-20
Be joyful in God, all you lands

Additional Reading
Genesis 8:13-19
The flood waters subside

Hymn: Alleluia! Sing to Jesus, ELW 392

Beloved God, you send Jesus to us that we might know your peace. Calm our troubled hearts and lead us out of fear and into courage. May the peace you give our hearts find its way into our trembling world.

Sunday, May 14, 2023
Sixth Sunday of Easter

Matthias, Apostle transferred to May 15

John 14:15-21
Christ our advocate

[Jesus said,] "If you love me, you will keep my commandments. And I will ask the Father, and he will give you another Advocate, to be with you forever. This is the Spirit of truth, whom the world cannot receive, because it neither sees him nor knows him. You know him, because he abides with you, and he will be in you." (John 14:15-17)

Psalm

Psalm 66:8-20
Be joyful in God, all you lands

Additional Readings

Acts 17:22-31
Paul's message to the Athenians

1 Peter 3:13-22
The days of Noah, a sign of baptism

Hymn: O Spirit of Life, ELW 405

Almighty and ever-living God, you hold together all things in heaven and on earth. In your great mercy receive the prayers of all your children, and give to all the world the Spirit of your truth and peace, through Jesus Christ, our Savior and Lord, who lives and reigns with you and the Holy Spirit, one God, now and forever.

Monday, May 15, 2023
Matthias, Apostle (transferred)

Luke 6:12-16
Jesus calls the Twelve

Now during those days [Jesus] went out to the mountain to pray; and he spent the night in prayer to God. And when day came, he called his disciples and chose twelve of them, whom he also named apostles: Simon, whom he named Peter, and his brother Andrew, and James, and John, and Philip, and Bartholomew, and Matthew, and Thomas, and James son of Alphaeus, and Simon, who was called the Zealot, and Judas son of James, and Judas Iscariot, who became a traitor. (Luke 6:12-16)

Psalm
Psalm 56
I am bound by the vow I made to you

Additional Readings
Isaiah 66:1-2
Heaven is God's throne, earth is God's footstool

Acts 1:15-26
The apostles cast lots for Matthias

Hymn: The Church of Christ, in Every Age, ELW 729

Almighty God, you chose your faithful servant Matthias to be numbered among the twelve. Grant that your church may always be taught and guided by faithful and true pastors, through Jesus Christ our shepherd, who lives and reigns with you and the Holy Spirit, one God, now and forever.

Tuesday, May 16, 2023
Week of Easter 6

1 Peter 3:8-12
Seek peace and pursue it

Finally, all of you, have unity of spirit, sympathy, love for one another, a tender heart, and a humble mind. Do not repay evil for evil or abuse for abuse; but, on the contrary, repay with a blessing. It is for this that you were called—that you might inherit a blessing. For
"Those who desire life
    and desire to see good days,
let them keep their tongues from evil
    and their lips from speaking deceit;
let them turn away from evil and do good;
    let them seek peace and pursue it.
For the eyes of the Lord are on the righteous,
    and his ears are open to their prayer.
But the face of the Lord is against those who do evil." (1 Peter 3:8-12)

Psalm
Psalm 93
God reigns above the floods

Additional Reading
Deuteronomy 5:22-33
Moses delivers God's commandments

Hymn: Spirit, Open My Heart, ACS 1043

Righteous God, so occupy our tongues in praising you that we have no time to use them in evil ways and deceitful speech. Turn us from evil that we might not put ourselves against you.

Wednesday, May 17, 2023
Week of Easter 6

John 16:16-24
A little while, and you shall see

[Jesus said,] "A little while, and you will no longer see me, and again a little while, and you will see me." Then some of his disciples said to one another, "What does he mean by saying to us, 'A little while, and you will no longer see me, and again a little while, and you will see me'; and 'Because I am going to the Father'?" They said, "What does he mean by this 'a little while'? We do not know what he is talking about." Jesus knew that they wanted to ask him, so he said to them, "Are you discussing among yourselves what I meant when I said, 'A little while, and you will no longer see me, and again a little while, and you will see me'? Very truly, I tell you, you will weep and mourn, but the world will rejoice; you will have pain, but your pain will turn into joy." (John 16:16-20)

Psalm
Psalm 93
God reigns above the floods

Additional Reading
Deuteronomy 31:1-13
Moses promises God's presence

Hymn: Lord, Thee I Love with All My Heart, ELW 750

God, be with us in our deep and profound confusion. Open our hearts and minds for at least a little while, that we may attend to your words.

Thursday, May 18, 2023
Ascension of Our Lord

Erik, King of Sweden, martyr, died 1160

Luke 24:44-53

Christ present in all times and places

Then [Jesus] opened [the disciples'] minds to understand the scriptures, and he said to them, "Thus it is written, that the Messiah is to suffer and to rise from the dead on the third day, and that repentance and forgiveness of sins is to be proclaimed in his name to all nations, beginning from Jerusalem. You are witnesses of these things. And see, I am sending upon you what my Father promised; so stay here in the city until you have been clothed with power from on high." (Luke 24:45-49)

Psalm

Psalm 47
God has gone up with a shout

Additional Readings

Acts 1:1-11
Jesus sends the apostles

Ephesians 1:15-23
Seeing the risen and ascended Christ

Hymn: A Hymn of Glory Let Us Sing! ELW 393

Almighty God, your blessed Son, our Savior Jesus Christ, ascended far above all heavens that he might fill all things. Mercifully give us faith to trust that, as he promised, he abides with us on earth to the end of time, who lives and reigns with you and the Holy Spirit, one God, now and forever.

Friday, May 19, 2023
Week of Easter 6

Ephesians 2:1-7

Seated in the heavenly places with Christ

But God, who is rich in mercy, out of the great love with which he loved us even when we were dead through our trespasses, made us alive together with Christ—by grace you have been saved—and raised us up with him and seated us with him in the heavenly places in Christ Jesus, so that in the ages to come he might show the immeasurable riches of his grace in kindness toward us in Christ Jesus. (Eph. 2:4-7)

Psalm

Psalm 93
Praise to God who reigns

Additional Reading

2 Kings 2:1-12
Elijah ascends in a chariot of fire

Hymn: Rejoice, for Christ Is King! ELW 430

God of our salvation, hope of all the earth, in you we have immeasurable riches which we could never obtain on our own. Help us to treasure your abundant mercy, love, and grace all the days of our lives.

Saturday, May 20, 2023
Week of Easter 6

2 Kings 2:13-15
The spirit rests on Elisha

[Elisha] picked up the mantle of Elijah that had fallen from him, and went back and stood on the bank of the Jordan. He took the mantle of Elijah that had fallen from him, and struck the water, saying, "Where is the LORD, the God of Elijah?" When he had struck the water, the water was parted to the one side and to the other, and Elisha went over.

When the company of prophets who were at Jericho saw him at a distance, they declared, "The spirit of Elijah rests on Elisha." They came to meet him and bowed to the ground before him. (2 Kings 2:13-15)

Psalm
Psalm 93
Praise to God who reigns

Additional Reading
John 8:21-30
Jesus speaks of going to the Father

Hymn: Give to Our God Immortal Praise! ELW 848

Holy Lord, you call your servants to tasks that feel beyond us. Guide us to pick up the mantle of people who have come before us, that we also might become bearers of your spirit, opening ways forward where none currently exist.

Sunday, May 21, 2023
Seventh Sunday of Easter

Helena, mother of Constantine, died around 330

John 17:1-11

Christ's prayer for his disciples

[Jesus prayed,] "I have made your name known to those whom you gave me from the world. They were yours, and you gave them to me, and they have kept your word. Now they know that everything you have given me is from you; for the words that you gave to me I have given to them, and they have received them and know in truth that I came from you; and they have believed that you sent me. I am asking on their behalf; I am not asking on behalf of the world, but on behalf of those whom you gave me, because they are yours. All mine are yours, and yours are mine; and I have been glorified in them. And now I am no longer in the world, but they are in the world, and I am coming to you. Holy Father, protect them in your name that you have given me, so that they may be one, as we are one." (John 17:6-11)

Psalm

Psalm 68:1-10, 32-35
Sing to God

Additional Readings

Acts 1:6-14
Jesus' companions at prayer

1 Peter 4:12-14; 5:6-11
God sustains those who suffer

Hymn: Lord, Who the Night You Were Betrayed, ELW 463

O God of glory, your Son Jesus Christ suffered for us and ascended to your right hand. Unite us with Christ and each other in suffering and in joy, that all the world may be drawn into your bountiful presence, through Jesus Christ, our Savior and Lord, who lives and reigns with you and the Holy Spirit, one God, now and forever.

Monday, May 22, 2023
Week of Easter 7

Psalm 99
Priests and people praise God

The LORD is king; let the peoples tremble!
>He sits enthroned upon the cherubim; let the earth quake!

The LORD is great in Zion;
>he is exalted over all the peoples.

Let them praise your great and awesome name.
>Holy is he!

Mighty King, lover of justice,
>you have established equity;

you have executed justice
>and righteousness in Jacob.

Extol the LORD our God;
>worship at his footstool.

>Holy is he! (Ps. 99:1-5)

Additional Readings

Leviticus 9:1-11, 22-24
The high priest Aaron offers sacrifice

1 Peter 4:1-6
Live by the will of God

Hymn: Oh, Worship the King, ELW 842

Lover of justice, our world is deeply divided and injustice rules on all sides. Come and establish your reign among us, that all who suffer may know relief and eyes soaked in tears might be wiped dry.

Tuesday, May 23, 2023
Week of Easter 7

1 Peter 4:7-11
Be good stewards of grace

The end of all things is near; therefore be serious and discipline yourselves for the sake of your prayers. Above all, maintain constant love for one another, for love covers a multitude of sins. Be hospitable to one another without complaining. Like good stewards of the manifold grace of God, serve one another with whatever gift each of you has received. Whoever speaks must do so as one speaking the very words of God; whoever serves must do so with the strength that God supplies, so that God may be glorified in all things through Jesus Christ. To him belong the glory and the power forever and ever. Amen. (1 Peter 4:7-11)

Psalm
Psalm 99
Priests and people praise God

Additional Reading
Numbers 16:41-50
The high priest Aaron makes atonement

Hymn: We All Are One in Mission, ELW 576

Giver of manifold grace, may the multitude of gifts you have showered upon us be used to serve the world. Your word is our strength and you alone are our glory. Enable us to reflect that in active love.

Wednesday, May 24, 2023
Week of Easter 7

Nicolaus Copernicus, died 1543; Leonhard Euler, died 1783; scientists

1 Kings 8:54-65
Solomon offers sacrifice

Then the king, and all Israel with him, offered sacrifice before the LORD. Solomon offered as sacrifices of well-being to the LORD twenty-two thousand oxen and one hundred twenty thousand sheep. So the king and all the people of Israel dedicated the house of the LORD. The same day the king consecrated the middle of the court that was in front of the house of the LORD; for there he offered the burnt offerings and the grain offerings and the fat pieces of the sacrifices of well-being, because the bronze altar that was before the LORD was too small to receive the burnt offerings and the grain offerings and the fat pieces of the sacrifices of well-being.

So Solomon held the festival at that time, and all Israel with him—a great assembly, people from Lebo-hamath to the Wadi of Egypt—before the LORD our God, seven days. (1 Kings 8:62-65)

Psalm
Psalm 99
Priests and people praise God

Additional Reading
John 3:31-36
The Son and the Father

Hymn: Jesus Shall Reign, ELW 434

King of love, you compassionately sent your Son to us that we might have life and have it in abundance. Let the sacrifice of our praise be pleasing in your sight and lead to well-being for all.

Thursday, May 25, 2023
Week of Easter 7

Psalm 33:12-22
Our help and our shield

Truly the eye of the LORD is on those who fear him,
    on those who hope in his steadfast love,
to deliver their soul from death,
    and to keep them alive in famine.

Our soul waits for the LORD;
    he is our help and shield.
Our heart is glad in him,
    because we trust in his holy name.
Let your steadfast love, O LORD, be upon us,
    even as we hope in you. (Ps. 33:18-22)

Additional Readings
Exodus 19:1-9a
The covenant at Sinai

Acts 2:1-11
The giving of the Spirit

Hymn: Jesus Lives, My Sure Defense, ELW 621

Gracious God, you extend steadfast love in abundance to this world. Be with all those caught in famine, that food might be provided and the earth itself renewed. May you always be our hope in desperate times.

Friday, May 26, 2023
Week of Easter 7

Romans 8:14-17
Led by the Spirit of God

For all who are led by the Spirit of God are children of God. For you did not receive a spirit of slavery to fall back into fear, but you have received a spirit of adoption. When we cry, "Abba! Father!" it is that very Spirit bearing witness with our spirit that we are children of God, and if children, then heirs, heirs of God and joint heirs with Christ—if, in fact, we suffer with him so that we may also be glorified with him. (Rom. 8:14-17)

Psalm
Psalm 33:12-22
Our help and our shield

Additional Reading
Exodus 19:16-25
Moses and Aaron meet the Lord

Hymn: We All Believe in One True God, ELW 411

Abba, Father, we cry to you as your beloved children. Help us to rest confidently in the assurance of your care. You provide us with a generous inheritance, that all our needs might be satisfied in you.

Saturday, May 27, 2023
Vigil of Pentecost

John Calvin, renewer of the church, died 1564

John 7:37-39
Jesus, the true living water

On the last day of the festival, the great day, while Jesus was standing there, he cried out, "Let anyone who is thirsty come to me, and let the one who believes in me drink. As the scripture has said, 'Out of the believer's heart shall flow rivers of living water.'" Now he said this about the Spirit, which believers in him were to receive; for as yet there was no Spirit, because Jesus was not yet glorified. (John 7:37-39)

Psalm
Psalm 33:12-22
Our help and our shield

Additional Readings
Exodus 19:1-9a
The covenant at Sinai

Romans 8:14-17, 22-27
Praying with the Spirit

Hymn: Come, Holy Ghost, God and Lord, ELW 395

Almighty and ever-living God, you fulfilled the promise of Easter by sending the gift of your Holy Spirit. Look upon your people gathered in prayer, open to receive the Spirit's flame. May it come to rest in our hearts and heal the divisions of word and tongue, that with one voice and one song we may praise your name in joy and thanksgiving; through Jesus Christ, our Savior and Lord, who lives and reigns with you and the Holy Spirit, one God, now and forever.

Pentecost

Christians pray to God "in the power of the Spirit." The gifts of the Spirit are faith, hope, and love. Whenever two or more gather in Jesus' name, the Spirit is present. At every baptism and communion, we pray for the Spirit's presence to forgive and strengthen, inspire and refresh. In the household, we pray for the Spirit's guidance, for the deepening of faith, hope, and love, for the patience and wisdom to live in peace with each other and our neighbors.

Table Prayer for Pentecost

Blessed are you, O Lord our God,
you gather the whole world into the Spirit of your Son.
You have given us food for another day:
blessed be God forever!
We beg you to pour out food for the needy,
that all peoples and languages may praise your name,
through Jesus Christ our Lord. Amen.

Thanksgiving for the Holy Spirit

Use this prayer during the week following Pentecost Sunday.

O Spirit of God, seek us;
Good Spirit, pray with us;
Spirit of counsel, inform us;
Spirit of might, free us;
Spirit of truth, enlighten us;
Spirit of Christ, raise us;
O Holy Spirit, dwell in us. Amen.

Sunday, May 28, 2023
Day of Pentecost

John 20:19-23
The Spirit poured out

When it was evening on that day, the first day of the week, and the doors of the house where the disciples had met were locked for fear of the Jews, Jesus came and stood among them and said, "Peace be with you." After he said this, he showed them his hands and his side. Then the disciples rejoiced when they saw the Lord. Jesus said to them again, "Peace be with you. As the Father has sent me, so I send you." When he had said this, he breathed on them and said to them, "Receive the Holy Spirit. If you forgive the sins of any, they are forgiven them; if you retain the sins of any, they are retained." (John 20:19-23)

Psalm
Psalm 104:24-34, 35b
Renewing the face of the earth

Additional Readings
Acts 2:1-21
Filled with the Spirit

1 Corinthians 12:3b-13
Varieties of gifts, the same Spirit

Hymn: O Spirit All-Embracing, ACS 944

O God, on this day you open the hearts of your faithful people by sending into us your Holy Spirit. Direct us by the light of that Spirit, that we may have a right judgment in all things and rejoice at all times in your peace, through Jesus Christ, your Son and our Lord, who lives and reigns with you and the Holy Spirit, one God, now and forever.

Monday, May 29, 2023
Time after Pentecost

Jiří Třanovský, hymnwriter, died 1637

Psalm 104:24-34, 35b
Renewing the face of the earth

O LORD, how manifold are your works!
>   In wisdom you have made them all;
>   the earth is full of your creatures. . . .

These all look to you
>   to give them their food in due season;
when you give to them, they gather it up;
>   when you open your hand, they are filled with good things.
When you hide your face, they are dismayed;
>   when you take away their breath, they die
>   and return to their dust.
When you send forth your spirit, they are created;
>   and you renew the face of the ground. (Ps. 104:24, 27-30)

Additional Readings

Joel 2:18-29
The promised spirit of God

Romans 8:18-24
We have the first fruits of the Spirit

Hymn: All Creatures, Worship God Most High! ELW 835

Fount of every blessing, we look to you not simply for our own needs, but so that all of humanity might have daily bread. Teach us to hunger for your justice, that the whole world might be renewed.

Tuesday, May 30, 2023
Time after Pentecost

Romans 8:26-27
Praying in the Spirit

Likewise the Spirit helps us in our weakness; for we do not know how to pray as we ought, but that very Spirit intercedes with sighs too deep for words. And God, who searches the heart, knows what is the mind of the Spirit, because the Spirit intercedes for the saints according to the will of God. (Rom. 8:26-27)

Psalm
Psalm 104:24-34, 35b
Renewing the face of the earth

Additional Reading
Ezekiel 39:7-8, 21-29
The promised spirit of God

Hymn: Eternal Spirit of the Living Christ, ELW 402

Word of life, at times we are so overwhelmed that we cannot even express our own dismay. Enable us to live in solidarity with the Spirit, who enters troubled souls that their cries might be heard in your presence.

Wednesday, May 31, 2023
Visit of Mary to Elizabeth

Luke 1:39-57
Mary greets Elizabeth

In those days Mary set out and went with haste to a Judean town in
the hill country, where she entered the house of Zechariah and greeted
Elizabeth. When Elizabeth heard Mary's greeting, the child leaped in
her womb. And Elizabeth was filled with the Holy Spirit and exclaimed
with a loud cry, "Blessed are you among women, and blessed is the fruit
of your womb." (Luke 1:39-42)

Psalm
Psalm 113
God, the helper of the needy

Additional Readings
1 Samuel 2:1-10
Hannah's thanksgiving

Romans 12:9-16b
*Rejoice with those who
rejoice*

Hymn: Unexpected and Mysterious, ELW 258

*Mighty God, by whose grace Elizabeth rejoiced with Mary and greeted her
as the mother of the Lord: look with favor on your lowly servants that, with
Mary, we may magnify your holy name and rejoice to acclaim her Son as
our Savior, who lives and reigns with you and the Holy Spirit, one God, now
and forever.*

Prayer List for June

_____

_____

_____

_____

_____

_____

_____

_____

_____

_____

Thursday, June 1, 2023
Time after Pentecost

Justin, martyr at Rome, died around 165

Psalm 8
How exalted is your name

O LORD, our Sovereign,
>   how majestic is your name in all the earth!

You have set your glory above the heavens.
>   Out of the mouths of babes and infants
you have founded a bulwark because of your foes,
>   to silence the enemy and the avenger.

When I look at your heavens, the work of your fingers,
>   the moon and the stars that you have established;
what are human beings that you are mindful of them,
>   mortals that you care for them?

Yet you have made them a little lower than God,
>   and crowned them with glory and honor. (Ps. 8:1-5)

Additional Readings

Job 38:1-11
Creation story from Job

2 Timothy 1:8-12a
Grace revealed in Christ

Hymn: Many and Great, O God, ELW 837

O God, ruler of the universe, we give you thanks for creating us in your image and calling us to be stewards of your creation. Fill us with awe that we may glorify you forever and ever.

Friday, June 2, 2023
Time after Pentecost

2 Timothy 1:12b-14
The treasure of the triune God

I am not ashamed, for I know the one in whom I have put my trust, and I am sure that he is able to guard until that day what I have entrusted to him. Hold to the standard of sound teaching that you have heard from me, in the faith and love that are in Christ Jesus. Guard the good treasure entrusted to you, with the help of the Holy Spirit living in us. (2 Tim. 1:12b-14)

Psalm
Psalm 8
How exalted is your name

Additional Reading
Job 38:12-21
Creation story from Job

Hymn: Praise the Almighty! ELW 877

O God, giver of every perfect gift, you promise to be present with us in the treasures of your word and sacraments. Inspire us to believe these simple gifts are plentiful enough to see us through this day.

Saturday, June 3, 2023
Time after Pentecost

The Martyrs of Uganda, died 1886
John XXIII, Bishop of Rome, died 1963

John 14:15-17
Father, Son, Spirit

[Jesus said,] "If you love me, you will keep my commandments. And I will ask the Father, and he will give you another Advocate, to be with you forever. This is the Spirit of truth, whom the world cannot receive, because it neither sees him nor knows him. You know him, because he abides with you, and he will be in you." (John 14:15-17)

Psalm
Psalm 8
How exalted is your name

Additional Reading
Job 38:22-38
Creation story from Job

Hymn: Father Most Holy, ELW 415

Dear God, you have sustained your people throughout the ages. Embrace us with your enduring love that we may walk in your ways and share your goodness with all those we meet this day.

Time after Pentecost
Summer

The weeks and months following the Day of Pentecost coincide with the natural seasons of summer, autumn, and late autumn/November. Christian communities refer to this time in different ways. Whatever term is used to describe the many weeks between Pentecost and Christ the King (the last Sunday of the year), the seasons and calendars of North America offer some distinctive periods through which we may shape prayer in the household.

The Day of Pentecost is celebrated close to the end of the school year. A connection exists between graduations/new beginnings and our prayer for the Spirit's guidance in new endeavors. For many people, the months of June, July, and August signal a slightly altered schedule attuned to the weather, harvests, and vacations. Summer months offer their unique grace to those who spend time in discerning the many images which link the scriptures and the patient growth of the seed in the soil.

Table Prayer for Summer

The earth is the LORD's and all that is in it,
the world, and those who live in it. (Ps. 24:1)

All here gathered, food from the land,
all is gift from your gracious hand.
Feed us today; feed all those who hunger;
teach us to feed one another.
We ask this in the name of the one who is our bread, Jesus Christ.
Amen.

Sunday, June 4, 2023
The Holy Trinity

Matthew 28:16-20

Living in the community of the Trinity

Now the eleven disciples went to Galilee, to the mountain to which Jesus had directed them. When they saw him, they worshiped him; but some doubted. And Jesus came and said to them, "All authority in heaven and on earth has been given to me. Go therefore and make disciples of all nations, baptizing them in the name of the Father and of the Son and of the Holy Spirit, and teaching them to obey everything that I have commanded you. And remember, I am with you always, to the end of the age." (Matt. 28:16-20)

Psalm

Psalm 8
How exalted is your name

Additional Readings

Genesis 1:1—2:4a
Creation of the heavens and the earth

2 Corinthians 13:11-13
Paul's farewell

Hymn: Womb of Life and Source of Being, ACS 948

God of heaven and earth, before the foundation of the universe and the beginning of time you are the triune God: Author of creation, eternal Word of salvation, life-giving Spirit of wisdom. Guide us to all truth by your Spirit, that we may proclaim all that Christ has revealed and rejoice in the glory he shares with us. Glory and praise to you, Father, Son, and Holy Spirit, now and forever.

Monday, June 5, 2023
Time after Pentecost

Boniface, Bishop of Mainz, missionary to Germany, martyr, died 754

Psalm 29
Praise the glory of God

Ascribe to the Lord, O heavenly beings,
　　ascribe to the Lord glory and strength.
Ascribe to the Lord the glory of his name;
　　worship the Lord in holy splendor. . . .

The Lord sits enthroned over the flood;
　　the Lord sits enthroned as king forever.
May the Lord give strength to his people!
　　May the Lord bless his people with peace! (Ps. 29:1-2, 10-11)

Additional Readings
Job 38:39—39:12
Creation story from Job

1 Corinthians 12:1-3
Faith is a gift of the Spirit

Hymn: Oh, That I Had a Thousand Voices, ELW 833

*O God of beauty, you invite us to gaze at the stars and behold your glory.
Dazzle us with your splendor, that in all we see and do this day we might
revel in your power and rest in your peace.*

Tuesday, June 6, 2023
Time after Pentecost

1 Corinthians 12:4-13
The Spirit in the community

For just as the body is one and has many members, and all the members of the body, though many, are one body, so it is with Christ. For in the one Spirit we were all baptized into one body—Jews or Greeks, slaves or free—and we were all made to drink of one Spirit. (1 Cor. 12:12-13)

Psalm
Psalm 29
Praise the glory of God

Additional Reading
Job 39:13-25
Creation story from Job

Hymn: O Living Breath of God, ELW 407

Wondrous God, you bless all your children with breathtaking skills and talents, insights and passions. Take from us the spirit of jealousy and enchant us with all the diverse gifts that form the body of Christ.

Wednesday, June 7, 2023
Time after Pentecost

Seattle, chief of the Duwamish Confederacy, died 1866

John 14:25-26
Father, Son, Spirit

[Jesus said,] "I have said these things to you while I am still with you. But the Advocate, the Holy Spirit, whom the Father will send in my name, will teach you everything, and remind you of all that I have said to you." (John 14:25-26)

Psalm
Psalm 29
Praise the glory of God

Additional Reading
Job 39:26—40:5
Creation story from Job; Job's response

Hymn: Come, Gracious Spirit, Heavenly Dove, ELW 404

Astonishing God, Father, Son, and Holy Spirit, draw us near to you that we may hear your voice, be touched by your love, and accept your invitation to join the dance of the Trinity.

Thursday, June 8, 2023
Time after Pentecost

Psalm 50:7-15
The salvation of God

"Hear, O my people, and I will speak,
    O Israel, I will testify against you.
    I am God, your God. . . .

Offer to God a sacrifice of thanksgiving,
    and pay your vows to the Most High.
Call on me in the day of trouble;
    I will deliver you, and you shall glorify me." (Ps. 50:7, 14-15)

Additional Readings
Lamentations 1:7-11
Jerusalem becomes unclean

2 Peter 2:17-22
The world's entanglements

Hymn: O God beyond All Praising, ELW 880

God of comfort, you plead with us to stand before you even when we are dismayed and enraged. Grant that, captivated by your soothing presence, we may offer you unending sacrifices of praise and thanksgiving.

Friday, June 9, 2023
Time after Pentecost

Columba, died 597; Aidan, died 651; Bede, died 735; renewers of the church

Acts 28:1-10
Paul in Malta heals Publius

Now in the neighborhood of that place were lands belonging to the leading man of the island, named Publius, who received us and entertained us hospitably for three days. It so happened that the father of Publius lay sick in bed with fever and dysentery. Paul visited him and cured him by praying and putting his hands on him. After this happened, the rest of the people on the island who had diseases also came and were cured. They bestowed many honors on us, and when we were about to sail, they put on board all the provisions we needed. (Acts 28:7-10)

Psalm
Psalm 50:7-15
The salvation of God

Additional Reading
Lamentations 3:40-58
Let us return to God

Hymn: Come, Ye Disconsolate, ELW 607

Merciful God, through the ages you have healed the sick and uplifted the weary. Embolden us to come to you in times of need, trusting that you can make all things new.

Saturday, June 10, 2023
Time after Pentecost

Matthew 9:27-34

Jesus heals those who are blind or mute

As Jesus went on from there, two blind men followed him, crying loudly, "Have mercy on us, Son of David!" When he entered the house, the blind men came to him; and Jesus said to them, "Do you believe that I am able to do this?" They said to him, "Yes, Lord." Then he touched their eyes and said, "According to your faith let it be done to you." And their eyes were opened. Then Jesus sternly ordered them, "See that no one knows of this." But they went away and spread the news about him throughout that district. (Matt. 9:27-31)

Psalm

Psalm 50:7-15
The salvation of God

Additional Reading

Exodus 34:1-9
Moses makes new tablets

Hymn: We Come to You for Healing, Lord, ELW 617

Gracious God, you yearn to touch us with your mercy. Empower us to believe that, as you gave sight to the two men who were blind, you can also heal us from all that troubles us.

Matthew 9:9-13, 18-26

Christ heals a woman and raises a girl

As Jesus was walking along, he saw a man called Matthew sitting at the tax booth; and he said to him, "Follow me." And he got up and followed him.

And as he sat at dinner in the house, many tax collectors and sinners came and were sitting with him and his disciples. When the Pharisees saw this, they said to his disciples, "Why does your teacher eat with tax collectors and sinners?" But when he heard this, he said, "Those who are well have no need of a physician, but those who are sick. Go and learn what this means, 'I desire mercy, not sacrifice.' For I have come to call not the righteous but sinners." (Matt. 9:9-13)

Psalm

Psalm 50:7-15
The salvation of God

Additional Readings

Hosea 5:15—6:6
God desires steadfast love

Romans 4:13-25
The faith of Abraham

Hymn: Come, Follow Me, the Savior Spake, ELW 799

O God, you are the source of life and the ground of our being. By the power of your Spirit bring healing to this wounded world, and raise us to the new life of your Son, Jesus Christ, our Savior and Lord.

Monday, June 12, 2023
Barnabas, Apostle (transferred)

Acts 11:19-30; 13:1-3
Barnabas and Saul are set apart

Now in the church at Antioch there were prophets and teachers:
Barnabas, Simeon who was called Niger, Lucius of Cyrene, Manaen
a member of the court of Herod the ruler, and Saul. While they were
worshiping the Lord and fasting, the Holy Spirit said, "Set apart for me
Barnabas and Saul for the work to which I have called them." Then after
fasting and praying they laid their hands on them and sent them off.
(Acts 13:1-3)

Psalm

Psalm 112
Happy are the God-fearing

Additional Readings

Isaiah 42:5-12
*The Lord calls us in
righteousness*

Matthew 10:7-16
Jesus sends out the Twelve

Hymn: Spread, Oh, Spread, Almighty Word, ELW 663

*We praise you, O God, for the life of your faithful servant Barnabas, who,
seeking not his own renown but the well-being of your church, gave generously of his life and possessions for the relief of the poor and the spread of
the gospel. Grant that we may follow his example and by our actions give
glory to you, Father, Son, and Holy Spirit, now and forever.*

Tuesday, June 13, 2023
Time after Pentecost

Hosea 8:11-14; 10:1-2
God rejects Israel's sacrifice

When Ephraim multiplied altars to expiate sin,
    they became to him altars for sinning.
Though I write for him the multitude of my instructions,
    they are regarded as a strange thing.
Though they offer choice sacrifices,
    though they eat flesh,
    the LORD does not accept them.
Now he will remember their iniquity,
    and punish their sins;
    they shall return to Egypt.
Israel has forgotten his Maker,
    and built palaces;
and Judah has multiplied fortified cities;
    but I will send a fire upon his cities,
    and it shall devour his strongholds. (Hosea 8:11-14)

Psalm
Psalm 40:1-8
God's will, not sacrifice

Additional Reading
Hebrews 13:1-16
Sacrifices pleasing to God

Hymn: Take My Life, That I May Be, ELW 583/685

God of infinite generosity, the angels sing of your glory. Kindle in us the gift of music-making, that as we listen to the voices of people who are poor and suffering, we might hear the melodies of heaven.

Wednesday, June 14, 2023
Time after Pentecost

Basil the Great, Bishop of Caesarea, died 379; Gregory, Bishop of Nyssa,
died around 385; Gregory of Nazianzus, Bishop of Constantinople,
died around 389; Macrina, teacher, died around 379

Psalm 40:1-8
God's will, not sacrifice

Happy are those who make
>the LORD their trust,
who do not turn to the proud,
>to those who go astray after false gods.
You have multiplied, O LORD my God,
>your wondrous deeds and your thoughts toward us;
>none can compare with you.
Were I to proclaim and tell of them,
>they would be more than can be counted.

Sacrifice and offering you do not desire,
>but you have given me an open ear.
Burnt offering and sin offering
>you have not required.
Then I said, "Here I am;
>in the scroll of the book it is written of me.
I delight to do your will, O my God;
>your law is within my heart." (Ps. 40:4-8)

Additional Readings

Hosea 14:1-9
God will be merciful to Israel

Matthew 12:1-8
Mercy, not sacrifice

Hymn: O God, Who Gives Us Life, ACS 1086

*Affectionate God, fill us with the warmth of your love that we may radiate
the gifts of your tenderness on everyone we meet this day.*

Thursday, June 15, 2023
Time after Pentecost

Exodus 4:18-23
Moses called to Egypt

And the LORD said to Moses, "When you go back to Egypt, see that you perform before Pharaoh all the wonders that I have put in your power; but I will harden his heart, so that he will not let the people go. Then you shall say to Pharaoh, 'Thus says the LORD: Israel is my firstborn son. I said to you, "Let my son go that he may worship me." But you refused to let him go; now I will kill your firstborn son.'" (Exod. 4:21-23)

Psalm
Psalm 100
We are God's people

Additional Reading
Hebrews 3:1-6
Moses a servant, Christ a son

Hymn: Wade in the Water, ELW 459

O God, defender of the oppressed and deliverer of the enslaved, you watch over your tormented children in every generation. Lead all those who are crossing the raging waters of oppression into the tranquil oasis of freedom.

Friday, June 16, 2023
Time after Pentecost

Exodus 4:27-31
Aaron called to Moses' side

The LORD said to Aaron, "Go into the wilderness to meet Moses." So he went; and he met him at the mountain of God and kissed him. Moses told Aaron all the words of the LORD with which he had sent him, and all the signs with which he had charged him. Then Moses and Aaron went and assembled all the elders of the Israelites. Aaron spoke all the words that the LORD had spoken to Moses, and performed the signs in the sight of the people. The people believed; and when they heard that the LORD had given heed to the Israelites and that he had seen their misery, they bowed down and worshiped. (Exod. 4:27-31)

Psalm
Psalm 100
We are God's people

Additional Reading
Acts 7:35-43
Israel doubts Moses, prevails upon Aaron

Hymn: God Is Here! ELW 526

God of the universe, by your word you create beauty from chaos, hope from despair, and life from death. Fill us with your Spirit, that we may be amazed by your resurrection power and praise your holy name forever.

Saturday, June 17, 2023
Time after Pentecost

Emanuel Nine, martyrs, died 2015

Mark 7:1-13
Moses' witness spurned by religious leaders

Then [Jesus] said to [the Pharisees], "You have a fine way of rejecting the commandment of God in order to keep your tradition! For Moses said, 'Honor your father and your mother'; and, 'Whoever speaks evil of father or mother must surely die.' But you say that if anyone tells father or mother, 'Whatever support you might have had from me is Corban' (that is, an offering to God)—then you no longer permit doing anything for a father or mother, thus making void the word of God through your tradition that you have handed on. And you do many things like this." (Mark 7:9-13)

Psalm
Psalm 100
We are God's people

Additional Reading
Exodus 6:28—7:13
Moses and Aaron before Pharaoh

Hymn: Salvation unto Us Has Come, ELW 590

God of the holy mountain, you entrust your people with the law that we might love you and live together in peace. We humbly confess our failure to live as you desire and implore you to free us from the devastation of our sins.

Sunday, June 18, 2023
Time after Pentecost

Matthew 9:35—10:8 [9-23]
The sending of the Twelve

These twelve [disciples] Jesus sent out with the following instructions: "Go nowhere among the Gentiles, and enter no town of the Samaritans, but go rather to the lost sheep of the house of Israel. As you go, proclaim the good news, 'The kingdom of heaven has come near.' Cure the sick, raise the dead, cleanse the lepers, cast out demons. You received without payment; give without payment." (Matt. 10:5-8)

Psalm

Psalm 100
We are God's people

Additional Readings

Exodus 19:2-8a
The covenant with Israel at Sinai

Romans 5:1-8
While we were sinners, Christ died for us

Hymn: The Son of God, Our Christ, ELW 584

God of compassion, you have opened the way for us and brought us to yourself. Pour your love into our hearts, that, overflowing with joy, we may freely share the blessings of your realm and faithfully proclaim the good news of your Son, Jesus Christ, our Savior and Lord.

Monday, June 19, 2023
Time after Pentecost

Psalm 105:1-11, 37-45
God saves the chosen people

So he brought his people out with joy,
>   his chosen ones with singing.
He gave them the lands of the nations,
>   and they took possession of the wealth of the peoples,
that they might keep his statutes
>   and observe his laws.
Praise the LORD! (Ps. 105:43-45)

Additional Readings
Joshua 1:1-11
God calls Joshua

1 Thessalonians 3:1-5
Timothy is sent to Thessalonica

Hymn: Sing with All the Saints in Glory, ELW 426

Ever-guiding God, you lead us from danger to safety, from chaos to serenity. Grant that we may trust your promise of everlasting life in all the dangers we face and make us confident that you are with us always.

Tuesday, June 20, 2023
Time after Pentecost

2 Thessalonians 2:13—3:5
The life of those chosen by God

But we must always give thanks to God for you, brothers and sisters beloved by the Lord, because God chose you as the first fruits for salvation through sanctification by the Spirit and through belief in the truth. For this purpose he called you through our proclamation of the good news, so that you may obtain the glory of our Lord Jesus Christ. So then, brothers and sisters, stand firm and hold fast to the traditions that you were taught by us, either by word of mouth or by our letter. (2 Thess. 2:13-15)

Psalm
Psalm 105:1-11, 37-45
God saves the chosen people

Additional Reading
1 Samuel 3:1-9
God calls Samuel

Hymn: Lord Jesus Christ, Be Present Now, ELW 527

Precious Savior, you are present with us in bread, wine, water, and the word. Comfort us with these gifts of heaven and arouse us to share them with those we are called to serve.

Wednesday, June 21, 2023
Time after Pentecost

Onesimos Nesib, translator, evangelist, died 1931

Proverbs 4:10-27
Choosing the way of wisdom

Hear, my child, and accept my words,
    that the years of your life may be many.
I have taught you the way of wisdom;
    I have led you in the paths of uprightness.
When you walk, your step will not be hampered;
    and if you run, you will not stumble.
Keep hold of instruction; do not let go;
    guard her, for she is your life. (Prov. 4:10-13)

Psalm
Psalm 105:1-11, 37-45
God saves the chosen people

Additional Reading
Luke 6:12-19
Jesus chooses the apostles

Hymn: Beloved, God's Chosen, ELW 648

Omnipotent God, you bless us with your words of eternal life. Inflame in us your Spirit's fire that we may walk boldly as your people, trusting that you are with us as we announce your goodness to everyone.

Thursday, June 22, 2023
Time after Pentecost

Psalm 69:7-10 [11-15] 16-18
Draw near to me

Answer me, O LORD, for your steadfast love is good;
    according to your abundant mercy, turn to me.
Do not hide your face from your servant,
    for I am in distress—make haste to answer me.
Draw near to me, redeem me,
    set me free because of my enemies. (Ps. 69:16-18)

Additional Readings
Jeremiah 18:12-17
Israel's stubborn idolatry

Hebrews 2:5-9
Exaltation through abasement

Hymn: In the Midst of Earthly Life, ACS 1026

Gracious God, you promise to be at our side in all seasons of life. Enliven our prayers that we may tell you what weighs heavily on our hearts and listen for your heavenly wisdom and divine favor.

Friday, June 23, 2023
Time after Pentecost

Jeremiah 18:18-23

A plot against Jeremiah

Give heed to me, O LORD,
>   and listen to what my adversaries say!
Is evil a recompense for good?
>   Yet they have dug a pit for my life.
Remember how I stood before you
>   to speak good for them,
>   to turn away your wrath from them.
Therefore give their children over to famine;
>   hurl them out to the power of the sword,
let their wives become childless and widowed.
>   May their men meet death by pestilence,
>   their youths be slain by the sword in battle.
May a cry be heard from their houses,
>   when you bring the marauder suddenly upon them!
For they have dug a pit to catch me,
>   and laid snares for my feet. (Jer. 18:19-22)

Psalm

Psalm 69:7-10 [11-15] 16-18
Draw near to me

Additional Reading

Acts 5:17-26
The apostles are persecuted

Hymn: Forgive Our Sins As We Forgive, ELW 605

O vigilant God, you promise to watch over us when our enemies surround us. Teach us to cry out boldly to you when fear paralyzes us, and protect us always from all the terrors of the night.

Saturday, June 24, 2023
John the Baptist

Luke 1:57-67 [68-80]
The birth and naming of John

On the eighth day [Elizabeth and her neighbors and relatives] came to circumcise the child, and they were going to name him Zechariah after his father. But his mother said, "No; he is to be called John." They said to her, "None of your relatives has this name." Then they began motioning to his father to find out what name he wanted to give him. He asked for a writing tablet and wrote, "His name is John." And all of them were amazed. Immediately his mouth was opened and his tongue freed, and he began to speak, praising God. (Luke 1:59-64)

Psalm

Psalm 141
My eyes are turned to God

Additional Readings

Malachi 3:1-4
My messenger, a refiner and purifier

Acts 13:13-26
The gospel for the descendants of Abraham

Hymn: Blessed Be the God of Israel, ELW 250

Almighty God, by your gracious providence your servant John the Baptist was born to Elizabeth and Zechariah. Grant to your people the wisdom to see your purpose and the openness to hear your will, that the light of Christ may increase in us, through Jesus Christ, our Savior and Lord, who lives and reigns with you and the Holy Spirit, one God, now and forever.

Sunday, June 25, 2023
Time after Pentecost

Presentation of the Augsburg Confession, 1530
Philipp Melanchthon, renewer of the church, died 1560

Matthew 10:24-39
The cost of discipleship

[Jesus said,] "Whoever loves father or mother more than me is not worthy of me; and whoever loves son or daughter more than me is not worthy of me; and whoever does not take up the cross and follow me is not worthy of me. Those who find their life will lose it, and those who lose their life for my sake will find it." (Matt. 10:37-39)

Psalm
Psalm 69:7-10 [11-15] 16-18
Draw near to me

Additional Readings
Jeremiah 20:7-13
The prophet must speak

Romans 6:1b-11
Buried and raised with Christ in baptism

Hymn: Take Up Your Cross, the Savior Said, ELW 667

Teach us, good Lord God, to serve you as you deserve, to give and not to count the cost, to fight and not to heed the wounds, to toil and not to seek for rest, to labor and not to ask for reward, except that of knowing that we do your will, through Jesus Christ, our Savior and Lord.

Monday, June 26, 2023
Time after Pentecost

Psalm 6
Prayer for deliverance

O LORD, do not rebuke me in your anger,
>   or discipline me in your wrath.
Be gracious to me, O LORD, for I am languishing;
>   O LORD, heal me, for my bones are shaking with terror.
My soul also is struck with terror,
>   while you, O LORD—how long?

Turn, O LORD, save my life;
>   deliver me for the sake of your steadfast love.
For in death there is no remembrance of you;
>   in Sheol who can give you praise? (Ps. 6:1-5)

Additional Readings
Micah 7:1-7
The corruption of the people

Revelation 2:1-7
Remember from what you have fallen

Hymn: O God, Our Help in Ages Past, ELW 632

Merciful God, you deliver your blessed children from the snares of death.
Spare us from the wrath of your judgment, and gather us at your mercy
table where we might savor the bread of heaven and the cup of salvation.

Tuesday, June 27, 2023
Time after Pentecost

Cyril, Bishop of Alexandria, died 444

Revelation 2:8-11
The faithful receive the crown of life

"And to the angel of the church in Smyrna write: These are the words of the first and the last, who was dead and came to life:

"I know your affliction and your poverty, even though you are rich. I know the slander on the part of those who say that they are Jews and are not, but are a synagogue of Satan. Do not fear what you are about to suffer. Beware, the devil is about to throw some of you into prison so that you may be tested, and for ten days you will have affliction. Be faithful until death, and I will give you the crown of life. Let anyone who has an ear listen to what the Spirit is saying to the churches. Whoever conquers will not be harmed by the second death." (Rev. 2:8-11)

Psalm
Psalm 6
Prayer for deliverance

Additional Reading
Jeremiah 26:1-12
Prophecy against Jerusalem

Hymn: Deep River, ACS 951

Compassionate God, you are near to us in all our trials. When our enemies persecute us, may we stand fast, trusting that you will place the crown of glory on our heads forever and ever.

Wednesday, June 28, 2023
Time after Pentecost

Irenaeus, Bishop of Lyons, died around 202

Matthew 10:5-23

Jesus speaks about persecution

[Jesus said to the twelve disciples,] "See, I am sending you out like sheep into the midst of wolves; so be wise as serpents and innocent as doves. Beware of them, for they will hand you over to councils and flog you in their synagogues; and you will be dragged before governors and kings because of me, as a testimony to them and the Gentiles. When they hand you over, do not worry about how you are to speak or what you are to say; for what you are to say will be given to you at that time; for it is not you who speak, but the Spirit of your Father speaking through you." (Matt. 10:16-20)

Psalm

Psalm 6
Prayer for deliverance

Additional Reading

Jeremiah 38:1-13
Jeremiah imprisoned and released

Hymn: O God, My Faithful God, ELW 806

O good Shepherd, you promise to watch over us as we endure the battles of this world. Embolden us to walk faithfully amid the powerful and to speak confidently of your love to every suffering soul.

Thursday, June 29, 2023
Peter and Paul, Apostles

John 21:15-19

Jesus says to Peter: Tend my sheep

When [the disciples] had finished breakfast, Jesus said to Simon Peter, "Simon son of John, do you love me more than these?" He said to him, "Yes, Lord; you know that I love you." Jesus said to him, "Feed my lambs." A second time he said to him, "Simon son of John, do you love me?" He said to him, "Yes, Lord; you know that I love you." Jesus said to him, "Tend my sheep." He said to him the third time, "Simon son of John, do you love me?" Peter felt hurt because he said to him the third time, "Do you love me?" And he said to him, "Lord, you know everything; you know that I love you." Jesus said to him, "Feed my sheep." (John 21:15-17)

Psalm

Psalm 87:1-3, 5-7
Glorious things are spoken of you

Additional Readings

Acts 12:1-11
Peter released from prison

2 Timothy 4:6-8, 17-18
The good fight of faith

Hymn: Lord, You Give the Great Commission, ELW 579

Almighty God, we praise you that your blessed apostles Peter and Paul glorified you by their martyrdoms. Grant that your church throughout the world may always be instructed by their teaching and example, be knit together in unity by your Spirit, and ever stand firm upon the one foundation who is Jesus Christ our Lord, for he lives and reigns with you and the Holy Spirit, one God, now and forever.

Friday, June 30, 2023
Time after Pentecost

Galatians 5:7-12
Beware of false teachers

You were running well; who prevented you from obeying the truth? Such persuasion does not come from the one who calls you. A little yeast leavens the whole batch of dough. I am confident about you in the Lord that you will not think otherwise. But whoever it is that is confusing you will pay the penalty. But my friends, why am I still being persecuted if I am still preaching circumcision? In that case the offense of the cross has been removed. I wish those who unsettle you would castrate themselves! (Gal. 5:7-12)

Psalm
Psalm 89:1-4, 15-18
I sing of your love

Additional Reading
Jeremiah 25:8-14
Captivity of Israel foretold

Hymn: Strengthen for Service, Lord, ELW 497

O patient God, you have endured the foolishness of your children in every generation. Be patient with us when we go astray and draw us back into your fold where you promise to protect us forever.

Prayer List for July

_____

_____

_____

_____

_____

_____

_____

_____

_____

_____

Saturday, July 1, 2023
Time after Pentecost

Catherine Winkworth, died 1878; John Mason Neale, died 1866; hymn translators

Jeremiah 28:1-4

Hananiah prophesies falsely

In that same year, at the beginning of the reign of King Zedckiah of Judah, in the fifth month of the fourth year, the prophet Hananiah son of Azzur, from Gibeon, spoke to me in the house of the LORD, in the presence of the priests and all the people, saying, "Thus says the LORD of hosts, the God of Israel: I have broken the yoke of the king of Babylon. Within two years I will bring back to this place all the vessels of the LORD's house, which King Nebuchadnezzar of Babylon took away from this place and carried to Babylon. I will also bring back to this place King Jeconiah son of Jehoiakim of Judah, and all the exiles from Judah who went to Babylon, says the LORD, for I will break the yoke of the king of Babylon." (Jer. 28:1-4)

Psalm

Psalm 89:1-4, 15-18
I sing of your love

Additional Reading

Luke 17:1-4
Causing little ones to stumble

Hymn: God of Grace and God of Glory, ELW 705

Word of life, thank you for prophets who speak your truth. Guard us from those who offer false promises in place of your sometimes-painful vision, so that we might act faithfully.

Sunday, July 2, 2023
Time after Pentecost

Matthew 10:40-42

Welcome Christ in those Christ sends

[Jesus said to his disciples,] "Whoever welcomes you welcomes me, and whoever welcomes me welcomes the one who sent me. Whoever welcomes a prophet in the name of a prophet will receive a prophet's reward; and whoever welcomes a righteous person in the name of a righteous person will receive the reward of the righteous; and whoever gives even a cup of cold water to one of these little ones in the name of a disciple—truly I tell you, none of these will lose their reward." (Matt. 10:40-42)

Psalm

Psalm 89:1-4, 15-18
I sing of your love

Additional Readings

Jeremiah 28:5-9
Test of a true prophet

Romans 6:12-23
No longer under law but under grace

Hymn: O Christ, Your Heart, Compassionate, ELW 722

O God, you direct our lives by your grace, and your words of justice and mercy reshape the world. Mold us into a people who welcome your word and serve one another through Jesus Christ, our Savior and Lord.

Monday, July 3, 2023
Thomas, Apostle

John 14:1-7
Jesus, the way, the truth, the life

Thomas said to [Jesus], "Lord, we do not know where you are going. How can we know the way?" Jesus said to him, "I am the way, and the truth, and the life. No one comes to the Father except through me. If you know me, you will know my Father also. From now on you do know him and have seen him." (John 14:5-7)

Psalm
Psalm 136:1-4, 23-26
God's mercy endures forever

Additional Readings
Judges 6:36-40
God affirms Gideon's calling

Ephesians 4:11-16
The body of Christ has various gifts

Hymn: Come, My Way, My Truth, My Life, ELW 816

Ever-living God, you strengthened your apostle Thomas with firm and certain faith in the resurrection of your Son. Grant that we too may confess our faith in Jesus Christ, our Lord and our God, who lives and reigns with you and the Holy Spirit, one God, now and forever.

Tuesday, July 4, 2023
Time after Pentecost

1 John 4:1-6
Testing the spirits

Beloved, do not believe every spirit, but test the spirits to see whether they are from God; for many false prophets have gone out into the world. By this you know the Spirit of God: every spirit that confesses that Jesus Christ has come in the flesh is from God, and every spirit that does not confess Jesus is not from God. And this is the spirit of the antichrist, of which you have heard that it is coming; and now it is already in the world. (1 John 4:1-3)

Psalm
Psalm 119:161-168
Loving God's law

Additional Reading
1 Kings 21:17-29
Elijah confronts Ahab

Hymn: Let Us Ever Walk with Jesus, ELW 802

Wise One, you know we are inclined to mistake lies for truth and evil for good. By your Holy Spirit, help us measure the claims of unholy voices against your grace proclaimed in Jesus.

Wednesday, July 5, 2023
Time after Pentecost

Matthew 11:20-24
Jesus prophesies against the cities

Then [Jesus] began to reproach the cities in which most of his deeds of power had been done, because they did not repent. "Woe to you, Chorazin! Woe to you, Bethsaida! For if the deeds of power done in you had been done in Tyre and Sidon, they would have repented long ago in sackcloth and ashes. But I tell you, on the day of judgment it will be more tolerable for Tyre and Sidon than for you.
And you, Capernaum,
     will you be exalted to heaven?
          No, you will be brought down to Hades.

For if the deeds of power done in you had been done in Sodom, it would have remained until this day. But I tell you that on the day of judgment it will be more tolerable for the land of Sodom than for you." (Matt. 11:20-24)

Psalm
Psalm 119:161-168
Loving God's law

Additional Reading
Jeremiah 18:1-11
Jeremiah at the potter's wheel

Hymn: Mine Eyes Have Seen the Glory, ELW 890

Relentless God, thank you for constantly pursuing your disobedient people through powerful miracles and fiery judgments. Open our wayward hearts to your determined mercy, so that we might return to you.

Thursday, July 6, 2023
Time after Pentecost

Jan Hus, martyr, died 1415

Psalm 145:8-14
God is full of compassion

The LORD is gracious and merciful,
> slow to anger and abounding in steadfast love.
The LORD is good to all,
> and his compassion is over all that he has made.

All your works shall give thanks to you, O LORD,
> and all your faithful shall bless you.
They shall speak of the glory of your kingdom,
> and tell of your power,
to make known to all people your mighty deeds,
> and the glorious splendor of your kingdom. (Ps. 145:8-12)

Additional Readings
Zechariah 1:1-6
Israel urged to repent

Romans 7:1-6
Dying to the law through Christ

Hymn: Thine the Amen, ELW 826

Gracious God, your faithful love rains down daily on all creation. Enable our thanks and praise to overflow, so that every living thing may be in awe of your glory and flourish under your rule.

Friday, July 7, 2023
Time after Pentecost

Zechariah 2:6-13
Exiles are the apple of God's eye

Up, up! Flee from the land of the north, says the LORD; for I have spread you abroad like the four winds of heaven, says the LORD. Up! Escape to Zion, you that live with daughter Babylon. For thus said the LORD of hosts (after his glory sent me) regarding the nations that plundered you: Truly, one who touches you touches the apple of my eye. See now, I am going to raise my hand against them, and they shall become plunder for their own slaves. Then you will know that the LORD of hosts has sent me. Sing and rejoice, O daughter Zion! For lo, I will come and dwell in your midst, says the LORD. (Zech. 2:6-10)

Psalm
Psalm 145:8-14
God is full of compassion

Additional Reading
Romans 7:7-20
Sin and the law kill us

Hymn: Let Streams of Living Justice, ELW 710

Freeing God, because you call us the apple of your eye, you liberate us from every form of bondage. Raise us up in the power of your loving spirit, so that we may free others from fear, violence, and injustice.

Saturday, July 8, 2023
Time after Pentecost

Luke 10:21-24

Jesus rejoices in the Holy Spirit

At that same hour Jesus rejoiced in the Holy Spirit and said, "I thank you, Father, Lord of heaven and earth, because you have hidden these things from the wise and the intelligent and have revealed them to infants; yes, Father, for such was your gracious will. All things have been handed over to me by my Father; and no one knows who the Son is except the Father, or who the Father is except the Son and anyone to whom the Son chooses to reveal him."

Then turning to the disciples, Jesus said to them privately, "Blessed are the eyes that see what you see! For I tell you that many prophets and kings desired to see what you see, but did not see it, and to hear what you hear, but did not hear it." (Luke 10:21-24)

Psalm

Psalm 145:8-14
God is full of compassion

Additional Reading

Zechariah 4:1-7
By my Spirit, says God

Hymn: O God of Mercy, God of Light, ELW 714

Almighty God, thank you for dethroning haughty people through the humble ways of Jesus. When we seek status through our own achievements, lead us to kneel in solidarity with people who are in misery.

Sunday, July 9, 2023
Time after Pentecost

Matthew 11:16-19, 25-30
The yoke of discipleship

[Jesus said,] "Come to me, all you that are weary and are carrying heavy burdens, and I will give you rest. Take my yoke upon you, and learn from me; for I am gentle and humble in heart, and you will find rest for your souls. For my yoke is easy, and my burden is light." (Matt. 11:28-30)

Psalm
Psalm 145:8-14
God is full of compassion

Additional Readings
Zechariah 9:9-12
The king comes in peace

Romans 7:15-25a
The struggle within the self

Hymn: Come, Bring Your Burdens to God, ACS 1009

You are great, O God, and greatly to be praised. You have made us for yourself, and our hearts are restless until they rest in you. Grant that we may believe in you, call upon you, know you, and serve you through your Son, Jesus Christ, our Savior and Lord.

Monday, July 10, 2023
Time after Pentecost

Psalm 131
I rest like a weaned child on God

O LORD, my heart is not lifted up,
    my eyes are not raised too high;
I do not occupy myself with things
    too great and too marvelous for me.
But I have calmed and quieted my soul,
    like a weaned child with its mother;
    my soul is like the weaned child that is with me.

O Israel, hope in the LORD
    from this time on and forevermore. (Ps. 131:1-3)

Additional Readings
Jeremiah 27:1-11, 16-22
Jeremiah wears the evil yoke

Romans 1:18-25
The guilt of humankind

Hymn: Come Down, O Love Divine, ELW 804

Mothering God, thank you for adopting us as your children. Embrace us with your peace when we tremble before the state of the world, so that we trust you are powerfully at work on behalf of your little ones.

Tuesday, July 11, 2023
Time after Pentecost

Benedict of Nursia, Abbot of Monte Cassino, died around 540

Jeremiah 28:10-17

Hananiah breaks Jeremiah's yoke

Then the prophet Hananiah took the yoke from the neck of the prophet Jeremiah, and broke it. And Hananiah spoke in the presence of all the people, saying, "Thus says the LORD: This is how I will break the yoke of King Nebuchadnezzar of Babylon from the neck of all the nations within two years." At this, the prophet Jeremiah went his way.

Sometime after the prophet Hananiah had broken the yoke from the neck of the prophet Jeremiah, the word of the LORD came to Jeremiah: Go, tell Hananiah, Thus says the LORD: You have broken wooden bars only to forge iron bars in place of them! For thus says the LORD of hosts, the God of Israel: I have put an iron yoke on the neck of all these nations so that they may serve King Nebuchadnezzar of Babylon, and they shall indeed serve him; I have even given him the wild animals. (Jer. 28:10-14)

Psalm
Psalm 131
I rest like a weaned child on God

Additional Reading
Romans 3:1-8
The faithfulness of God

Hymn: O God of Every Nation, ELW 713

God of truth, your prophet Jeremiah announced that no one can defy your will forever. When lies and injustice seem to triumph, renew our belief that Jesus' resurrection guarantees that even death will yield to your righteous rule.

Wednesday, July 12, 2023
Time after Pentecost

Nathan Söderblom, Bishop of Uppsala, died 1931

Jeremiah 13:1-11

Jeremiah's loincloth

Then the word of the LORD came to me: Thus says the LORD: Just so I will ruin the pride of Judah and the great pride of Jerusalem. This evil people, who refuse to hear my words, who stubbornly follow their own will and have gone after other gods to serve them and worship them, shall be like this loincloth, which is good for nothing. For as the loincloth clings to one's loins, so I made the whole house of Israel and the whole house of Judah cling to me, says the LORD, in order that they might be for me a people, a name, a praise, and a glory. But they would not listen. (Jer. 13:8-11)

Psalm

Psalm 131
I rest like a weaned child on God

Additional Reading

John 13:1-17
Jesus washes the disciples' feet

Hymn: Abide with Me, ELW 629

Merciful God, you cleanse us from our sins through Jesus' righteousness, yet we ignore your voice and pursue our proud desires. Wash us again in your grace, so that our lives might glorify your name alone.

Thursday, July 13, 2023
Time after Pentecost

Psalm 65:[1-8] 9-13
Your paths overflow with plenty

You visit the earth and water it,
    you greatly enrich it;
the river of God is full of water;
    you provide the people with grain,
    for so you have prepared it.
You water its furrows abundantly,
    settling its ridges,
softening it with showers,
    and blessing its growth.
You crown the year with your bounty;
    your wagon tracks overflow with richness.
The pastures of the wilderness overflow,
    the hills gird themselves with joy,
the meadows clothe themselves with flocks,
    the valleys deck themselves with grain,
    they shout and sing together for joy. (Ps. 65:9-13)

Additional Readings

Isaiah 48:1-5
What God declared long ago

Romans 2:12-16
God judges secret thoughts

Hymn: The Earth Adorned in Verdant Robe, ACS 1068

Astonishing Creator, we do not deserve this abundant earth, yet you provide it to us. We rejoice in your goodness. Help us to faithfully tend your gifts of waters, wilderness, and meadows.

Romans 15:14-21

Sanctified by the Holy Spirit

I myself feel confident about you, my brothers and sisters, that you yourselves are full of goodness, filled with all knowledge, and able to instruct one another. Nevertheless on some points I have written to you rather boldly by way of reminder, because of the grace given me by God to be a minister of Christ Jesus to the Gentiles in the priestly service of the gospel of God, so that the offering of the Gentiles may be acceptable, sanctified by the Holy Spirit. In Christ Jesus, then, I have reason to boast of my work for God. (Rom. 15:14-17)

Psalm

Psalm 65:[1-8] 9-13
Your paths overflow with plenty

Additional Reading

Isaiah 48:6-11
You will hear new, hidden things

Hymn: Founded on Faith, ACS 1048

Gracious God, thank you for calling Christ-like ministers to deepen people's knowledge and practice of the faith. Keep us open to their instruction, so that your Holy Spirit may overflow into the world.

Saturday, July 15, 2023
Time after Pentecost

Isaiah 52:1-6
Sold, redeemed without money

For thus says the LORD: You were sold for nothing, and you shall be redeemed without money. For thus says the Lord GOD: Long ago, my people went down into Egypt to reside there as aliens; the Assyrian, too, has oppressed them without cause. Now therefore what am I doing here, says the LORD, seeing that my people are taken away without cause? Their rulers howl, says the LORD, and continually, all day long, my name is despised. Therefore my people shall know my name; therefore in that day they shall know that it is I who speak; here am I. (Isa. 52:3-6)

Psalm
Psalm 65:[1-8] 9-13
Your paths overflow with plenty

Additional Reading
John 12:44-50
I have come as light into the world

Hymn: When the Poor Ones, ELW 725

O God, you spoke and we were created. You speak again and your lost people are made new. We praise your liberation of Israel and your salvation of all nations through Christ. Help us to honor you forever.

Sunday, July 16, 2023
Time after Pentecost

Matthew 13:1-9, 18-23
The parable of the sower and the seed

[Jesus] told [the crowd] many things in parables, saying: "Listen! A sower went out to sow. And as he sowed, some seeds fell on the path, and the birds came and ate them up. Other seeds fell on rocky ground, where they did not have much soil, and they sprang up quickly, since they had no depth of soil. But when the sun rose, they were scorched; and since they had no root, they withered away. Other seeds fell among thorns, and the thorns grew up and choked them. Other seeds fell on good soil and brought forth grain, some a hundredfold, some sixty, some thirty. Let anyone with ears listen!" (Matt. 13:3-9)

Psalm
Psalm 65:[1-8] 9-13
Your paths overflow with plenty

Additional Readings
Isaiah 55:10-13
The growth of the word

Romans 8:1-11
Living according to the Spirit

Hymn: Lord, Let My Heart Be Good Soil, ELW 512

Almighty God, we thank you for planting in us the seed of your word. By your Holy Spirit help us to receive it with joy, live according to it, and grow in faith and hope and love, through Jesus Christ, our Savior and Lord.

Monday, July 17, 2023
Time after Pentecost

Bartolomé de Las Casas, missionary to the Indies, died 1566

Psalm 92
The righteous as a tree

The righteous flourish like the palm tree,
> and grow like a cedar in Lebanon.
They are planted in the house of the LORD;
> they flourish in the courts of our God.
In old age they still produce fruit;
> they are always green and full of sap,
showing that the LORD is upright;
> he is my rock, and there is no unrighteousness in him. (Ps. 92:12-15)

Additional Readings

Leviticus 26:3-20
A rich and a poor harvest

1 Thessalonians 4:1-8
A life pleasing to God

Hymn: My Hope Is Built on Nothing Less, ELW 596/597

Gracious Gardener, you plant us where we can flourish at any age. Water us with your forgiving spirit, so that our relationships with others might bear the fruits of justice and peace.

Tuesday, July 18, 2023
Time after Pentecost

Ephesians 4:17—5:2
The old life and the new

Let no evil talk come out of your mouths, but only what is useful for building up, as there is need, so that your words may give grace to those who hear. And do not grieve the Holy Spirit of God, with which you were marked with a seal for the day of redemption. Put away from you all bitterness and wrath and anger and wrangling and slander, together with all malice, and be kind to one another, tenderhearted, forgiving one another, as God in Christ has forgiven you. (Eph. 4:29-32)

Psalm
Psalm 92
The righteous as a tree

Additional Reading
Deuteronomy 28:1-14
The blessings of obedience

Hymn: God, When Human Bonds Are Broken, ELW 603

Tender Heart, you grieve when our evil talk burns down our households and your church. Quench our bitterness and malice. Renew our trust in Jesus, so that our lives might witness to his lovingkindness and forgiveness.

Wednesday, July 19, 2023
Time after Pentecost

Proverbs 11:23-30
The fruit of righteousness

Whoever diligently seeks good seeks favor,
    but evil comes to the one who searches for it.
Those who trust in their riches will wither,
    but the righteous will flourish like green leaves.
Those who trouble their households will inherit wind,
    and the fool will be servant to the wise.
The fruit of the righteous is a tree of life,
    but violence takes lives away. (Prov. 11:27-30)

Psalm
Psalm 92
The righteous as a tree

Additional Reading
Matthew 13:10-17
The purpose of parables

Hymn: Be Thou My Vision, ELW 793

Lover of souls, you promise us abundant life in you. Help us to reject our ways of violence and greed, so that we may live fully in Jesus' resurrection life.

Thursday, July 20, 2023
Time after Pentecost

Psalm 86:11-17
Teach me your way

Teach me your way, O LORD,
>   that I may walk in your truth;
>   give me an undivided heart to revere your name.
I give thanks to you, O LORD my God, with my whole heart,
>   and I will glorify your name forever.
For great is your steadfast love toward me;
>   you have delivered my soul from the depths of Sheol. (Ps. 86:11-13)

Additional Readings
Isaiah 41:21-29
The futility of idols

Hebrews 2:1-9
Warning to pay attention

Hymn: O Master, Let Me Walk with You, ELW 818

O Lord, thank you for delivering us from every trouble. Guide us along your way that reveals the truth of your life-giving love. Overcome the doubts in our hearts, so that we praise your name wholeheartedly.

Friday, July 21, 2023
Time after Pentecost

Hebrews 6:13-20
The certainty of God's promises

When God made a promise to Abraham, because he had no one greater by whom to swear, he swore by himself, saying, "I will surely bless you and multiply you." And thus Abraham, having patiently endured, obtained the promise. (Heb. 6:13-15)

Psalm
Psalm 86:11-17
Teach me your way

Additional Reading
Isaiah 44:9-17
Those who make idols are nothing

Hymn: The God of Abraham Praise, ELW 831

Faithful God, thank you for keeping your promise to bless your people abundantly. When scarcity tempts us to doubt your power, reassure us with Abraham's example, so that we also may endure to the end.

Saturday, July 22, 2023
Mary Magdalene, Apostle

John 20:1-2, 11-18
Mary Magdalene meets Jesus in the garden

Jesus said to [Mary Magdalene], "Woman, why are you weeping? Whom are you looking for?" Supposing him to be the gardener, she said to him, "Sir, if you have carried him away, tell me where you have laid him, and I will take him away." Jesus said to her, "Mary!" She turned and said to him in Hebrew, "Rabbouni!" (which means Teacher). Jesus said to her, "Do not hold on to me, because I have not yet ascended to the Father. But go to my brothers and say to them, 'I am ascending to my Father and your Father, to my God and your God.'" Mary Magdalene went and announced to the disciples, "I have seen the Lord"; and she told them that he had said these things to her. (John 20:15-18)

Psalm
Psalm 73:23-28
I will speak of all God's works

Additional Readings
Ruth 1:6-18
Ruth stays with Naomi

Acts 13:26-33a
The raising of Jesus fulfills God's promise

Hymn: Signs and Wonders, ELW 672

Almighty God, your Son first entrusted the apostle Mary Magdalene with the joyful news of his resurrection. Following the example of her witness, may we proclaim Christ as our living Lord and one day see him in glory, for he lives and reigns with you and the Holy Spirit, one God, now and forever.

Sunday, July 23, 2023
Time after Pentecost

Birgitta of Sweden, renewer of the church, died 1373

Matthew 13:24-30, 36-43
The parable of the weeds

[Jesus] put before [the disciples] another parable: "The kingdom of heaven may be compared to someone who sowed good seed in his field; but while everybody was asleep, an enemy came and sowed weeds among the wheat, and then went away. So when the plants came up and bore grain, then the weeds appeared as well. And the slaves of the householder came and said to him, 'Master, did you not sow good seed in your field? Where, then, did these weeds come from?' He answered, 'An enemy has done this.' The slaves said to him, 'Then do you want us to go and gather them?' But he replied, 'No; for in gathering the weeds you would uproot the wheat along with them. Let both of them grow together until the harvest; and at harvest time I will tell the reapers, Collect the weeds first and bind them in bundles to be burned, but gather the wheat into my barn.'" (Matt. 13:24-30)

Psalm
Psalm 86:11-17
Teach me your ways

Additional Readings
Isaiah 44:6-8
There is no other God

Romans 8:12-25
The revealing of the children of God

Hymn: The Reign of God, like Farmer's Field, ACS 952

Faithful God, most merciful judge, you care for your children with firmness and compassion. By your Spirit nurture us who live in your kingdom, that we may be rooted in the way of your Son, Jesus Christ, our Savior and Lord.

Monday, July 24, 2023
Time after Pentecost

Psalm 75
God's judgment

We give thanks to you, O God;
    we give thanks; your name is near.
People tell of your wondrous deeds.

At the set time that I appoint
    I will judge with equity.
When the earth totters, with all its inhabitants,
    it is I who keep its pillars steady. (Ps. 75:1-3)

Additional Readings
Nahum 1:1-13
The wrath and mercy of God

Revelation 14:12-20
The harvest at the end of time

Hymn: How Great Thou Art, ELW 856

Sovereign God, as you set the seasons you also set the time to judge the world with equity. Help us praise your providence, even when evil rages around us, so that we follow Jesus steadfastly until he comes in glory.

Tuesday, July 25, 2023
James, Apostle

Mark 10:35-45

Whoever wishes to be great must serve

James and John, the sons of Zebedee, came forward to Jesus and said to him, "Teacher, we want you to do for us whatever we ask of you." And he said to them, "What is it you want me to do for you?" And they said to him, "Grant us to sit, one at your right hand and one at your left, in your glory." But Jesus said to them, "You do not know what you are asking. Are you able to drink the cup that I drink, or be baptized with the baptism that I am baptized with?" They replied, "We are able." Then Jesus said to them, "The cup that I drink you will drink; and with the baptism with which I am baptized, you will be baptized; but to sit at my right hand or at my left is not mine to grant, but it is for those for whom it has been prepared." (Mark 10:35-40)

Psalm

Psalm 7:1-10
God, my shield and defense

Additional Readings

1 Kings 19:9-18
Elijah hears God amid silence

Acts 11:27—12:3a
James is killed by Herod

Hymn: Will You Let Me Be Your Servant, ELW 659

Gracious God, we remember before you today your servant and apostle James, the first among the twelve to be martyred for the name of Jesus Christ. Pour out on the leaders of your church that spirit of self-denying service which is the true mark of authority among your people, through Jesus Christ our servant, who lives and reigns with you and the Holy Spirit, one God, now and forever.

Wednesday, July 26, 2023
Time after Pentecost

Daniel 12:1-13

The righteous will shine

"At that time Michael, the great prince, the protector of your people, shall arise. There shall be a time of anguish, such as has never occurred since nations first came into existence. But at that time your people shall be delivered, everyone who is found written in the book. Many of those who sleep in the dust of the earth shall awake, some to everlasting life, and some to shame and everlasting contempt. Those who are wise shall shine like the brightness of the sky, and those who lead many to righteousness, like the stars forever and ever. But you, Daniel, keep the words secret and the book sealed until the time of the end. Many shall be running back and forth, and evil shall increase." (Dan. 12:1-4)

Psalm

Psalm 75
God's judgment

Additional Reading

Matthew 12:15-21
God's chosen servant

Hymn: I'm So Glad Jesus Lifted Me, ELW 860

Resurrecting God, in Christ you have already begun the world's end, where anguish yields to joy because death yields to life. Make us radiant in this good news, so that your will to set right the world shines through us.

Thursday, July 27, 2023
Time after Pentecost

Psalm 119:129-136
Light and understanding

Your decrees are wonderful;
    therefore my soul keeps them.
The unfolding of your words gives light;
    it imparts understanding to the simple.
With open mouth I pant,
    because I long for your commandments.
Turn to me and be gracious to me,
    as is your custom toward those who love your name.
Keep my steps steady according to your promise,
    and never let iniquity have dominion over me. (Ps. 119:129-133)

Additional Readings

1 Kings 1:28-37
Solomon designated as king

1 Corinthians 4:14-20
Reign of God depends not on talk but power

Hymn: Let All Things Now Living, ELW 881

Holy Lawgiver, thank you for the gift of your commandments! Give us grace to love and understand your law, so we may walk humbly, steadily, and joyfully by the light of your wisdom.

Friday, July 28, 2023
Time after Pentecost

Johann Sebastian Bach, died 1750; Heinrich Schütz, died 1672;
George Frederick Handel, died 1759; musicians

Acts 7:44-53

Solomon's temple cannot contain God

[Stephen spoke:] "Our ancestors had the tent of testimony in the wilderness, as God directed when he spoke to Moses, ordering him to make it according to the pattern he had seen. Our ancestors in turn brought it in with Joshua when they dispossessed the nations that God drove out before our ancestors. And it was there until the time of David, who found favor with God and asked that he might find a dwelling place for the house of Jacob. But it was Solomon who built a house for him. Yet the Most High does not dwell in houses made with human hands." (Acts 7:44-48a)

Psalm
Psalm 119:129-136
Light and understanding

Additional Reading
1 Kings 1:38-48
Solomon more famous than David

Hymn: Built on a Rock, ELW 652

God of the universe, though no house can fully contain you, you meet us wherever two or three gather in your name. Continue hallowing our assemblies as we acknowledge your desire to dwell within us.

Saturday, July 29, 2023
Time after Pentecost

Mary, Martha, and Lazarus of Bethany
Olaf, King of Norway, martyr, died 1030

1 Kings 2:1-4

David's instructions to Solomon

When David's time to die drew near, he charged his son Solomon, saying: "I am about to go the way of all the earth. Be strong, be courageous, and keep the charge of the LORD your God, walking in his ways and keeping his statutes, his commandments, his ordinances, and his testimonies, as it is written in the law of Moses, so that you may prosper in all that you do and wherever you turn. Then the LORD will establish his word that he spoke concerning me: 'If your heirs take heed to their way, to walk before me in faithfulness with all their heart and with all their soul, there shall not fail you a successor on the throne of Israel.'" (1 Kings 2:1-4)

Psalm

Psalm 119:129-136
Light and understanding

Additional Reading

Matthew 12:38-42
Something greater than Solomon is here

Hymn: Lord of All Nations, Grant Me Grace, ELW 716

God of the ages, you charge each generation not only to keep faith in you, but to hand on that faith to their children. Bless parents, teachers, and pastors as they work to form the next generation's faith in Christ.

Sunday, July 30, 2023
Time after Pentecost

Matthew 13:31-33, 44-52

Parables of the reign of heaven

[Jesus] told [the disciples] another parable: "The kingdom of heaven is like yeast that a woman took and mixed in with three measures of flour until all of it was leavened." . . .

"The kingdom of heaven is like treasure hidden in a field, which someone found and hid; then in his joy he goes and sells all that he has and buys that field.

"Again, the kingdom of heaven is like a merchant in search of fine pearls; on finding one pearl of great value, he went and sold all that he had and bought it." (Matt. 13:33, 44-46)

Psalm

Psalm 119:129-136
Light and understanding

Additional Readings

1 Kings 3:5-12
Solomon's prayer for wisdom

Romans 8:26-39
Nothing can separate us from God's love

Hymn: You Are the Way, ELW 758

Beloved and sovereign God, through the death and resurrection of your Son you bring us into your kingdom of justice and mercy. By your Spirit, give us your wisdom, that we may treasure the life that comes from Jesus Christ, our Savior and Lord.

Monday, July 31, 2023
Time after Pentecost

Psalm 119:121-128
Give me understanding

I am your servant; give me understanding,
    so that I may know your decrees.
It is time for the LORD to act,
    for your law has been broken.
Truly I love your commandments
    more than gold, more than fine gold.
Truly I direct my steps by all your precepts;
    I hate every false way. (Ps. 119:125-128)

Additional Readings
1 Kings 3:16-28
Solomon's wisdom in judgment

James 3:13-18
Two kinds of wisdom

Hymn: O Word of God Incarnate, ELW 514

Perfect Creator, your word does what it says, and your word's creation is life. Deepen our understanding of your will, so that our actions match our confession that Jesus is your life-giving word for us.

Prayer List for August

_____

_____

_____

_____

_____

_____

_____

_____

_____

_____

Tuesday, August 1, 2023
Time after Pentecost

1 Kings 4:29-34
God gave Solomon wisdom

God gave Solomon very great wisdom, discernment, and breadth of understanding as vast as the sand on the seashore, so that Solomon's wisdom surpassed the wisdom of all the people of the east, and all the wisdom of Egypt. He was wiser than anyone else, wiser than Ethan the Ezrahite, and Heman, Calcol, and Darda, children of Mahol; his fame spread throughout all the surrounding nations. He composed three thousand proverbs, and his songs numbered a thousand and five. He would speak of trees, from the cedar that is in the Lebanon to the hyssop that grows in the wall; he would speak of animals, and birds, and reptiles, and fish. People came from all the nations to hear the wisdom of Solomon; they came from all the kings of the earth who had heard of his wisdom. (1 Kings 4:29-34)

Psalm
Psalm 119:121-128
Give me understanding

Additional Reading
Ephesians 6:10-18
The allegory of the armor of God

Hymn: Lord Jesus, You Shall Be My Song, ELW 808

All-wise God, illumine our minds with your wisdom, enhance our creativity, and stir up our imaginations. You have created a wonderful cosmos. Enable us to share it with others.

Wednesday, August 2, 2023
Time after Pentecost

Proverbs 1:1-7, 20-33
The call of wisdom

Wisdom cries out in the street;
> in the squares she raises her voice.
At the busiest corner she cries out;
> at the entrance of the city gates she speaks:
"How long, O simple ones, will you love being simple?
How long will scoffers delight in their scoffing
> and fools hate knowledge?
Give heed to my reproof;
I will pour out my thoughts to you;
> I will make my words known to you." (Prov. 1:20-23)

Psalm
Psalm 119:121-128
Give me understanding

Additional Reading
Mark 4:30-34
Jesus' use of parables

Hymn: We Eat the Bread of Teaching, ELW 518

Wisdom-bearer, you are full of great counsel. We apologize for when we have scoffed at you. Grant us respect for the gift of your thoughts and words. Guard our mouths, O God, that we may not sin against you.

Thursday, August 3, 2023
Time after Pentecost

Psalm 145:8-9, 14-21
You open wide your hand

The LORD upholds all who are falling,
>   and raises up all who are bowed down.
The eyes of all look to you,
>   and you give them their food in due season.
You open your hand,
>   satisfying the desire of every living thing. (Ps. 145:14-16)

Additional Readings

Proverbs 10:1-5
The righteous will not go hungry

Philippians 4:10-15
Being well fed and yet hungry

Hymn: O Bread of Life from Heaven, ELW 480

God our provider, you are everything that we need. We stretch out our hands to you, knowing that you are pleased to save us. Help us to find rest in you.

Friday, August 4, 2023
Time after Pentecost

Isaiah 51:17-23
Drink no more from the bowl of wrath

Therefore hear this, you who are wounded,
    who are drunk, but not with wine:
Thus says your Sovereign, the LORD,
    your God who pleads the cause of his people:
See, I have taken from your hand the cup of staggering;
you shall drink no more
    from the bowl of my wrath.
And I will put it into the hand of your tormentors,
    who have said to you,
    "Bow down, that we may walk on you";
and you have made your back like the ground
    and like the street for them to walk on. (Isa. 51:21-23)

Psalm
Psalm 145:8-9, 14-21
You open wide your hand

Additional Reading
Romans 9:6-13
True descendants of Abraham

Hymn: All Are Welcome, ELW 641

Gracious God, thank you for your sacrificial love. Inspire us to build a beloved and global community where all are welcome, safe, and free. May we always see you in the face of the stranger.

Saturday, August 5, 2023
Time after Pentecost

Isaiah 44:1-5

God's blessing on Israel

But now hear, O Jacob my servant,
    Israel whom I have chosen!
Thus says the LORD who made you,
    who formed you in the womb and will help you:
Do not fear, O Jacob my servant,
    Jeshurun whom I have chosen.
For I will pour water on the thirsty land,
    and streams on the dry ground;
I will pour my spirit upon your descendants,
    and my blessing on your offspring.
They shall spring up like a green tamarisk,
    like willows by flowing streams.
This one will say, "I am the LORD's,"
    another will be called by the name of Jacob,
yet another will write on the hand, "The LORD's,"
    and adopt the name of Israel. (Isa. 44:1-5)

Psalm

Psalm 145:8-9, 14-21
You open wide your hand

Additional Reading

Matthew 7:7-11
Bread and stones

Hymn: Bread of Life, Our Host and Meal, ELW 464

Maternal God, we go from your womb to the cries of your rejoicing. You cradle us, naming us beloved and well-pleasing children. We are always safe in your loving arms.

Sunday, August 6, 2023
Time after Pentecost

Matthew 14:13-21

Jesus feeds 5000

Then [Jesus] ordered the crowds to sit down on the grass. Taking the five loaves and the two fish, he looked up to heaven, and blessed and broke the loaves, and gave them to the disciples, and the disciples gave them to the crowds. And all ate and were filled; and they took up what was left over of the broken pieces, twelve baskets full. And those who ate were about five thousand men, besides women and children. (Matt. 14:19-21)

Psalm
Psalm 145:8-9, 14-21
You open wide your hand

Additional Readings

Isaiah 55:1-5
Eat and drink what truly satisfies

Romans 9:1-5
The glory of God's people in Israel

Hymn: Loaves Were Broken, Words Were Spoken, ACS 966

Glorious God, your generosity waters the world with goodness, and you cover creation with abundance. Awaken in us a hunger for the food that satisfies both body and spirit, and with this food fill all the starving world; through your Son, Jesus Christ, our Savior and Lord.

Monday, August 7, 2023
Time after Pentecost

Psalm 78:1-8, 17-29
God fed the people with manna

Yet he commanded the skies above,
 and opened the doors of heaven;
he rained down on them manna to eat,
 and gave them the grain of heaven.
Mortals ate of the bread of angels;
 he sent them food in abundance. (Ps. 78:23-25)

Additional Readings
Deuteronomy 8:1-10
God will feed the people

Romans 1:8-15
A harvest among the Gentiles

Hymn: Break Now the Bread of Life, ELW 515

God of life, how generously you feed us. Your love is bread upon our tongues and your grace is the sweetest wine. Help us to share these gifts extravagantly with others.

Tuesday, August 8, 2023
Time after Pentecost

Dominic, founder of the Order of Preachers (Dominicans), died 1221

Acts 2:37-47

The believers breaking bread

Awe came upon everyone, because many wonders and signs were being done by the apostles. All who believed were together and had all things in common; they would sell their possessions and goods and distribute the proceeds to all, as any had need. Day by day, as they spent much time together in the temple, they broke bread at home and ate their food with glad and generous hearts, praising God and having the goodwill of all the people. And day by day the Lord added to their number those who were being saved. (Acts 2:43-47)

Psalm
Psalm 78:1-8, 17-29
God fed the people with manna

Additional Reading
Deuteronomy 26:1-15
A tithe from God's harvest

Hymn: Draw Us in the Spirit's Tether, ELW 470

Communing God, you inspire the church to be your hands and feet in a world that desperately needs your presence. Create in us such a grace-filled community that all will want to join in fellowship with you.

Wednesday, August 9, 2023
Time after Pentecost

Exodus 16:2-15, 31-35
God feeds the people manna

The whole congregation of the Israelites complained against Moses and Aaron in the wilderness. The Israelites said to them, "If only we had died by the hand of the LORD in the land of Egypt, when we sat by the fleshpots and ate our fill of bread; for you have brought us out into this wilderness to kill this whole assembly with hunger."

Then the LORD said to Moses, "I am going to rain bread from heaven for you, and each day the people shall go out and gather enough for that day. In that way I will test them, whether they will follow my instruction or not." (Exod. 16:2-4)

Psalm
Psalm 78:1-8, 17-29
God fed the people with manna

Additional Reading
Matthew 15:32-39
Jesus feeds 4000

Hymn: Glorious Things of You Are Spoken, ELW 647

Patient One, you are the provider of our daily bread. Forgive us for our self-indulgent pity parties and lack of gratitude. Teach us to praise you, in our words and actions, for your benevolent generosity toward us.

Thursday, August 10, 2023
Time after Pentecost

Lawrence, deacon, martyr, died 258

Psalm 85:8-13
I will listen to God

Let me hear what God the LORD will speak,
    for he will speak peace to his people,
    to his faithful, to those who turn to him in their hearts.
Surely his salvation is at hand for those who fear him,
    that his glory may dwell in our land.

Steadfast love and faithfulness will meet;
    righteousness and peace will kiss each other.
Faithfulness will spring up from the ground,
    and righteousness will look down from the sky.
The LORD will give what is good,
    and our land will yield its increase.
Righteousness will go before him,
    and will make a path for his steps. (Ps. 85:8-13)

Additional Readings

1 Kings 18:1-16
God promises relief from drought

Acts 17:10-15
The good news is shared

Hymn: Lord, Speak to Us, That We May Speak, ELW 676

Speak, Lord, for your words are life. We long to hear from you. We inhale your steadfast love and faithfulness. We exhale your righteousness and peace. Speak to us, that we may share good news.

Friday, August 11, 2023
Time after Pentecost

Clare, Abbess of San Damiano, died 1253

Acts 18:24-28

A new disciple preaches

Now there came to Ephesus a Jew named Apollos, a native of Alexandria. He was an eloquent man, well-versed in the scriptures. He had been instructed in the Way of the Lord; and he spoke with burning enthusiasm and taught accurately the things concerning Jesus, though he knew only the baptism of John. He began to speak boldly in the synagogue; but when Priscilla and Aquila heard him, they took him aside and explained the Way of God to him more accurately. And when he wished to cross over to Achaia, the believers encouraged him and wrote to the disciples to welcome him. On his arrival he greatly helped those who through grace had become believers, for he powerfully refuted the Jews in public, showing by the scriptures that the Messiah is Jesus. (Acts 18:24-28)

Psalm
Psalm 85:8-13
I will listen to God

Additional Reading
1 Kings 18:17-19, 30-40
God's flooded altar burns

Hymn: In Christ Called to Baptize, ELW 575

Spirit of fire, give us a burning enthusiasm to invite others to journey with us on the way. Set us alight with the awesome wonder of your story.

Saturday, August 12, 2023
Time after Pentecost

1 Kings 18:41-46
From drought to heavy rain

Elijah said to Ahab, "Go up, eat and drink; for there is a sound of rushing rain." So Ahab went up to eat and to drink. Elijah went up to the top of Carmel; there he bowed himself down upon the earth and put his face between his knees. He said to his servant, "Go up now, look toward the sea." He went up and looked, and said, "There is nothing." Then he said, "Go again seven times." At the seventh time he said, "Look, a little cloud no bigger than a person's hand is rising out of the sea." Then he said, "Go say to Ahab, 'Harness your chariot and go down before the rain stops you.'" In a little while the heavens grew black with clouds and wind; there was a heavy rain. Ahab rode off and went to Jezreel. But the hand of the LORD was on Elijah; he girded up his loins and ran in front of Ahab to the entrance of Jezreel. (1 Kings 18:41-46)

Psalm
Psalm 85:8-13
I will listen to God

Additional Reading
Matthew 16:1-4
The sign of Jonah

Hymn: Crashing Waters at Creation, ELW 455

Miracle-working God, drench us in living water, that our thirsty lives overflow with the promise of renewed vitality through you. Help us to believe your promise that we will never go thirsty again.

Sunday, August 13, 2023

Time after Pentecost

Florence Nightingale, died 1910; Clara Maass, died 1901; renewers of society

Matthew 14:22-33

Jesus walking on the sea

Immediately [Jesus] made the disciples get into the boat and go on ahead to the other side, while he dismissed the crowds. And after he had dismissed the crowds, he went up the mountain by himself to pray. When evening came, he was there alone, but by this time the boat, battered by the waves, was far from the land, for the wind was against them. And early in the morning he came walking toward them on the sea. But when the disciples saw him walking on the sea, they were terrified, saying, "It is a ghost!" And they cried out in fear. But immediately Jesus spoke to them and said, "Take heart, it is I; do not be afraid." (Matt. 14:22-27)

Psalm

Psalm 85:8-13
I will listen to God

Additional Readings

1 Kings 19:9-18
Elijah on Mount Horeb

Romans 10:5-15
The word of faith

Hymn: Calm to the Waves, ELW 794

O God our defender, storms rage around and within us and cause us to be afraid. Rescue your people from despair, deliver your sons and daughters from fear, and preserve us all in the faith of your Son, Jesus Christ, our Savior and Lord.

Monday, August 14, 2023
Time after Pentecost

Maximilian Kolbe, died 1941; Kaj Munk, died 1944; martyrs

Psalm 18:1-19
God saves from the waters

He reached down from on high, he took me;
    he drew me out of mighty waters.
He delivered me from my strong enemy,
    and from those who hated me;
    for they were too mighty for me.
They confronted me in the day of my calamity;
    but the Lord was my support.
He brought me out into a broad place;
    he delivered me, because he delighted in me. (Ps. 18:16-19)

Additional Readings

Genesis 7:11—8:5
God saves Noah from the flood

2 Peter 2:4-10
God judges and rescues

Hymn: God, Bless the Hands, ACS 1022

Saving God, you are our rescuer. We face perils at every turn and we cannot defend ourselves. Stretch out your hand and lift us up into your powerful arms. We are desperate to find rest in you.

Tuesday, August 15, 2023
Mary, Mother of Our Lord

Luke 1:46-55

Mary's thanksgiving

And Mary said,
"My soul magnifies the Lord,
and my spirit rejoices in God my Savior,
for he has looked with favor on the lowliness of his servant.
Surely, from now on all generations will call me blessed;
for the Mighty One has done great things for me,
and holy is his name." (Luke 1:46-49)

Psalm

Psalm 34:1-9
O magnify the Lord with me

Additional Readings

Isaiah 61:7-11
God will cause righteousness to spring up

Galatians 4:4-7
We are no longer slaves, but children

Hymn: No Wind at the Window, ACS 906

Almighty God, in choosing the virgin Mary to be the mother of your Son, you made known your gracious regard for the poor, the lowly, and the despised. Grant us grace to receive your word in humility, and so to be made one with your Son, Jesus Christ our Savior and Lord, who lives and reigns with you and the Holy Spirit, one God, now and forever.

Wednesday, August 16, 2023
Time after Pentecost

Matthew 8:23-27
Jesus stills the storm

And when [Jesus] got into the boat, his disciples followed him. A windstorm arose on the sea, so great that the boat was being swamped by the waves; but he was asleep. And they went and woke him up, saying, "Lord, save us! We are perishing!" And he said to them, "Why are you afraid, you of little faith?" Then he got up and rebuked the winds and the sea; and there was a dead calm. They were amazed, saying, "What sort of man is this, that even the winds and the sea obey him?" (Matt. 8:23-27)

Psalm
Psalm 18:1-19
God saves from the waters

Additional Reading
Job 36:24-33; 37:14-24
The waters of God's creation

Hymn: Jesus, Savior, Pilot Me, ELW 755

God, you are a strong deliverer. We are drowning in the storms of life. Wake now and save us. We are in over our heads. Increase our faith that you will both hear and answer our prayers.

Thursday, August 17, 2023
Time after Pentecost

Psalm 67
Let all the peoples praise God

May God be gracious to us and bless us
    and make his face to shine upon us,
that your way may be known upon earth,
    your saving power among all nations.
Let the peoples praise you, O God;
    let all the peoples praise you.

Let the nations be glad and sing for joy,
    for you judge the peoples with equity
    and guide the nations upon earth.
Let the peoples praise you, O God;
    let all the peoples praise you. (Ps. 67:1-5)

Additional Readings
Isaiah 45:20-25
All the ends of the earth shall be saved

Revelation 15:1-4
All nations will worship God

Hymn: Praise to the Lord, the Almighty, ELW 858

God, we praise you. There is nothing you cannot do. Grant us glad and blessed hearts as we raise a chorus of "Alleluias," making the power of your salvation known to all people.

Friday, August 18, 2023
Time after Pentecost

Isaiah 63:15-19

A plea for God's attention

Why, O LORD, do you make us stray from your ways
    and harden our heart, so that we do not fear you?
Turn back for the sake of your servants,
    for the sake of the tribes that are your heritage.
Your holy people took possession for a little while;
    but now our adversaries have trampled down your sanctuary.
We have long been like those whom you do not rule,
    like those not called by your name. (Isa. 63:17-19)

## Psalm	## Additional Reading
Psalm 67	**Acts 14:19-28**
Let all the peoples praise God	*God opens the door to Gentiles*

Hymn: By Gracious Powers, ELW 626

We are crushed down by the weight of despair, God. In mind, body, and spirit, we are wearier than we have ever been. By your gracious power, draw near to us, restore our hope, and help us live.

Saturday, August 19, 2023
Time after Pentecost

Isaiah 56:1-5

A covenant for all who obey

Thus says the LORD:
Maintain justice, and do what is right,
>for soon my salvation will come,
>>and my deliverance be revealed.

Happy is the mortal who does this,
>the one who holds it fast,
who keeps the sabbath, not profaning it,
>and refrains from doing any evil.

Do not let the foreigner joined to the LORD say,
>"The LORD will surely separate me from his people";
and do not let the eunuch say,
>"I am just a dry tree." (Isa. 56:1-3)

Psalm
Psalm 67
Let all the peoples praise God

Additional Reading
Matthew 14:34-36
Jesus heals the sick

Hymn: Let Justice Flow like Streams, ELW 717

God our deliverer, we confess that we are sinners. We are puffed up, thinking too highly of ourselves. We have oppressed others and averted our eyes from their needs. Turn us away from doing evil.

Sunday, August 20, 2023
Time after Pentecost

Bernard, Abbot of Clairvaux, died 1153

Matthew 15:[10-20] 21-28
The Canaanite woman's daughter is healed

[The Canaanite woman] came and knelt before [Jesus], saying, "Lord, help me." He answered, "It is not fair to take the children's food and throw it to the dogs." She said, "Yes, Lord, yet even the dogs eat the crumbs that fall from their masters' table." Then Jesus answered her, "Woman, great is your faith! Let it be done for you as you wish." And her daughter was healed instantly. (Matt. 15:25-28)

Psalm

Psalm 67
Let all the peoples praise God

Additional Readings

Isaiah 56:1, 6-8
A house of prayer for all people

Romans 11:1-2a, 29-32
God's mercy to all, Jew and Gentile

Hymn: We Come to You for Healing, Lord, ELW 617

God of all peoples, your arms reach out to embrace all those who call upon you. Teach us as disciples of your Son to love the world with compassion and constancy, that your name may be known throughout the earth, through Jesus Christ, our Savior and Lord.

Monday, August 21, 2023
Time after Pentecost

Psalm 87
Foreigners praise God in Zion

On the holy mount stands the city he founded;
> the LORD loves the gates of Zion
> more than all the dwellings of Jacob.
Glorious things are spoken of you,
> O city of God.

Among those who know me I mention Rahab and Babylon;
> Philistia too, and Tyre, with Ethiopia—
> "This one was born there," they say.

And of Zion it shall be said,
> "This one and that one were born in it";
> for the Most High himself will establish it. (Ps. 87:1-5)

Additional Readings
2 Kings 5:1-14
The foreigner Naaman is healed

Acts 15:1-21
The believing Jews accept the Gentiles

Hymn: Come, We That Love the Lord, ELW 625

Loving God, you have adopted us all as your children, creating one human family. Remove the barriers to our unity. Your love is big and wide enough that all may dwell safely in your city.

Tuesday, August 22, 2023
Time after Pentecost

Romans 11:13-29
God saves Jews and Gentiles

So that you may not claim to be wiser than you are, brothers and sisters, I want you to understand this mystery: a hardening has come upon part of Israel, until the full number of the Gentiles has come in. And so all Israel will be saved; as it is written,

> "Out of Zion will come the Deliverer;
>> he will banish ungodliness from Jacob."
> "And this is my covenant with them,
> when I take away their sins."

As regards the gospel they are enemies of God for your sake; but as regards election they are beloved, for the sake of their ancestors; for the gifts and the calling of God are irrevocable. (Rom. 11:25-29)

Psalm
Psalm 87
Foreigners praise God in Zion

Additional Reading
Isaiah 43:8-13
Let all the nations gather

Hymn: Alleluia! Sing to Jesus, ELW 392

Sacrificing God, we are redeemed and called to share your love with all people. Cast out all prejudice within us that we may know your way of peace.

Wednesday, August 23, 2023
Time after Pentecost

Matthew 8:1-13

Jesus heals many people

When [Jesus] entered Capernaum, a centurion came to him, appealing to him and saying, "Lord, my servant is lying at home paralyzed, in terrible distress." And he said to him, "I will come and cure him." The centurion answered, "Lord, I am not worthy to have you come under my roof; but only speak the word, and my servant will be healed. For I also am a man under authority, with soldiers under me; and I say to one, 'Go,' and he goes, and to another, 'Come,' and he comes, and to my slave, 'Do this,' and the slave does it." When Jesus heard him, he was amazed and said to those who followed him, "Truly I tell you, in no one in Israel have I found such faith." (Matt. 8:5-10)

Psalm
Psalm 87
Foreigners praise God in Zion

Additional Reading
Isaiah 66:18-23
All nations shall come to worship

Hymn: O Christ, the Healer, We Have Come, ELW 610

Great Physician, we know people who are wounded and who are carrying heavy burdens. Help us to extend your powerful healing to others in need this day.

Thursday, August 24, 2023
Bartholomew, Apostle

John 1:43-51
Jesus says: Follow me

When Jesus saw Nathanael coming toward him, he said of him, "Here is truly an Israelite in whom there is no deceit!" Nathanael asked him, "Where did you get to know me?" Jesus answered, "I saw you under the fig tree before Philip called you." Nathanael replied, "Rabbi, you are the Son of God! You are the King of Israel!" Jesus answered, "Do you believe because I told you that I saw you under the fig tree? You will see greater things than these." And he said to him, "Very truly, I tell you, you will see heaven opened and the angels of God ascending and descending upon the Son of Man." (John 1:47-51)

Psalm
Psalm 12
A plea for help in evil times

Additional Readings
Exodus 19:1-6
Israel is God's priestly kingdom

1 Corinthians 12: 27-31a
The body of Christ

Hymn: O God, My Faithful God, ELW 806

Almighty and everlasting God, you gave to your apostle Bartholomew grace truly to believe and courageously to preach your word. Grant that your church may proclaim the good news to the ends of the earth, through Jesus Christ, our Savior and Lord, who lives and reigns with you and the Holy Spirit, one God, now and forever.

Friday, August 25, 2023
Time after Pentecost

Ezekiel 31:15-18
Israel like the cedars of Lebanon

Thus says the Lord GOD: On the day it went down to Sheol I closed the deep over it and covered it; I restrained its rivers, and its mighty waters were checked. I clothed Lebanon in gloom for it, and all the trees of the field fainted because of it. I made the nations quake at the sound of its fall, when I cast it down to Sheol with those who go down to the Pit; and all the trees of Eden, the choice and best of Lebanon, all that were well watered, were consoled in the world below. They also went down to Sheol with it, to those killed by the sword, along with its allies, those who lived in its shade among the nations.

Which among the trees of Eden was like you in glory and in greatness? Now you shall be brought down with the trees of Eden to the world below; you shall lie among the uncircumcised, with those who are killed by the sword. This is Pharaoh and all his horde, says the Lord GOD. (Ezek. 31:15-18)

Psalm
Psalm 138
Your love endures forever

Additional Reading
2 Corinthians 10:12-18
Let those who boast, boast in the Lord

Hymn: Light Dawns on a Weary World, ELW 726

Compassionate One, thank you that we are not given what we deserve. Though we wander through forsaken lands, you go before us, leading us home to you.

Saturday, August 26, 2023
Time after Pentecost

Ezekiel 36:33-38
A desolate land becomes like Eden

Thus says the Lord GOD: On the day that I cleanse you from all your iniquities, I will cause the towns to be inhabited, and the waste places shall be rebuilt. The land that was desolate shall be tilled, instead of being the desolation that it was in the sight of all who passed by. And they will say, "This land that was desolate has become like the garden of Eden; and the waste and desolate and ruined towns are now inhabited and fortified." Then the nations that are left all around you shall know that I, the LORD, have rebuilt the ruined places, and replanted that which was desolate; I, the LORD, have spoken, and I will do it. (Ezek. 36:33-36)

Psalm
Psalm 138
Your love endures forever

Additional Reading
Matthew 16:5-12
Bread as a sign of other things

Hymn: Come, Ye Disconsolate, ELW 607

Creator God, out of great darkness you caused Eden to spring forth. We have wandered far from safety. From ruinous places, gather us home to your fertile and healing lands.

Sunday, August 27, 2023

Time after Pentecost

Matthew 16:13-20

The profession of Peter's faith

[Jesus said to the disciples,] "But who do you say that I am?" Simon Peter answered, "You are the Messiah, the Son of the living God." And Jesus answered him, "Blessed are you, Simon son of Jonah! For flesh and blood has not revealed this to you, but my Father in heaven. And I tell you, you are Peter, and on this rock I will build my church, and the gates of Hades will not prevail against it. I will give you the keys of the kingdom of heaven, and whatever you bind on earth will be bound in heaven, and whatever you loose on earth will be loosed in heaven." (Matt. 16:15-19)

Psalm

Psalm 138
Your love endures forever

Additional Readings

Isaiah 51:1-6
God's enduring salvation

Romans 12:1-8
One body in Christ, with gifts that differ

Hymn: Christ Is Made the Sure Foundation, ELW 645

O God, with all your faithful followers of every age, we praise you, the rock of our life. Be our strong foundation and form us into the body of your Son, that we may gladly minister to all the world, through Jesus Christ, our Savior and Lord.

Monday, August 28, 2023
Time after Pentecost

Augustine, Bishop of Hippo, died 430

Moses the Black, monk, martyr, died around 400

Psalm 18:1-3, 20-32
God the rock

I love you, O Lord, my strength.

The Lord is my rock, my fortress, and my deliverer,

> my God, my rock in whom I take refuge,

> my shield, and the horn of my salvation, my stronghold.

I call upon the Lord, who is worthy to be praised,

> so I shall be saved from my enemies. (Ps. 18:1-3)

Additional Readings

1 Samuel 7:3-13
Samuel raises the Ebenezer stone

Romans 2:1-11
The righteous judgment of God

Hymn: How Sweet the Name of Jesus Sounds, ELW 620

Almighty One, you save us from the glittery lights of self-indulgence and greed. You ransom us from ourselves. Thank you for your willingness to rescue and deliver us.

Tuesday, August 29, 2023
Time after Pentecost

Romans 11:33-36

The riches, wisdom, and knowledge of God

O the depth of the riches and wisdom and knowledge of God! How unsearchable are his judgments and how inscrutable his ways!
"For who has known the mind of the Lord?
Or who has been his counselor?"
"Or who has given a gift to him,
to receive a gift in return?"
For from him and through him and to him are all things. To him be the glory forever. Amen. (Rom. 11:33-36)

Psalm
Psalm 18:1-3, 20-32
God the rock

Additional Reading
Deuteronomy 32:18-20, 28-39
Praise the rock that is God

Hymn: He Comes to Us as One Unknown, ELW 737

Wise One, you know all things and nothing catches you by surprise. May we abide in your presence, enraptured by the richness of your knowledge.

Wednesday, August 30, 2023
Time after Pentecost

Isaiah 28:14-22
God lays a cornerstone in Zion

Therefore hear the word of the LORD, you scoffers
　　who rule this people in Jerusalem.
Because you have said, "We have made a covenant with death,
　　and with Sheol we have an agreement;
when the overwhelming scourge passes through
　　it will not come to us;
for we have made lies our refuge,
　　and in falsehood we have taken shelter";
therefore thus says the Lord GOD,
See, I am laying in Zion a foundation stone,
　　a tested stone,
a precious cornerstone, a sure foundation:
　　"One who trusts will not panic." (Isa. 28:14-16)

Psalm
Psalm 18:1-3, 20-32
God the rock

Additional Reading
Matthew 26:6-13
A woman anoints Jesus

Hymn: Oh, Praise the Gracious Power, ELW 651

You are our strong foundation, O God. Even when we feel shaken, we can always find stability in you. You are the rock of our salvation. Help us cling to you.

Thursday, August 31, 2023
Time after Pentecost

Psalm 26:1-8
Your love is before my eyes

Vindicate me, O Lord,
>   for I have walked in my integrity,
>   and I have trusted in the Lord without wavering.
Prove me, O Lord, and try me;
>   test my heart and mind.
For your steadfast love is before my eyes,
>   and I walk in faithfulness to you. (Ps. 26:1-3)

Additional Readings
Jeremiah 14:13-18
Denunciation of lying prophets

Ephesians 5:1-6
Do not be deceived by empty words

Hymn: We Praise You, O God, ELW 870

God, you are the steadfast lover of our souls. It is our deepest desire to walk with you in an honest and faithful fashion. Guide us in our ways.

Prayer List for September

_____

_____

_____

_____

_____

_____

_____

_____

_____

Time after Pentecost
Autumn

The days of early autumn (September and October) herald the resumption of a more regular schedule: school begins, church education programs commence, and the steady rhythms of work are accompanied by cooling breezes and the changing colors of the landscape. During these months, various crops are harvested and appear on roadside stands and in grocery stores. In many countries the harvest days of September and October are marked with prayer, feasting, and special care for the poor and hungry.

Table Prayer for Autumn

We praise you and bless you, O God,
for autumn days,
and for the gifts of this table.
Grant us grace to share your goodness,
until all people are fed by the harvest of the earth.
We ask this through Christ our Lord. Amen.

Friday, September 1, 2023
Time after Pentecost

2 Thessalonians 2:7-12
Refusal to love the truth

For the mystery of lawlessness is already at work, but only until the one who now restrains it is removed. And then the lawless one will be revealed, whom the Lord Jesus will destroy with the breath of his mouth, annihilating him by the manifestation of his coming. The coming of the lawless one is apparent in the working of Satan, who uses all power, signs, lying wonders, and every kind of wicked deception for those who are perishing, because they refused to love the truth and so be saved. For this reason God sends them a powerful delusion, leading them to believe what is false, so that all who have not believed the truth but took pleasure in unrighteousness will be condemned. (2 Thess. 2:7-12)

Psalm
Psalm 26:1-8
Your love is before my eyes

Additional Reading
Jeremiah 15:1-9
The consequences of sin

Hymn: Abide, O Dearest Jesus, ELW 539

God, your dream for this beloved world is not condemnation, but salvation. Release us from insistence on our own ways. Write your word on our hearts, so that we are not deceived by lies but love the truth.

Saturday, September 2, 2023
Time after Pentecost

Nikolai Frederik Severin Grundtvig, bishop, renewer of the church, died 1872

Jeremiah 15:10-14
Jeremiah's complaint to God

Woe is me, my mother, that you ever bore me, a man of strife and contention to the whole land! I have not lent, nor have I borrowed, yet all of them curse me. The LORD said: Surely I have intervened in your life for good, surely I have imposed enemies on you in a time of trouble and in a time of distress. Can iron and bronze break iron from the north?

Your wealth and your treasures I will give as plunder, without price, for all your sins, throughout all your territory. I will make you serve your enemies in a land that you do not know, for in my anger a fire is kindled that shall burn forever. (Jer. 15:10-14)

Psalm
Psalm 26:1-8
Your love is before my eyes

Additional Reading
Matthew 8:14-17
Jesus heals many at Peter's house

Hymn: If You But Trust in God to Guide You, ELW 769

We are heartsick, homesick, and wounded in spirit, dear God. Thank you for giving us your very self—attentive, steadfast love embodied in Jesus. Daily save us from our sins. Strengthen us with your healing power.

Sunday, September 3, 2023
Time after Pentecost

Matthew 16:21-283
The rebuke to Peter

From that time on, Jesus began to show his disciples that he must go to Jerusalem and undergo great suffering at the hands of the elders and chief priests and scribes, and be killed, and on the third day be raised. And Peter took him aside and began to rebuke him, saying, "God forbid it, Lord! This must never happen to you." But he turned and said to Peter, "Get behind me, Satan! You are a stumbling block to me; for you are setting your mind not on divine things but on human things." (Matt. 16:21-23)

Psalm
Psalm 26:1-8
Your love is before my eyes

Additional Readings
Jeremiah 15:15-21
God fortifies the prophet

Romans 12:9-21
Live in harmony

Hymn: Take Up Your Cross, the Savior Said, ELW 667

O God, we thank you for your Son who chose the path of suffering for the sake of the world. Humble us by his example, point us to the path of obedience, and give us strength to follow your commands, through Jesus Christ, our Savior and Lord.

Monday, September 4, 2023
Time after Pentecost

Psalm 17
The righteous shall see God

I call upon you, for you will answer me, O God;
   incline your ear to me, hear my words.
Wondrously show your steadfast love,
   O savior of those who seek refuge
   from their adversaries at your right hand.

Guard me as the apple of the eye;
   hide me in the shadow of your wings,
from the wicked who despoil me,
   my deadly enemies who surround me. (Ps. 17:6-9)

Additional Readings
2 Samuel 11:2-26
David sins

Revelation 3:1-6
Wake up to your faithlessness

Hymn: What Wondrous Love Is This, ELW 666

Savior of all who seek refuge, your strong, steady wings shelter every living thing. When we forget your faithfulness, show us again your steadfast love. Draw us near to you and awaken us to the wonder of your grace.

Tuesday, September 5, 2023
Time after Pentecost

Revelation 3:7-13
Facing the hour of trial

"And to the angel of the church in Philadelphia write:
These are the words of the holy one, the true one,
> who has the key of David,
> who opens and no one will shut,
>> who shuts and no one opens. . . .

Because you have kept my word of patient endurance, I will keep you from the hour of trial that is coming on the whole world to test the inhabitants of the earth. I am coming soon; hold fast to what you have, so that no one may seize your crown. If you conquer, I will make you a pillar in the temple of my God; you will never go out of it. I will write on you the name of my God, and the name of the city of my God, the new Jerusalem that comes down from my God out of heaven, and my own new name." (Rev. 3:7, 10-12)

Psalm
Psalm 17
The righteous shall see God

Additional Reading
2 Samuel 11:27b—12:15
Nathan rebukes David

Hymn: Just As I Am, without One Plea, ELW 592

God, you have named us beloved. When we fear the future, remind us that your love is our beginning and our end. In times of trial, hold us fast, heed our cries, and deliver us from evil.

Wednesday, September 6, 2023
Time after Pentecost

Jeremiah 17:5-18
The vindication of the righteous

Thus says the LORD:
Cursed are those who trust in mere mortals
    and make mere flesh their strength,
    whose hearts turn away from the LORD.
They shall be like a shrub in the desert,
    and shall not see when relief comes.
They shall live in the parched places of the wilderness,
    in an uninhabited salt land.

Blessed are those who trust in the LORD,
    whose trust is the LORD.
They shall be like a tree planted by water,
    sending out its roots by the stream.
It shall not fear when heat comes,
    and its leaves shall stay green;
in the year of drought it is not anxious,
    and it does not cease to bear fruit. (Jer. 17:5-8)

Psalm
Psalm 17
The righteous shall see God

Additional Reading
Matthew 12:22-32
Jesus comes to cast out Satan

Hymn: Come to Me, All Pilgrims Thirsty, ELW 777

Living Water, you provide for our every need and enliven us to bear fruit for the sake of hungry neighbors near and far. Cast out all fears that make us wither and wilt. Keep us green and growing.

Thursday, September 7, 2023
Time after Pentecost

Psalm 119:33-40
The path of your commandments

Teach me, O LORD, the way of your statutes,
    and I will observe it to the end.
Give me understanding, that I may keep your law
    and observe it with my whole heart.
Lead me in the path of your commandments,
    for I delight in it.
Turn my heart to your decrees,
    and not to selfish gain. (Ps. 119:33-36)

Additional Readings
Ezekiel 24:1-14
God judges unrepentant Israel

2 Corinthians 12:11-21
Sinners warned but unrepentant

Hymn: O God of Light, ELW 507

Divine Teacher, your way is the way of justice and your path the path of truth. For the sake of Christ, have mercy on us. Lead your beloved. Turn us again and always to you.

Friday, September 8, 2023
Time after Pentecost

Romans 10:15b-21
God reaches out to erring Israel

As it is written, "How beautiful are the feet of those who bring good news!" But not all have obeyed the good news; for Isaiah says, "Lord, who has believed our message?" So faith comes from what is heard, and what is heard comes through the word of Christ. (Rom. 10:15b-17)

Psalm
Psalm 119:33-40
The path of your commandments

Additional Reading
Ezekiel 24:15-27
God opens the prophet's mouth

Hymn: O God, Whose Word Well-Planted, ACS 975

Abiding God, through Jesus Christ the good news of your enduring love has come to dwell in this broken, weary world. Inspire us to be beautiful messengers of your abundant grace, even in seasons of sorrow.

Saturday, September 9, 2023
Time after Pentecost

Peter Claver, priest, missionary to Colombia, died 1654

Ezekiel 33:1-6
The prophet's vocation

The word of the LORD came to me: O Mortal, speak to your people and say to them, If I bring the sword upon a land, and the people of the land take one of their number as their sentinel; and if the sentinel sees the sword coming upon the land and blows the trumpet and warns the people; then if any who hear the sound of the trumpet do not take warning, and the sword comes and takes them away, their blood shall be upon their own heads. They heard the sound of the trumpet and did not take warning; their blood shall be upon themselves. But if they had taken warning, they would have saved their lives. But if the sentinel sees the sword coming and does not blow the trumpet, so that the people are not warned, and the sword comes and takes any of them, they are taken away in their iniquity, but their blood I will require at the sentinel's hand. (Ezek. 33:1-6)

Psalm
Psalm 119:33-40
The path of your commandments

Additional Reading
Matthew 23:29-36
The martyrdom of the prophets

Hymn: Evening and Morning, ELW 761

Your word, O God, is our salvation. Yet we continue to crucify your prophets, safeguarding our own privilege. Open not only our ears, O God, but also our hearts and minds, that all creation might live.

Sunday, September 10, 2023
Time after Pentecost

Matthew 18:15-20

Reconciliation in the community of faith

[Jesus said to the disciples,] "If another member of the church sins against you, go and point out the fault when the two of you are alone. If the member listens to you, you have regained that one. But if you are not listened to, take one or two others along with you, so that every word may be confirmed by the evidence of two or three witnesses. If the member refuses to listen to them, tell it to the church; and if the offender refuses to listen even to the church, let such a one be to you as a Gentile and a tax collector." (Matt. 18:15-17)

Psalm
Psalm 119:33-40
The path of your commandments

Additional Readings
Ezekiel 33:7-11
The prophet's responsibility

Romans 13:8-14
Live honorably as in the day

Hymn: Forgive Our Sins As We Forgive, ELW 605

O Lord God, enliven and preserve your church with your perpetual mercy. Without your help, we mortals will fail; remove far from us everything that is harmful, and lead us toward all that gives life and salvation, through Jesus Christ, our Savior and Lord.

Monday, September 11, 2023
Time after Pentecost

Psalm 119:65-72
The law humbles me

You have dealt well with your servant,
>   O LORD, according to your word.
Teach me good judgment and knowledge,
>   for I believe in your commandments.
Before I was humbled I went astray,
>   but now I keep your word. (Ps. 119:65-67)

Additional Readings

Leviticus 4:27-31; 5:14-16
Atoning for sin in the community

1 Peter 2:11-17
Live as servants of God

Hymn: O Word of God Incarnate, ELW 514

God, in all times and in all places you are good. Still, we mourn our dead. Still, we lament injustice. Still, we defend our sin and fail to love as you would have us love. Forgive us and free us.

Tuesday, September 12, 2023
Time after Pentecost

Romans 13:1-7
Obeying authority

Let every person be subject to the governing authorities; for there is no authority except from God, and those authorities that exist have been instituted by God. Therefore whoever resists authority resists what God has appointed, and those who resist will incur judgment. For rulers are not a terror to good conduct, but to bad. Do you wish to have no fear of the authority? Then do what is good, and you will receive its approval; for it is God's servant for your good. But if you do what is wrong, you should be afraid, for the authority does not bear the sword in vain! It is the servant of God to execute wrath on the wrongdoer. (Rom. 13:1-4)

Psalm
Psalm 119:65-72
The law humbles me

Additional Reading
Deuteronomy 17:2-13
Punishment for sin in community

Hymn: What God Ordains Is Good Indeed, ELW 776

Governing God, thank you for raising up elected officials who serve our communities with courageous awareness and bold imagination. Inspire this world's leaders to pursue justice, disrupt implicit bias, and confront systemic racism for the flourishing of all people.

Wednesday, September 13, 2023
Time after Pentecost

John Chrysostom, Bishop of Constantinople, died 407

Matthew 21:18-22
Jesus teaches about praying in faith

In the morning, when [Jesus] returned to the city, he was hungry. And seeing a fig tree by the side of the road, he went to it and found nothing at all on it but leaves. Then he said to it, "May no fruit ever come from you again!" And the fig tree withered at once. When the disciples saw it, they were amazed, saying, "How did the fig tree wither at once?" Jesus answered them, "Truly I tell you, if you have faith and do not doubt, not only will you do what has been done to the fig tree, but even if you say to this mountain, 'Be lifted up and thrown into the sea,' it will be done. Whatever you ask for in prayer with faith, you will receive." (Matt. 21:18-22)

Psalm
Psalm 119:65-72
The law humbles me

Additional Reading
Leviticus 16:1-5, 20-28
The scapegoat cleanses the community

Hymn: Lord, Teach Us How to Pray Aright, ELW 745

God, you yearn for us to be well. When seasons change and doubts assail, you carry our burdens and hear our prayers. Assure us of your steadfast love, as near to us as the autumn air we breathe.

Thursday, September 14, 2023
Holy Cross Day

John 3:13-17
The Son of Man will be lifted up

[Jesus said to Nicodemus,] "No one has ascended into heaven except the one who descended from heaven, the Son of Man. And just as Moses lifted up the serpent in the wilderness, so must the Son of Man be lifted up, that whoever believes in him may have eternal life.

"For God so loved the world that he gave his only Son, so that everyone who believes in him may not perish but may have eternal life.

"Indeed, God did not send the Son into the world to condemn the world, but in order that the world might be saved through him." (John 3:13-17)

Psalm

Psalm 98:1-4
The Lord has done marvelous things

Additional Readings

Numbers 21:4b-9
A bronze serpent in the wilderness

1 Corinthians 1:18-24
The cross is the power of God

Hymn: Lift High the Cross, ELW 660

Almighty God, your Son Jesus Christ was lifted high upon the cross so that he might draw the whole world to himself. To those who look upon the cross, grant your wisdom, healing, and eternal life, through Jesus Christ, our Savior and Lord, who lives and reigns with you and the Holy Spirit, one God, now and forever.

Friday, September 15, 2023
Time after Pentecost

Genesis 41:53—42:17

Joseph acts harshly against his brothers

But Joseph said to [his brothers], "It is just as I have said to you; you are spies! Here is how you shall be tested: as Pharaoh lives, you shall not leave this place unless your youngest brother comes here! Let one of you go and bring your brother, while the rest of you remain in prison, in order that your words may be tested, whether there is truth in you; or else, as Pharaoh lives, surely you are spies." And he put them all together in prison for three days. (Gen. 42:14-17)

Psalm
Psalm 103:[1-7] 8-13
God's compassion and mercy

Additional Reading
Acts 7:9-16
Joseph's family is fed in Egypt

Hymn: Lord of Glory, You Have Bought Us, ELW 707

Compassionate God, you forgive when we cannot yet forgive. You see the end when we are stuck in the painful, messy middle. Lead us in the way of abundant mercy. Feed us with your amazing grace.

Saturday, September 16, 2023
Time after Pentecost

Cyprian, Bishop of Carthage, martyr, died around 258

Matthew 6:7-15

Forgiving one another

[Jesus taught his disciples,]
"Pray then in this way:
Our Father in heaven,
hallowed be your name.
Your kingdom come.
Your will be done,
on earth as it is in heaven.
Give us this day our daily bread.
And forgive us our debts,
as we also have forgiven our debtors.
And do not bring us to the time of trial,
but rescue us from the evil one." (Matt. 6:9-13)

Psalm
Psalm 103:[1-7] 8-13
God's compassion and mercy

Additional Reading
Genesis 45:1-20
Joseph forgives his brothers

Hymn: Our Father, God in Heaven Above, ELW 746/747

Creator God, faithful provider, you anticipate our needs and are attentive to our truest hungers. Look on all creation with love. Protect and preserve this planet from human negligence and greed. Lead us to abundant life for all.

Sunday, September 17, 2023
Time after Pentecost

Hildegard, Abbess of Bingen, died 1179

Matthew 18:21-35

A parable of forgiveness

Then Peter came and said to [Jesus], "Lord, if another member of the church sins against me, how often should I forgive? As many as seven times?" Jesus said to him, "Not seven times, but, I tell you, seventy-seven times." (Matt. 18:21-22)

Psalm

Psalm 103:[1-7] 8-13
God's compassion and mercy

Additional Readings

Genesis 50:15-21
Joseph reconciles with his brothers

Romans 14:1-12
When brothers and sisters judge each other

Hymn: Our Father, We Have Wandered, ELW 606

O Lord God, merciful judge, you are the inexhaustible fountain of forgiveness. Replace our hearts of stone with hearts that love and adore you, that we may delight in doing your will, through Jesus Christ, our Savior and Lord.

Monday, September 18, 2023
Time after Pentecost

Dag Hammarskjöld, renewer of society, died 1961

Psalm 133
How good it is to live in unity

How very good and pleasant it is
　　when kindred live together in unity!
It is like the precious oil on the head,
　　running down upon the beard,
on the beard of Aaron,
　　running down over the collar of his robes.
It is like the dew of Hermon,
　　which falls on the mountains of Zion.
For there the LORD ordained his blessing,
　　life forevermore. (Ps. 133:1-3)

Additional Readings
Genesis 48:8-22　　　　　　　**Hebrews 11:23-29**
Jacob blesses Joseph's sons　　　*The faith of Moses*

Hymn: Behold, How Pleasant, ELW 649

Shepherding God, what we imagine to be beyond redemption is never lost to you. Where families are dysfunctional and fractured, bring new life from the ashes of burned bridges and charred dreams. Hold our lives with tender mercy.

Tuesday, September 19, 2023
Time after Pentecost

Romans 14:13—15:2

Building up each other

Let us therefore no longer pass judgment on one another, but resolve instead never to put a stumbling block or hindrance in the way of another. I know and am persuaded in the Lord Jesus that nothing is unclean in itself; but it is unclean for anyone who thinks it unclean. If your brother or sister is being injured by what you eat, you are no longer walking in love. Do not let what you eat cause the ruin of one for whom Christ died. So do not let your good be spoken of as evil. For the kingdom of God is not food and drink but righteousness and peace and joy in the Holy Spirit. The one who thus serves Christ is acceptable to God and has human approval. Let us then pursue what makes for peace and for mutual upbuilding. (Rom. 14:13-19)

Psalm
Psalm 133
How good it is to live in unity

Additional Reading
Genesis 49:29—50:14
Honoring Jacob's burial wishes

Hymn: Beloved, God's Chosen, ELW 648

Divine Architect of peace and joy, you have created us to live in community. Make us resolute in building up one another. Let all that we do spring from the faith of Christ at work within us.

Wednesday, September 20, 2023
Time after Pentecost

Genesis 50:22-26
Joseph dies

So Joseph remained in Egypt, he and his father's household; and Joseph lived one hundred ten years. Joseph saw Ephraim's children of the third generation; the children of Machir son of Manasseh were also born on Joseph's knees.

Then Joseph said to his brothers, "I am about to die; but God will surely come to you, and bring you up out of this land to the land that he swore to Abraham, to Isaac, and to Jacob." So Joseph made the Israelites swear, saying, "When God comes to you, you shall carry up my bones from here." And Joseph died, being one hundred ten years old; he was embalmed and placed in a coffin in Egypt. (Gen. 50:22-26)

Psalm
Psalm 133
How good it is to live in unity

Additional Reading
Mark 11:20-25
Forgiveness for those who forgive

Hymn: Children of the Heavenly Father, ELW 781

Holy One, in life and in death you carry us in your gentle arms. With you, we are never alone. In days of grief and loss, assure your beloved children that you hold us securely.

Thursday, September 21, 2023
Matthew, Apostle and Evangelist

Matthew 9:9-13
Jesus calls to Matthew: Follow me

As Jesus was walking along, he saw a man called Matthew sitting at the tax booth; and he said to him, "Follow me." And he got up and followed him.

And as he sat at dinner in the house, many tax collectors and sinners came and were sitting with him and his disciples. When the Pharisees saw this, they said to his disciples, "Why does your teacher eat with tax collectors and sinners?" But when he heard this, he said, "Those who are well have no need of a physician, but those who are sick. Go and learn what this means, 'I desire mercy, not sacrifice.' For I have come to call not the righteous but sinners." (Matt. 9:9-13)

Psalm
Psalm 119:33-40
Give me understanding

Additional Readings
Ezekiel 2:8—3:11
A prophet to the house of Israel

Ephesians 2:4-10
By grace you have been saved

Hymn: Jesus Calls Us; o'er the Tumult, ELW 696

Almighty God, your Son our Savior called a despised tax collector to become one of his apostles. Help us, like Matthew, to respond to the transforming call of Jesus Christ, who lives and reigns with you and the Holy Spirit, one God, now and forever.

Friday, September 22, 2023
Time after Pentecost

2 Corinthians 13:5-10

Correction that builds up

But we pray to God that you may not do anything wrong—not that we may appear to have met the test, but that you may do what is right, though we may seem to have failed. For we cannot do anything against the truth, but only for the truth. For we rejoice when we are weak and you are strong. This is what we pray for, that you may become perfect. So I write these things while I am away from you, so that when I come, I may not have to be severe in using the authority that the Lord has given me for building up and not for tearing down. (2 Cor. 13:7-10)

Psalm
Psalm 145:1-8
God is slow to anger

Additional Reading
Nahum 2:3-13
Nineveh under siege

Hymn: Just a Closer Walk with Thee, ELW 697

Even as you rage against injustice, O God, you abound in steadfast love. For the sake of the gospel, examine our lives and transform our failures. Build us up through the love of Christ dwelling in us.

Saturday, September 23, 2023
Time after Pentecost

Zephaniah 2:13-15
Judgment on Nineveh

And he will stretch out his hand against the north,
 and destroy Assyria;
and he will make Nineveh a desolation,
 a dry waste like the desert.
Herds shall lie down in it,
 every wild animal;
the desert owl and the screech owl
 shall lodge on its capitals;
the owl shall hoot at the window,
 the raven croak on the threshold;
 for its cedar work will be laid bare.
Is this the exultant city
 that lived secure,
that said to itself,
 "I am, and there is no one else"? (Zeph. 2:13-15a)

Psalm
Psalm 145:1-8
God is slow to anger

Additional Reading
Matthew 19:23-30
The last will be first

Hymn: All Who Love and Serve Your City, ELW 724

Persistent God, you alone are God. Free us from false security that depends on our own capacity. Destroy our idols. Reverse our expectations. Help us dare to trust that all things all possible through you.

Matthew 20:1-16

The parable of the vineyard workers

[Jesus said:] "But [the landowner] replied to one of [the laborers], 'Friend, I am doing you no wrong; did you not agree with me for the usual daily wage? Take what belongs to you and go; I choose to give to this last the same as I give to you. Am I not allowed to do what I choose with what belongs to me? Or are you envious because I am generous?' So the last will be first, and the first will be last." (Matt. 20:13-16)

Psalm

Psalm 145:1-8
God is slow to anger

Additional Readings

Jonah 3:10 — 4:11
God's concern for Nineveh

Philippians 1:21-30
Standing firm in the gospel

Hymn: Praise and Thanksgiving, ELW 689

Almighty and eternal God, you show perpetual lovingkindness to us your servants. Because we cannot rely on our own abilities, grant us your merciful judgment, and train us to embody the generosity of your Son, Jesus Christ, our Savior and Lord.

Monday, September 25, 2023
Time after Pentecost

Psalm 106:1-12
God's mercy

Praise the LORD!
>O give thanks to the LORD, for he is good;
>for his steadfast love endures forever.

Who can utter the mighty doings of the LORD,
>or declare all his praise?

Happy are those who observe justice,
>who do righteousness at all times.

Remember me, O LORD, when you show favor to your people;
>help me when you deliver them;

that I may see the prosperity of your chosen ones,
>that I may rejoice in the gladness of your nation,
>that I may glory in your heritage. (Ps. 106:1-5)

Additional Readings
Genesis 27:1-29
The younger son gets the blessing

Romans 16:1-16
Diverse women and men are coworkers in Christ

Hymn: Praise and Thanks and Adoration, ELW 783

God, you are good! At all times and in all places, we praise you. With sun and stars, fields and forests, limestone bluffs and winding rivers, we marvel at your abiding presence! Remember us and bless us with your love.

Tuesday, September 26, 2023
Time after Pentecost

Romans 16:17-20
A warning about troublemakers

I urge you, brothers and sisters, to keep an eye on those who cause dissensions and offenses, in opposition to the teaching that you have learned; avoid them. For such people do not serve our Lord Christ, but their own appetites, and by smooth talk and flattery they deceive the hearts of the simple-minded. For while your obedience is known to all, so that I rejoice over you, I want you to be wise in what is good and guileless in what is evil. The God of peace will shortly crush Satan under your feet. The grace of our Lord Jesus Christ be with you. (Rom. 16:17-20)

Psalm
Psalm 106:1-12
God's mercy

Additional Reading
Genesis 28:10-17
God blesses the runaway Jacob

Hymn: Lord, Take My Hand and Lead Me, ELW 767

Almighty God, already you have led this world to freedom. Still, we wait for the fullness of your reign. Keep us from falling prey to false claims and illusory hope. Remind us of your promises. Shield us with your grace.

Wednesday, September 27, 2023
Time after Pentecost

Matthew 18:1-5
True greatness

At that time the disciples came to Jesus and asked, "Who is the greatest in the kingdom of heaven?" He called a child, whom he put among them, and said, "Truly I tell you, unless you change and become like children, you will never enter the kingdom of heaven. Whoever becomes humble like this child is the greatest in the kingdom of heaven. Whoever welcomes one such child in my name welcomes me." (Matt. 18:1-5)

Psalm
Psalm 106:1-12
God's mercy

Additional Reading
Isaiah 41:1-13
God will be with the last

Hymn: Cradling Children in His Arm, ELW 444

Vulnerable and victorious God, you confound our understandings and expectations. Thank you for honoring children, naming them as teachers and leaders. Help adults—especially in your church—to welcome, affirm, and celebrate children as you do.

Thursday, September 28, 2023
Time after Pentecost

Psalm 25:1-9
God's compassion and love

Make me to know your ways, O LORD;
    teach me your paths.
Lead me in your truth, and teach me,
    for you are the God of my salvation;
    for you I wait all day long.

Be mindful of your mercy, O LORD, and of your steadfast love,
    for they have been from of old.
Do not remember the sins of my youth or my transgressions;
    according to your steadfast love remember me,
    for your goodness' sake, O LORD! (Ps. 25:4-7)

Psalm
Ezekiel 12:17-28
God's judgment is timely

Additional Reading
James 4:11-16
We do not know what tomorrow will bring

Hymn: Oh, That the Lord Would Guide My Ways, ELW 772

God, you are trustworthy. Where you lead, we can follow without fear. Fulfill your word among us today. Replace judgment with spacious, stretching curiosity. One day at a time, free us from shame and teach us to love.

Friday, September 29, 2023
Michael and All Angels

Revelation 12:7-12

Michael defeats Satan in a cosmic battle

And war broke out in heaven; Michael and his angels fought against the dragon. The dragon and his angels fought back, but they were defeated, and there was no longer any place for them in heaven. The great dragon was thrown down, that ancient serpent, who is called the Devil and Satan, the deceiver of the whole world—he was thrown down to the earth, and his angels were thrown down with him. (Rev. 12:7-9)

Psalm

Psalm 103:1-5, 20-22
Bless the Lord, you angels

Additional Readings

Daniel 10:10-14; 12:1-3
Michael shall arise

Luke 10:17-20
Jesus gives his followers authority

Hymn: How Shall I Sing That Majesty, ACS 1095

Everlasting God, you have wonderfully established the ministries of angels and mortals. Mercifully grant that as Michael and the angels contend against the cosmic forces of evil, so by your direction they may help and defend us here on earth, through your Son, Jesus Christ our Lord, who lives and reigns with you and the Holy Spirit, one God whom we worship and praise with angels and archangels and all the company of heaven, now and forever.

Saturday, September 30, 2023
Time after Pentecost

Jerome, translator, teacher, died 420

Ezekiel 18:19-24

A child does not suffer for a parent's sin

Yet you say, "Why should not the son suffer for the iniquity of the father?" When the son has done what is lawful and right, and has been careful to observe all my statutes, he shall surely live. The person who sins shall die. A child shall not suffer for the iniquity of a parent, nor a parent suffer for the iniquity of a child; the righteousness of the righteous shall be his own, and the wickedness of the wicked shall be his own. (Ezek. 18:19-20)

Psalm
Psalm 25:1-9
God's compassion and love

Additional Reading
Mark 11:27-33
Jesus' authority is questioned

Hymn: Christ, Whose Glory Fills the Skies, ELW 553

God of every generation, your will for all creation is life. In Jesus you have the final, grace-full word. Lift our spirits. In the end, and already now, our salvation is secure. Your love never ends.

Prayer List for October

_____

_____

_____

_____

_____

_____

_____

_____

_____

Philippians 1:15-21

A parable of doing God's will

[Jesus said,] "What do you think? A man had two sons; he went to the first and said, 'Son, go and work in the vineyard today.' He answered, 'I will not'; but later he changed his mind and went. The father went to the second and said the same; and he answered, 'I go, sir'; but he did not go. Which of the two did the will of his father?" They said, "The first." Jesus said to them, "Truly I tell you, the tax collectors and the prostitutes are going into the kingdom of God ahead of you. For John came to you in the way of righteousness and you did not believe him, but the tax collectors and the prostitutes believed him; and even after you saw it, you did not change your minds and believe him." (Matt. 21:28-32)

Psalm

Psalm 25:1-9
God's compassion and love

Additional Readings

Ezekiel 18:1-4, 25-32
The fairness of God's way

Philippians 2:1-13
Christ humbled to the point of death

Hymn: All My Hope on God Is Founded, ELW 757

God of love, giver of life, you know our frailties and failings. Give us your grace to overcome them, keep us from those things that harm us, and guide us in the way of salvation, through Jesus Christ, our Savior and Lord.

Monday, October 2, 2023
Time after Pentecost

Psalm 28
Prayer to do God's will

Blessed be the LORD,
> for he has heard the sound of my pleadings.
The LORD is my strength and my shield;
> in him my heart trusts;
so I am helped, and my heart exults,
> and with my song I give thanks to him.

The LORD is the strength of his people;
> he is the saving refuge of his anointed.
O save your people, and bless your heritage;
> be their shepherd, and carry them forever. (Ps. 28:6-9)

Additional Readings

Judges 14:1-20
Samson's riddle explained

Philippians 1:3-14
Paul prays for the Philippians

Hymn: All Depends on Our Possessing, ELW 589

Lord our protector, when we pray, we know you listen. As you have always heard and helped us in the past, we ask you to shelter us and care for us in our hard times now.

Tuesday, October 3, 2023
Time after Pentecost

Philippians 1:15-21
Christ is proclaimed regardless of the motive

Some proclaim Christ from envy and rivalry, but others from goodwill. These proclaim Christ out of love, knowing that I have been put here for the defense of the gospel; the others proclaim Christ out of selfish ambition, not sincerely but intending to increase my suffering in my imprisonment. What does it matter? Just this, that Christ is proclaimed in every way, whether out of false motives or true; and in that I rejoice. (Phil. 1:15-18b)

Psalm
Psalm 28
Prayer to do God's will

Additional Reading
Judges 16:1-22
Samson asked about his strength

Hymn: Jesus Lives, My Sure Defense, ELW 621

Christ our joy, we are so glad when you are proclaimed in this world, for whatever the reason. The good news of your love and grace endures, no matter who the messenger may be. May your name be praised!

Wednesday, October 4, 2023
Time after Pentecost

Francis of Assisi, renewer of the church, died 1226
Theodor Fliedner, renewer of society, died 1864

See page 421 for a blessing for pets and animals, often used on or near the October 4 commemoration of Francis of Assisi.

Judges 16:23-31
Samson prays to do God's will

Then Samson called to the LORD and said, "Lord GOD, remember me and strengthen me only this once, O God, so that with this one act of revenge I may pay back the Philistines for my two eyes." And Samson grasped the two middle pillars on which the house rested, and he leaned his weight against them, his right hand on the one and his left hand on the other. Then Samson said, "Let me die with the Philistines." He strained with all his might; and the house fell on the lords and all the people who were in it. So those he killed at his death were more than those he had killed during his life. Then his brothers and all his family came down and took him and brought him up and buried him between Zorah and Eshtaol in the tomb of his father Manoah. He had judged Israel twenty years. (Judg. 16:28-31)

Psalm
Psalm 28
Prayer to do God's will

Additional Reading
Matthew 9:2-8
Jesus' authority to forgive and heal

Hymn: Lead On, O King Eternal! ELW 805

Lord, you use us in our strength, as well as our weakness. We surrender to your will and ask that you give us what we need to overcome evil and bring justice and peace.

Thursday, October 5, 2023
Time after Pentecost

Psalm 80:7-15
Look down from heaven, O God

Restore us, O God of hosts;
  let your face shine, that we may be saved.

You brought a vine out of Egypt;
  you drove out the nations and planted it.
You cleared the ground for it;
  it took deep root and filled the land. . . .

Turn again, O God of hosts;
  look down from heaven, and see;
have regard for this vine,
  the stock that your right hand planted. (Ps. 80:7-9, 14-15)

Additional Readings
Jeremiah 2:14-22
The choice vine becomes degenerate

Colossians 2:16-23
Hold fast to Christ, the head

Hymn: Like the Murmur of the Dove's Song, ELW 403

Creating and nurturing God, you are the source of all life, including our lives. Remember us and care for us, the vines you planted, as we face life's storms. Keep us safe and watch over us always.

Friday, October 6, 2023
Time after Pentecost

William Tyndale, translator, martyr, died 1536

Philippians 2:14-18; 3:1-4a

Boast only in Jesus Christ

Do all things without murmuring and arguing, so that you may be blameless and innocent, children of God without blemish in the midst of a crooked and perverse generation, in which you shine like stars in the world. It is by your holding fast to the word of life that I can boast on the day of Christ that I did not run in vain or labor in vain. But even if I am being poured out as a libation over the sacrifice and the offering of your faith, I am glad and rejoice with all of you—and in the same way you also must be glad and rejoice with me. (Phil. 2:14-18)

Psalm
Psalm 80:7-15
Look down from heaven, O God

Additional Reading
Jeremiah 2:23-37
Israel shall be shamed

Hymn: O Savior, Precious Savior, ELW 820

God, we are your beloved children. Help us to care for one another and to reflect your amazing love in a world that needs it more than ever. We rejoice to know that we can share your goodness and mercy with everyone we encounter.

Saturday, October 7, 2023
Time after Pentecost

Henry Melchior Muhlenberg, pastor in North America, died 1787

Jeremiah 6:1-10

Gleaning a remnant from the vine

Thus says the Lord of hosts:
Glean thoroughly as a vine
    the remnant of Israel;
like a grape-gatherer, pass your hand again
    over its branches.

To whom shall I speak and give warning,
    that they may hear?
See, their ears are closed,
    they cannot listen.
The word of the Lord is to them an object of scorn;
    they take no pleasure in it. (Jer. 6:9-10)

Psalm
Psalm 80:7-15
Look down from heaven, O God

Additional Reading
John 7:40-52
Some accept, others reject Jesus Christ

Hymn: Dearest Jesus, at Your Word, ELW 520

Lord, even in our sinfulness, you see us as worth saving. May we respond to your loving care by blossoming. May we be open and receptive to your nourishing and healing word, and never turn away from you.

Sunday, October 8, 2023
Time after Pentecost

Matthew 21:33-46
The parable of the vineyard owner's son

Jesus said to [the chief priests and elders], "Have you never read in the scriptures:
'The stone that the builders rejected
    has become the cornerstone;
this was the Lord's doing,
    and it is amazing in our eyes'?
Therefore I tell you, the kingdom of God will be taken away from you and given to a people that produces the fruits of the kingdom. The one who falls on this stone will be broken to pieces; and it will crush anyone on whom it falls."

When the chief priests and the Pharisees heard his parables, they realized that he was speaking about them. They wanted to arrest him, but they feared the crowds, because they regarded him as a prophet. (Matt. 21:42-46)

Psalm
Psalm 80:7-15
Look down from heaven, O God

Additional Readings
Isaiah 5:1-7
The song of the vineyard

Philippians 3:4b-14
Nothing surpasses knowing Christ

Hymn: Build Us Up, Lord, ELW 670

Beloved God, from you come all things that are good. Lead us by the inspiration of your Spirit to know those things that are right, and by your merciful guidance, help us to do them, through Jesus Christ, our Savior and Lord.

Monday, October 9, 2023
Time after Pentecost

Day of Thanksgiving (Canada)

A Blessing of the Household for Thanksgiving Day is provided on page 357.

Psalm 144
Prayer for blessing

Blessed be the LORD, my rock,
> who trains my hands for war, and my fingers for battle;

my rock and my fortress,
> my stronghold and my deliverer,

my shield, in whom I take refuge,
> who subdues the peoples under me.

O LORD, what are human beings that you regard them,
> or mortals that you think of them?

They are like a breath;
> their days are like a passing shadow. (Ps. 144:1-4)

Additional Readings
Ezekiel 19:10-14
A lament for Israel the vine

1 Peter 2:4-10
Christ the cornerstone

Hymn: My Hope Is Built on Nothing Less, ELW 596/597

God of the universe, it is a constant wonder that you even notice us humans. Yet you not only notice us; you love us, protect us, and guide us. Keep us ever mindful of all the gifts you give us.

Tuesday, October 10, 2023
Time after Pentecost

2 Corinthians 5:17-21
God reconciles us through Christ

So if anyone is in Christ, there is a new creation: everything old has passed away; see, everything has become new! All this is from God, who reconciled us to himself through Christ, and has given us the ministry of reconciliation; that is, in Christ God was reconciling the world to himself, not counting their trespasses against them, and entrusting the message of reconciliation to us. So we are ambassadors for Christ, since God is making his appeal through us; we entreat you on behalf of Christ, be reconciled to God. For our sake he made him to be sin who knew no sin, so that in him we might become the righteousness of God. (2 Cor. 5:17-21)

Psalm
Psalm 144
Prayer for blessing

Additional Reading
Isaiah 27:1-6
God will save Israel the vine

Hymn: Rise, Shine, You People! ELW 665

God our redeemer, thank you for becoming one with us and for bringing us to your heart, reconciled, forgiven, and made clean. Help us to be your messengers, sharing the incredible news of your saving grace.

Wednesday, October 11, 2023
Time after Pentecost

John 11:45-57

Critics plan to silence Jesus

Now the Passover of the Jews was near, and many went up from the country to Jerusalem before the Passover to purify themselves. They were looking for Jesus and were asking one another as they stood in the temple, "What do you think? Surely he will not come to the festival, will he?" Now the chief priests and the Pharisees had given orders that anyone who knew where Jesus was should let them know, so that they might arrest him. (John 11:55-57)

Psalm

Psalm 144
Prayer for blessing

Additional Reading

Song of Solomon 8:5-14
A love song for the vineyard

Hymn: Oh, Love, How Deep, ELW 322

Lord God, it is so hard to think about Jesus' betrayal, arrest, suffering, and death. It is so hard to realize that he was not recognized as the Messiah. Open our eyes to the reality of you all around us.

Thursday, October 12, 2023
Time after Pentecost

Psalm 23
You spread a table before me

Even though I walk through the darkest valley,
    I fear no evil;
for you are with me;
    your rod and your staff—they comfort me.

You prepare a table before me
    in the presence of my enemies;
you anoint my head with oil;
    my cup overflows.
Surely goodness and mercy shall follow me
    all the days of my life,
and I shall dwell in the house of the LORD
    my whole life long. (Ps. 23:4-6)

Additional Readings
Isaiah 22:1-8a
A futile cry to the mountains for help

1 Peter 5:1-5, 12-14
Stand fast, the chief shepherd is coming

Hymn: Savior, like a Shepherd Lead Us, ELW 789

Abundantly generous Lord, you fill our every need. With you there is nothing to fear from life's difficulties. May we be comforted by your loving presence with us every moment of our lives.

Friday, October 13, 2023
Time after Pentecost

James 4:4-10

Humble yourselves before God

Submit yourselves therefore to God. Resist the devil, and he will flee from you. Draw near to God, and he will draw near to you. Cleanse your hands, you sinners, and purify your hearts, you double-minded. Lament and mourn and weep. Let your laughter be turned into mourning and your joy into dejection. Humble yourselves before the Lord, and he will exalt you. (James 4:7-10)

Psalm

Psalm 23
You spread a table before me

Additional Reading

Isaiah 22:8b-14
False joy instead of repentance

Hymn: Before the Waters Nourished Earth, ACS 1049

God of surprises, when the world tells us to exalt ourselves, you ask us instead to be humble. It is by submitting to you that we are exalted. Thank you for drawing close and for delivering us from evil.

Saturday, October 14, 2023
Time after Pentecost

Isaiah 24:17-23
God judges the earth from Mount Zion

On that day the LORD will punish
    the host of heaven in heaven,
    and on earth the kings of the earth.
They will be gathered together
    like prisoners in a pit;
they will be shut up in a prison,
    and after many days they will be punished.
Then the moon will be abashed,
    and the sun ashamed;
for the LORD of hosts will reign
    on Mount Zion and in Jerusalem,
and before his elders he will manifest his glory. (Isa. 24:21-23)

Psalm
Psalm 23
You spread a table before me

Additional Reading
Mark 2:18-22
No fasting when the bridegroom is present

Hymn: Oh, Happy Day When We Shall Stand, ELW 441

Lord God, with your amazing grace and forgiveness we have nothing to fear in the end times. We give thanks for the promise of seeing the fullness of your glory and dwelling forever with you in your heavenly realm.

Sunday, October 15, 2023

Time after Pentecost

Teresa of Avila, teacher, renewer of the church, died 1582

Matthew 22:1-14

The parable of the unwelcome guest

[Jesus concluded the parable:] "But when the king came in to see the guests, he noticed a man there who was not wearing a wedding robe, and he said to him, 'Friend, how did you get in here without a wedding robe?' And he was speechless. Then the king said to the attendants, 'Bind him hand and foot, and throw him into the outer darkness, where there will be weeping and gnashing of teeth.' For many are called, but few are chosen." (Matt. 22:11-14)

Psalm

Psalm 23
You spread a table before me

Additional Readings

Isaiah 25:1-9
The feast of victory

Philippians 4:1-9
Rejoice in the Lord always

Hymn: All Who Hunger, Gather Gladly, ELW 461

Lord of the feast, you have prepared a table before all peoples and poured out your life with abundance. Call us again to your banquet. Strengthen us by what is honorable, just, and pure, and transform us into a people of righteousness and peace, through Jesus Christ, our Savior and Lord.

Monday, October 16, 2023
Time after Pentecost

Psalm 34
Taste and see

O taste and see that the LORD is good;
    happy are those who take refuge in him.
O fear the LORD, you his holy ones,
    for those who fear him have no want.
The young lions suffer want and hunger,
    but those who seek the LORD lack no good thing. (Ps. 34:8-10)

Additional Readings
Exodus 19:7-20
God meets Moses on the mountain

Jude 17-25
Prepare for the Lord's coming

Hymn: Taste and See, ELW 493

We know you are all goodness, sustaining God. With you we have everything we need. When we seek you, you are always there. Thank you for sheltering us from every storm that arises in life.

Tuesday, October 17, 2023
Time after Pentecost

Ignatius, Bishop of Antioch, martyr, died around 115

Amos 9:5-15
Sweet wine from the mountains

The time is surely coming, says the LORD,
> when the one who plows shall overtake the one who reaps,
> and the treader of grapes the one who sows the seed;
the mountains shall drip sweet wine,
> and all the hills shall flow with it.
I will restore the fortunes of my people Israel,
> and they shall rebuild the ruined cities and inhabit them;
they shall plant vineyards and drink their wine,
> and they shall make gardens and eat their fruit.
I will plant them upon their land,
> and they shall never again be plucked up
> out of the land that I have given them,

> > says the LORD your God. (Amos 9:13-15)

Psalm
Psalm 34
Taste and see

Additional Reading
Philippians 3:13—4:1
Hold fast to Christ

Hymn: Sing to the Lord of Harvest, ELW 694

Lord of the covenant, we believe that you rescue and restore your people. When we despair, remind us of your promises. Our troubles will end and we will come at last to the life of plenty that you prepare for us.

Wednesday, October 18, 2023
Luke, Evangelist

Luke 1:1-4; 24:44-53
Luke witnesses to the ministry of Jesus

Since many have undertaken to set down an orderly account of the events that have been fulfilled among us, just as they were handed on to us by those who from the beginning were eyewitnesses and servants of the word, I too decided, after investigating everything carefully from the very first, to write an orderly account for you, most excellent Theophilus, so that you may know the truth concerning the things about which you have been instructed. (Luke 1:1-4)

Psalm
Psalm 124
Our help is in God

Additional Readings
Isaiah 43:8-13
You are my witness

2 Timothy 4:5-11
The good fight of faith

Hymn: Come, Share the Spirit, ACS 1045

Almighty God, you inspired your servant Luke to reveal in his gospel the love and healing power of your Son. Give your church the same love and power to heal, and to proclaim your salvation to the nations to the glory of your name, through Jesus Christ, your Son, our healer, who lives and reigns with you and the Holy Spirit, one God, now and forever.

Thursday, October 19, 2023
Time after Pentecost

Psalm 96:1-9 [10-13]
God's glory among the nations

O sing to the LORD a new song;
>	sing to the LORD, all the earth.
Sing to the LORD, bless his name;
>	tell of his salvation from day to day.
Declare his glory among the nations,
>	his marvelous works among all the peoples.
For great is the LORD, and greatly to be praised;
>	he is to be revered above all gods. (Ps. 96:1-4)

Additional Readings
Judges 17:1-6
Before Israel had a king

3 John 9-12
Imitate what is good

Hymn: Earth and All Stars! ELW 731

O God, our hearts are full of joy, knowing that you are the Most High. You are the God of wonders, who blesses and saves us every day. May nothing keep us from singing your praises.

Friday, October 20, 2023
Time after Pentecost

1 Peter 5:1-5
Exemplary leadership

Now as an elder myself and a witness of the sufferings of Christ, as well as one who shares in the glory to be revealed, I exhort the elders among you to tend the flock of God that is in your charge, exercising the oversight, not under compulsion but willingly, as God would have you do it—not for sordid gain but eagerly. Do not lord it over those in your charge, but be examples to the flock. And when the chief shepherd appears, you will win the crown of glory that never fades away. (1 Peter 5:1-4)

Psalm
Psalm 96:1-9 [10-13]
God's glory among the nations

Additional Reading
Deuteronomy 17:14-20
The limitations of royal authority

Hymn: We All Are One in Mission, ELW 576

Inspiring Lord, you gave us the perfect example of servant leadership: your Son, Jesus Christ. May we lead others to you with open hearts and generous spirits, eager to share the joy that comes with life in you.

Saturday, October 21, 2023
Time after Pentecost

Isaiah 14:3-11

The king of Babylon will fall

When the LORD has given you rest from your pain and turmoil and the hard service with which you were made to serve, you will take up this taunt against the king of Babylon:

> How the oppressor has ceased!
>> How his insolence has ceased!
> The LORD has broken the staff of the wicked,
>> the scepter of rulers,
> that struck down the peoples in wrath
>> with unceasing blows,
> that ruled the nations in anger
>> with unrelenting persecution. (Isa. 14:3-6)

Psalm
Psalm 96:1-9 [10-13]
God's glory among the nations

Additional Reading
Matthew 14:1-12
King Herod's misuse of power

Hymn: O Day of Peace, ELW 711

God, give us strength when we suffer. God, give us hope when we are broken. God, give us comfort in the knowledge that you will not let evil stand, that you will free us from pain and bring us peace.

Sunday, October 22, 2023
Time after Pentecost

Matthew 22:15-22
A teaching about the emperor and God

But Jesus, aware of [the Pharisees'] malice, said, "Why are you putting me to the test, you hypocrites? Show me the coin used for the tax." And they brought him a denarius. Then he said to them, "Whose head is this, and whose title?" They answered, "The emperor's." Then he said to them, "Give therefore to the emperor the things that are the emperor's, and to God the things that are God's." When they heard this, they were amazed; and they left him and went away. (Matt. 22:18-22)

Psalm
Psalm 96:1-9 [10-13]
God's glory among the nations

Additional Readings
Isaiah 45:1-7
An earthly ruler works God's will

1 Thessalonians 1:1-10
Thanksgiving for the church at Thessalonica

Hymn: We Give Thee but Thine Own, ELW 686

Sovereign God, raise your throne in our hearts. Created by you, let us live in your image; created for you, let us act for your glory; redeemed by you, let us give you what is yours, through Jesus Christ, our Savior and Lord.

Monday, October 23, 2023
Time after Pentecost

James of Jerusalem, martyr, died around 62

Psalm 98

God reigns over the nations

O sing to the Lord a new song,
    for he has done marvelous things.
His right hand and his holy arm
    have gotten him victory.
The Lord has made known his victory;
    he has revealed his vindication in the sight of the nations.
He has remembered his steadfast love and faithfulness
    to the house of Israel.
All the ends of the earth have seen
    the victory of our God. (Ps. 98:1-3)

Additional Readings

Daniel 3:1-18
Three disobey Nebuchadnezzar

Revelation 18:1-10, 19-20
The fall of Babylon

Hymn: Oh, Sing to the Lord, ELW 822

Ever-faithful God, you never forget us. You are victorious over all the earth. Help us remember that your love always wins in the end. May we strive to be instruments of that beautiful and triumphant love in the world.

Tuesday, October 24, 2023
Time after Pentecost

Daniel 3:19-30
God saves three men in the furnace

Nebuchadnezzar then approached the door of the furnace of blazing fire and said, "Shadrach, Meshach, and Abednego, servants of the Most High God, come out! Come here!" So Shadrach, Meshach, and Abednego came out from the fire. And the satraps, the prefects, the governors, and the king's counselors gathered together and saw that the fire had not had any power over the bodies of those men; the hair of their heads was not singed, their tunics were not harmed, and not even the smell of fire came from them. Nebuchadnezzar said, "Blessed bc the God of Shadrach, Meshach, and Abednego, who has sent his angel and delivered his servants who trusted in him. They disobeyed the king's command and yielded up their bodies rather than serve and worship any god except their own God. Therefore I make a decree: Any people, nation, or language that utters blasphemy against the God of Shadrach, Meshach, and Abednego shall be torn limb from limb, and their houses laid in ruins; for there is no other god who is able to deliver in this way." (Dan. 3:26-29)

Psalm
Psalm 98
God reigns over the nations

Additional Reading
Revelation 18:21-24
Babylon will be found no more

Hymn: In a Deep, Unbounded Darkness, ACS 1093

Lord, you bring us through the spiritual fires of life and you protect us from harm. May we trust in your deliverance, and may we be fearless in worshiping you and sharing the news of your infinite power and mercy.

Wednesday, October 25, 2023
Time after Pentecost

Matthew 17:22-27
Jesus pays the temple tax

When [Jesus and the disciples] reached Capernaum, the collectors of the temple tax came to Peter and said, "Does your teacher not pay the temple tax?" He said, "Yes, he does." And when he came home, Jesus spoke of it first, asking, "What do you think, Simon? From whom do kings of the earth take toll or tribute? From their children or from others?" When Peter said, "From others," Jesus said to him, "Then the children are free. However, so that we do not give offense to them, go to the sea and cast a hook; take the first fish that comes up; and when you open its mouth, you will find a coin; take that and give it to them for you and me." (Matt. 17:24-27)

Psalm
Psalm 98
God reigns over the nations

Additional Reading
Daniel 6:1-28
Daniel disobeys King Darius

Hymn: Oh, Praise the Gracious Power, ELW 651

Wise Jesus, you taught your disciples well, sometimes using signs and wonders. May we learn those lessons and remember your timeless wisdom as we navigate through life.

Thursday, October 26, 2023
Time after Pentecost

Philipp Nicolai, died 1608; Johann Heermann, died 1647;
Paul Gerhardt, died 1676; hymnwriters

Psalm 1
Their delight is in the law

Happy are those
  who do not follow the advice of the wicked,
or take the path that sinners tread,
  or sit in the seat of scoffers;
but their delight is in the law of the Lord,
  and on his law they meditate day and night.
They are like trees
  planted by streams of water,
which yield their fruit in its season,
  and their leaves do not wither.
In all that they do, they prosper. (Ps. 1:1-3)

Additional Readings
Numbers 5:5-10   **Titus 1:5-16**
Restitution for wronged neighbors   *Troublemakers deny God*

Hymn: Sing Praise to God, the Highest Good, ELW 871

*Loving Lord, we thank you for always providing for us as we move through
life's seasons. Help us to focus on you, and not on the forces that oppose you.
We flourish with your tender care and need nothing else.*

Friday, October 27, 2023
Time after Pentecost

Titus 2:7-8, 11-15
A life devoted to good works

For the grace of God has appeared, bringing salvation to all, training us to renounce impiety and worldly passions, and in the present age to live lives that are self-controlled, upright, and godly, while we wait for the blessed hope and the manifestation of the glory of our great God and Savior, Jesus Christ. He it is who gave himself for us that he might redeem us from all iniquity and purify for himself a people of his own who are zealous for good deeds. (Titus 2:11-14)

Psalm
Psalm 1
Their delight is in the law

Additional Reading
Deuteronomy 9:25—10:5
The second set of commandments

Hymn: Strengthen for Service, Lord, ELW 497

God our destiny, may we wait for you in hope, and may living in that hope glorify you. You came to save and purify us. May we show our gratitude to you by loving and serving our neighbors.

Saturday, October 28, 2023
Simon and Jude, Apostles

John 14:21-27
Those who love Jesus will keep his word

[Jesus said,] "They who have my commandments and keep them are those who love me; and those who love me will be loved by my Father, and I will love them and reveal myself to them." Judas (not Iscariot) said to him, "Lord, how is it that you will reveal yourself to us, and not to the world?" Jesus answered him, "Those who love me will keep my word, and my Father will love them, and we will come to them and make our home with them. Whoever does not love me does not keep my words; and the word that you hear is not mine, but is from the Father who sent me." (John 14:21-24)

Psalm
Psalm 11
Take refuge in God

Additional Readings
Jeremiah 26:[1-6] 7-16
Jeremiah promises the judgment of God

1 John 4:1-6
Do not believe every spirit of this world

Hymn: Lord, Keep Us Steadfast in Your Word, ELW 517

O God, we thank you for the glorious company of the apostles, and especially on this day for Simon and Jude. We pray that, as they were faithful and zealous in your mission, so we may with ardent devotion make known the love and mercy of our Savior Jesus Christ, who lives and reigns with you and the Holy Spirit, one God, now and forever.

Sunday, October 29, 2023
Time after Pentecost

Matthew 22:34-46
Loving God and neighbor

When the Pharisees heard that [Jesus] had silenced the Sadducees, they gathered together, and one of them, a lawyer, asked him a question to test him. "Teacher, which commandment in the law is the greatest?" He said to him, "'You shall love the Lord your God with all your heart, and with all your soul, and with all your mind.' This is the greatest and first commandment. And a second is like it: 'You shall love your neighbor as yourself.' On these two commandments hang all the law and the prophets." (Matt. 22:34-40)

Psalm

Psalm 1
Their delight is in the law

Additional Readings

Leviticus 19:1-2, 15-18
Acts of justice

1 Thessalonians 2:1-8
The apostle's concern

Hymn: God's Work, Our Hands, ACS 1000

O Lord God, you are the holy lawgiver, you are the salvation of your people. By your Spirit renew us in your covenant of love, and train us to care tenderly for all our neighbors, through Jesus Christ, our Savior and Lord.

Monday, October 30, 2023
Time after Pentecost

Psalm 119:41-48
I will keep God's law

Let your steadfast love come to me, O LORD,
    your salvation according to your promise.
Then I shall have an answer for those who taunt me,
    for I trust in your word.
Do not take the word of truth utterly out of my mouth,
    for my hope is in your ordinances.
I will keep your law continually,
    forever and ever. (Ps. 119:41-44)

Additional Readings
Deuteronomy 6:1-9, 20-25
The great commandment

James 2:8-13
Fulfilling the royal law

Hymn: O Jesus, I Have Promised, ELW 810

God of all truth, help us to trust completely in you. We know you will never lead us astray and you will give us the courage we need to face a world that renounces you. Lord, we believe.

Tuesday, October 31, 2023
Reformation Day

John 8:31-36
The truth will set you free

Then Jesus said to the Jews who had believed in him, "If you continue in my word, you are truly my disciples; and you will know the truth, and the truth will make you free." They answered him, "We are descendants of Abraham and have never been slaves to anyone. What do you mean by saying, 'You will be made free'?"

Jesus answered them, "Very truly, I tell you, everyone who commits sin is a slave to sin. The slave does not have a permanent place in the household; the son has a place there forever. So if the Son makes you free, you will be free indeed." (John 8:31-36)

Psalm

Psalm 46
The God of Jacob is our stronghold

Additional Readings

Jeremiah 31:31-34
I will write my law in their hearts

Romans 3:19-28
Justified by God's grace as a gift

Hymn: A Mighty Fortress Is Our God, ELW 503/504/505

Gracious Father, we pray for your holy catholic church. Fill it with all truth and peace. Where it is corrupt, purify it; where it is in error, direct it; where in anything it is amiss, reform it; where it is right, strengthen it; where it is in need, provide for it; where it is divided, reunite it; for the sake of your Son, Jesus Christ, our Savior, who lives and reigns with you and the Holy Spirit, one God, now and forever.

Prayer List for November

Time after Pentecost
November

The month of November is unique in that it begins with All Saints Day (November 1) and ends with the feast of Christ the King (often the last Sunday of November). The Sunday and daily readings seem to extend the harvest, but in a new way: they speak of God's harvest of human beings into their heavenly home.

Perhaps it is no coincidence that November's scriptural emphasis on the consummation of all things in Christ is reflected in the landscape and the chilling temperatures. Yet in the midst of this turning of the seasons and the reminders of death's presence, Christians hold forth the central feast of the year: the death and resurrection of Christ present in baptism and the holy supper. In these last days of the church's year, Christians are invited to celebrate the reign of Christ, whose death on the cross has transformed our deaths into the gate of everlasting life.

Table Prayer for November

Stay with us, God of life,
as we share the bounty of this food and drink.
We give you thanks for those who have gone before us in faith.
Bring us, with them, to the harvest of everlasting life,
where all people will feast forever at your abundant table.
We ask this through Christ our Lord. Amen.

Remembering Those Who Have Died

Use this prayer in the home or at the grave.

O God, our help in ages past and our hope for years to come:
We give you thanks for all your faithful people
who have followed the light of your word throughout the centuries
into our time and place.

Here individual names may be spoken.

As we remember these people,
strengthen us to follow Christ through this world
until we are carried into the harvest of eternal life,
where suffering and death will be no more.
Hear our prayer in the name of the good and gracious shepherd,
Jesus Christ, our Savior and Lord. Amen.

or

With reverence and affection we remember before you,
O everlasting God,
all our departed friends and relatives.
Keep us in union with them here
through faith and love toward you,
that hereafter we may enter into your presence
and be numbered with those who serve you
and look upon your face in glory everlasting,
through your Son, Jesus Christ our Lord. Amen.

Wednesday, November 1, 2023
All Saints Day

Matthew 5:1-12

Blessed are the poor in spirit

[Jesus said to his disciples,] "Blessed are those who are persecuted for righteousness' sake, for theirs is the kingdom of heaven.

"Blessed are you when people revile you and persecute you and utter all kinds of evil against you falsely on my account. Rejoice and be glad, for your reward is great in heaven, for in the same way they persecuted the prophets who were before you." (Matt. 5:10-12)

Psalm

Psalm 34:1-10, 22
Fear the Lord, you saints

Additional Readings

Revelation 7:9-17
The multitude of heaven worship the Lamb

1 John 3:1-3
We are God's children

Hymn: Death Be Never Last, ACS 1030

Almighty God, you have knit your people together in one communion in the mystical body of your Son, Jesus Christ our Lord. Grant us grace to follow your blessed saints in lives of faith and commitment, and to know the inexpressible joys you have prepared for those who love you, through Jesus Christ, our Savior and Lord, who lives and reigns with you and the Holy Spirit, one God, now and forever.

Thursday, November 2, 2023
Time after Pentecost

Psalm 43
Send out your light and truth

O send out your light and your truth;
    let them lead me;
let them bring me to your holy hill
    and to your dwelling.
Then I will go to the altar of God,
    to God my exceeding joy;
and I will praise you with the harp,
      O God, my God. (Ps. 43:3-4)

Additional Readings
1 Samuel 2:27-36
Hope for a better priesthood

Romans 2:17-29
Real circumcision a matter of the heart

Hymn: Shine, Jesus, Shine, ELW 671

God of light and life, we thank you with glad and generous hearts for your guidance and insight. As our lives are enriched by your wisdom, help us to be for others an experience of your compassion and encouragement.

Friday, November 3, 2023
Time after Pentecost

Martín de Porres, renewer of society, died 1639

2 Peter 2:1-3
False prophets and their punishment

But false prophets also arose among the people, just as there will
be false teachers among you, who will secretly bring in destructive
opinions. They will even deny the Master who bought them—bringing
swift destruction on themselves. Even so, many will follow their
licentious ways, and because of these teachers the way of truth will be
maligned. And in their greed they will exploit you with deceptive words.
Their condemnation, pronounced against them long ago, has not been
idle, and their destruction is not asleep. (2 Peter 2:1-3)

Psalm
Psalm 43
Send out your light and truth

Additional Reading
Ezekiel 13:1-16
False prophets condemned

Hymn: Word of God, Come Down on Earth, ELW 510

God of truth, you make us aware of forces in our world that destroy the fabric of community. Nurture in us habits that nourish the common good so that we may embody the good news of the gospel.

Saturday, November 4, 2023
Time after Pentecost

Malachi 1:6—2:9
False and true priests

Oh, that someone among you would shut the temple doors, so that you would not kindle fire on my altar in vain! I have no pleasure in you, says the LORD of hosts, and I will not accept an offering from your hands. For from the rising of the sun to its setting my name is great among the nations, and in every place incense is offered to my name, and a pure offering; for my name is great among the nations, says the LORD of hosts. But you profane it when you say that the Lord's table is polluted, and the food for it may be despised. "What a weariness this is," you say, and you sniff at me, says the LORD of hosts. You bring what has been taken by violence or is lame or sick, and this you bring as your offering! Shall I accept that from your hand? says the LORD. (Mal. 1:10-13)

Psalm
Psalm 43
Send out your light and truth

Additional Reading
Matthew 23:13-28
Woe to the scribes and Pharisees

Hymn: God of Tempest, God of Whirlwind, ELW 400

In your name, O God, we pray for purity of heart and strength of purpose, so that no selfishness on our part may prevent us from knowing your will, and no reluctance prevent us from doing it.

Sunday, November 5, 2023
Time after Pentecost

Matthew 23:1-12

Humble yourselves

Then Jesus said to the crowds and to his disciples, "The scribes and the Pharisees sit on Moses' seat; therefore, do whatever they teach you and follow it; but do not do as they do, for they do not practice what they teach. They tie up heavy burdens, hard to bear, and lay them on the shoulders of others; but they themselves are unwilling to lift a finger to move them. They do all their deeds to be seen by others; for they make their phylacteries broad and their fringes long." (Matt. 23:1-5)

Psalm

Psalm 43
Send out your light and truth

Additional Readings

Micah 3:5-12
Judgment upon corrupt leaders

1 Thessalonians 2:9-13
The apostle's teaching

Hymn: Will You Let Me Be Your Servant, ELW 659

O God, generous and supreme, your loving Son lived among us, instructing us in the ways of humility and justice. Continue to ease our burdens, and lead us to serve alongside him, Jesus Christ, our Savior and Lord.

Monday, November 6, 2023
Time after Pentecost

Psalm 5
God blesses the righteous

Give ear to my words, O LORD;
　　give heed to my sighing.
Listen to the sound of my cry,
　　my King and my God,
　　for to you I pray.
O LORD, in the morning you hear my voice;
　　in the morning I plead my case to you, and watch. . . .

Lead me, O LORD, in your righteousness
　　because of my enemies;
　　make your way straight before me. (Ps. 5:1-3, 8)

Additional Readings

Jeremiah 5:18-31
Prophets and priests who mislead

1 Thessalonians 2:13-20
Words to the church

Hymn: Golden Breaks the Dawn, ELW 852

Gentle God, hear not only the prayers we offer with words but those we offer with sighs of frustration. Sustain us when we are weary, unclench us when we are uptight, and call forth our gifts for loving service.

Tuesday, November 7, 2023
Time after Pentecost

John Christian Frederick Heyer, died 1873; Bartholomaeus Ziegenbalg, died 1719;
Ludwig Nommensen, died 1918; missionaries

Lamentations 2:13-17
When prophets see false visions

What can I say for you, to what compare you,
O daughter Jerusalem?
To what can I liken you, that I may comfort you,
O virgin daughter Zion?
For vast as the sea is your ruin;
who can heal you? . . .

All who pass along the way
clap their hands at you;
they hiss and wag their heads
at daughter Jerusalem;
"Is this the city that was called
the perfection of beauty,
the joy of all the earth?" (Lam. 2:13, 15)

Psalm
Psalm 5
God blesses the righteous

Additional Reading
Acts 13:1-12
Paul and Barnabas confront a false prophet

Hymn: Jerusalem, My Happy Home, ELW 628

Even in our despair we can find you, O God. As we imagine a world that is healthier and holier for all, strengthen us to set our hearts where true joy can be found.

Wednesday, November 8, 2023
Time after Pentecost

Proverbs 16:21-33
The wise heart and persuasive lips

The wise of heart is called perceptive,
  and pleasant speech increases persuasiveness.
Wisdom is a fountain of life to one who has it,
  but folly is the punishment of fools.
The mind of the wise makes their speech judicious,
  and adds persuasiveness to their lips. (Prov. 16:21-23)

Psalm
Psalm 5
God blesses the righteous

Additional Reading
Matthew 15:1-9
Lips that misrepresent the heart

Hymn: Come and Seek the Ways of Wisdom, ACS 971

Generous God, you share your wisdom freely with us and constantly guide the work we most need to do. Give us humble and willing spirits so that we might be good receivers of your gracious gifts.

Thursday, November 9, 2023
Time after Pentecost

Psalm 70

You are my helper and deliverer

Be pleased, O God, to deliver me.
>   O Lord, make haste to help me!
Let those be put to shame and confusion
>   who seek my life.
Let those be turned back and brought to dishonor
>   who desire to hurt me.
Let those who say, "Aha, Aha!"
>   turn back because of their shame.

Let all who seek you
>   rejoice and be glad in you.
Let those who love your salvation
>   say evermore, "God is great!"
But I am poor and needy;
>   hasten to me, O God!
You are my help and my deliverer;
>   O Lord, do not delay! (Ps. 70:1-5)

Additional Readings

Amos 1:1—2:5
God judges Israel's neighbors

Revelation 8:6—9:12
The trumpet of God's judgment

Hymn: Immortal, Invisible, God Only Wise, ELW 834

God, come quick! Breathe into us new life! Nourish us in our innermost beings so we may meet the future with the joyful confidence of people who are in awe of your greatness and confident in your care.

Friday, November 10, 2023
Time after Pentecost

Amos 3:1-12
Israel's guilt and punishment

Proclaim to the strongholds in Ashdod,
> and to the strongholds in the land of Egypt,
and say, "Assemble yourselves on Mount Samaria,
> and see what great tumults are within it,
> and what oppressions are in its midst."
They do not know how to do right, says the LORD,
> those who store up violence and robbery in their strongholds.
Therefore thus says the Lord GOD:
An adversary shall surround the land,
> and strip you of your defense;
> and your strongholds shall be plundered. (Amos 3:9-11)

Psalm
Psalm 70
You are my helper and deliverer

Additional Reading
Revelation 9:13-21
Unrepentant humankind persists in sin

Hymn: My Life Flows On in Endless Song, ELW 763

Fill us with your discomfort, O God, when we see life out of alignment. Help us to face squarely the truths we would avoid. Give us the necessary courage to move decisively in the direction of your dreams.

Saturday, November 11, 2023
Time after Pentecost

Martin, Bishop of Tours, died 397
Søren Aabye Kierkegaard, teacher, died 1855

Matthew 24:1-14
Jesus foretells the end

When [Jesus] was sitting on the Mount of Olives, the disciples came to him privately, saying, "Tell us, when will this be, and what will be the sign of your coming and of the end of the age?" Jesus answered them, "Beware that no one leads you astray. For many will come in my name, saying, 'I am the Messiah!' and they will lead many astray. And you will hear of wars and rumors of wars; see that you are not alarmed; for this must take place, but the end is not yet." (Matt. 24:3-6)

Psalm
Psalm 70
You are my helper and deliverer

Additional Reading
Amos 4:6-13
Israel, prepare to meet your God

Hymn: Lord Christ, When First You Came to Earth, ELW 727

God of peace, remind us to breathe in the miracle of now. Make us attentive to good news, small victories, and the grace of what is always possible for us to be, to give, and to receive.

Sunday, November 12, 2023
Time after Pentecost

Matthew 25:1-13

Wise and foolish bridesmaids

[Jesus said to the disciples,] "Then the kingdom of heaven will be like this. Ten bridesmaids took their lamps and went to meet the bridegroom. Five of them were foolish, and five were wise. When the foolish took their lamps, they took no oil with them; but the wise took flasks of oil with their lamps." (Matt. 25:1-4)

Psalm

Psalm 70
You are my helper and deliverer

Additional Readings

Amos 5:18-24
Let justice roll down like waters

1 Thessalonians 4:13-18
The promise of the resurrection

Hymn: Keep Your Lamps Trimmed and Burning, ACS 949

O God of justice and love, you illumine our way through life with the words of your Son. Give us the light we need, and awaken us to the needs of others, through Jesus Christ, our Savior and Lord.

Monday, November 13, 2023
Time after Pentecost

Psalm 63
God is a rich feast

My soul is satisfied as with a rich feast,
    and my mouth praises you with joyful lips
when I think of you on my bed,
    and meditate on you in the watches of the night;
for you have been my help,
    and in the shadow of your wings I sing for joy.
My soul clings to you;
    your right hand upholds me. (Ps. 63:5-8)

Additional Readings
Amos 8:7-14
A famine of hearing God's word

1 Corinthians 14:20-25
They will not listen to me

Hymn: Thy Holy Wings, ELW 613

God of subtle and simple moments, help us to loosen up. Touch our hearts and make our spirits supple. Dispel our lingering fears. May we rest in your presence until we are renewed in body, mind, and spirit.

Tuesday, November 14, 2023
Time after Pentecost

1 Thessalonians 3:6-13
Stand firm in the faith

Now may our God and Father himself and our Lord Jesus direct our way to you. And may the Lord make you increase and abound in love for one another and for all, just as we abound in love for you. And may he so strengthen your hearts in holiness that you may be blameless before our God and Father at the coming of our Lord Jesus with all his saints. (1 Thess. 3:11-13)

Psalm
Psalm 63
God is a rich feast

Additional Reading
Joel 1:1-14
Call to repentance

Hymn: Blest Be the Tie That Binds, ELW 656

Energy of life, alive and at large in the world, nourish us with your love. Shape our passions into purposes and increase in us a longing for that day when your goodness shall soak into every corner of the universe.

Wednesday, November 15, 2023
Time after Pentecost

Matthew 24:29-35
My words will not pass away

[Jesus said to the disciples,] "From the fig tree learn its lesson: as soon as its branch becomes tender and puts forth its leaves, you know that summer is near. So also, when you see all these things, you know that he is near, at the very gates. Truly I tell you, this generation will not pass away until all these things have taken place. Heaven and earth will pass away, but my words will not pass away." (Matt. 24:32-35)

Psalm
Psalm 63
God is a rich feast

Additional Reading
Joel 3:9-21
Promise of a glorious future

Hymn: My Lord, What a Morning, ELW 438

Eternal God, from generation to generation you have used ordinary words to declare the good news of your love for the world. We pray that you will speak that eternal message through what we say and do.

Thursday, November 16, 2023
Time after Pentecost

Psalm 90:1-8 [9-11] 12

Number your days

LORD, you have been our dwelling place
    in all generations.
Before the mountains were brought forth,
    or ever you had formed the earth and the world,
    from everlasting to everlasting you are God.

You turn us back to dust,
    and say, "Turn back, you mortals."
For a thousand years in your sight
    are like yesterday when it is past,
    or like a watch in the night. (Ps. 90:1-4)

Additional Readings

Ezekiel 6:1-14
Judgment on idolatrous Israel

Revelation 16:1-7
God's judgments are true and just

Hymn: How Small Our Span of Life, ELW 636

God of past, present, and future: Our times are in your keeping. Give us the awareness to receive each moment as a gift and to enjoy the passage of time without clinging to the past or worrying excessively about the future.

Friday, November 17, 2023
Time after Pentecost

Elizabeth of Hungary, renewer of society, died 1231

Ezekiel 7:1-9

The end is upon us

The word of the LORD came to me: You, O mortal, thus says the Lord GOD to the land of Israel:

> An end! The end has come
> > upon the four corners of the land.
> Now the end is upon you,
> > I will let loose my anger upon you;
> I will judge you according to your ways,
> > I will punish you for all your abominations.
> My eye will not spare you, I will have no pity.
> > I will punish you for your ways,
> > while your abominations are among you.

Then you shall know that I am the LORD. (Ezek. 7:1-4)

Psalm
Psalm 90:1-8 [9-11] 12
Number your days

Additional Reading
Revelation 16:8-21
The judged curse God

Hymn: My God, How Wonderful Thou Art, ELW 863

Merciful God, forgive us those times when we ignored the invitations to wonder and partnership that you placed in our paths. Help us to discern the stirrings of your Spirit by which you reveal beginnings out of endings.

Saturday, November 18, 2023
Time after Pentecost

Matthew 12:43-45
From bad to worse

[Jesus said,] "When the unclean spirit has gone out of a person, it wanders through waterless regions looking for a resting place, but it finds none. Then it says, 'I will return to my house from which I came.' When it comes, it finds it empty, swept, and put in order. Then it goes and brings along seven other spirits more evil than itself, and they enter and live there; and the last state of that person is worse than the first. So will it be also with this evil generation." (Matt. 12:43-45)

Psalm
Psalm 90:1-8 [9-11] 12
Number your days

Additional Reading
Ezekiel 7:10-27
You shall know that the Lord is God

Hymn: Goodness Is Stronger than Evil, ELW 721

We confess, O God, that we cannot always keep our house in order. Center us in your deepest hopes for us, steady us through times of upheaval, and give us the courage to live as you would have us live.

Sunday, November 19, 2023
Time after Pentecost

Matthew 25:14-30

The story of the slaves entrusted with talents

[Jesus spoke a parable:] "Then the slave who had received the one talent also came forward, saying, 'Master, I knew that you were a harsh man, reaping where you did not sow, and gathering where you did not scatter seed; so I was afraid, and I went and hid your talent in the ground. Here you have what is yours.' But his master replied, 'You wicked and lazy slave! You knew, did you, that I reap where I did not sow, and gather where I did not scatter? Then you ought to have invested my money with the bankers, and on my return I would have received what was my own with interest. So take the talent from him, and give it to the one with the ten talents.'" (Matt. 25:24-28)

Psalm

Psalm 90:1-8 [9-11] 12
Number your days

Additional Readings

Zephaniah 1:7, 12-18
The day of the LORD

1 Thessalonians 5:1-11
Be alert for the day of the Lord

Hymn: God, Whose Giving Knows No Ending, ELW 678

Righteous God, our merciful master, you own the earth and all its peoples, and you give us all that we have. Inspire us to serve you with justice and wisdom, and prepare us for the joy of the day of your coming, through Jesus Christ, our Savior and Lord.

Monday, November 20, 2023
Time after Pentecost

Psalm 9:1-14
God's reward for the righteous

I will give thanks to the LORD with my whole heart;
>   I will tell of all your wonderful deeds.
I will be glad and exult in you;
>   I will sing praise to your name, O Most High.

When my enemies turned back,
>   they stumbled and perished before you.
For you have maintained my just cause;
>   you have sat on the throne giving righteous judgment. (Ps. 9:1-4)

Additional Readings
Zechariah 1:7-17
God's judgment and mercy

Romans 2:1-11
The righteous judgment of God

Hymn: O Beauty Ever Ancient, ACS 1100

What language shall we borrow to thank you, Creator God? You love us in every season of our lives. Empower us to turn graciously toward the world in all matters so that we might be instruments of your peace.

Tuesday, November 21, 2023
Time after Pentecost

Zechariah 2:1-5; 5:1-4
Visions of mercy and judgment

I looked up and saw a man with a measuring line in his hand. Then I asked, "Where are you going?" He answered me, "To measure Jerusalem, to see what is its width and what is its length." Then the angel who talked with me came forward, and another angel came forward to meet him, and said to him, "Run, say to that young man: Jerusalem shall be inhabited like villages without walls, because of the multitude of people and animals in it. For I will be a wall of fire all around it, says the LORD, and I will be the glory within it." (Zech. 2:1-5)

Psalm
Psalm 9:1-14
God's reward for the righteous

Additional Reading
1 Thessalonians 5:12-18
The Christian life

Hymn: Rejoice, Ye Pure in Heart, ELW 873/874

Almighty God, we seek the vision that you have for our future, and we seek ways to make that dream come true. May we discover the glory of your presence right where we live and move confidently in the direction of hope.

Wednesday, November 22, 2023
Time after Pentecost

Matthew 24:45-51
Parable of the unfaithful slave

[Jesus said,] "Who then is the faithful and wise slave, whom his master has put in charge of his household, to give the other slaves their allowance of food at the proper time? Blessed is that slave whom his master will find at work when he arrives. Truly I tell you, he will put that one in charge of all his possessions." (Matt. 24:45-47)

Psalm
Psalm 9:1-14
God's reward for the righteous

Additional Reading
Job 16:1-21
A lament about unjust punishment

Hymn: Lord Jesus, You Shall Be My Song, ELW 808

God of surprises, give us vibrant faith. Fill us with your spirit of hospitality. Inspire us with your wisdom, that we may be thoughtful and generous stewards of the resources you entrust to us.

Blessing of the Household for Thanksgiving Day

We gather this day to give thanks to God for the gifts of this land and its people, for God has been generous to us. As we ask God's blessing upon this food we share, may we be mindful of the lonely and the hungry.

As we prepare to offer thanks to God, let us listen to the words of scripture:

"I give thanks to my God always for you because of the grace of God that has been given you in Christ Jesus, for in every way you have been enriched in him, in speech and knowledge of every kind—just as the testimony of Christ has been strengthened among you—so that you are not lacking in any spiritual gift as you wait for the revealing of our Lord Jesus Christ. He will also strengthen you to the end, so that you may be blameless on the day of our Lord Jesus Christ." (1 Cor. 1:4-8)

Let us pray.
God most provident, we join all creation in offering you praise through Jesus Christ. For generations the people of this land have sung of your bounty. With them, we offer you thanksgiving for the rich harvest we have received at your hands. Bless us and this food that we share with grateful hearts. Continue to make our land fruitful and let our love for you be seen in our pursuit of justice and peace and in our generous response to those in need. We ask this through Christ our Lord. Amen.

May Christ, the living bread, bring us to the feast of eternal life. Amen.

Thursday, November 23, 2023
Time after Pentecost

Day of Thanksgiving (USA)
Clement, Bishop of Rome, died around 100; Miguel Agustín Pro, martyr, died 1927

Psalm 95:1-7a

We are the people of God's pasture

O come, let us sing to the LORD;
> let us make a joyful noise to the rock of our salvation!

Let us come into his presence with thanksgiving;
> let us make a joyful noise to him with songs of praise!

For the LORD is a great God,
> and a great King above all gods.

In his hand are the depths of the earth;
> the heights of the mountains are his also.

The sea is his, for he made it,
> and the dry land, which his hands have formed. (Ps. 95:1-5)

Additional Readings

1 Kings 22:13-23
Israel like sheep without a shepherd

Revelation 14:1-11
Fear God and give God glory

Hymn: O Christ, What Can It Mean for Us, ELW 431

With humble and grateful hearts, we give thanks to you, O God of generosity. Your lavish hospitality extends to the whole world and your peace is an unquenchable fountain of mercy. Help us to be compassionate as you are compassionate.

Friday, November 24, 2023
Time after Pentecost

Justus Falckner, died 1723; Jehu Jones, died 1852; William Passavant, died 1894; pastors in North America

Revelation 22:1-9
Worship God alone

Then the angel showed me the river of the water of life, bright as crystal, flowing from the throne of God and of the Lamb through the middle of the street of the city. On either side of the river is the tree of life with its twelve kinds of fruit, producing its fruit each month; and the leaves of the tree are for the healing of the nations. Nothing accursed will be found there any more. But the throne of God and of the Lamb will be in it, and his servants will worship him; they will see his face, and his name will be on their foreheads. And there will be no more night; they need no light of lamp or sun, for the Lord God will be their light, and they will reign forever and ever. (Rev. 22:1-5)

Psalm
Psalm 95:1-7a
We are the people of God's pasture

Additional Reading
1 Chronicles 17:1-15
David, shepherd and king of Israel

Hymn: Crown Him with Many Crowns, ELW 855

In your light, O God, we see visions of beauty and harmony. You have given us the capacity to imagine a world at its best and brightest. We ask you for the resilience to help in making that world come true.

Saturday, November 25, 2023
Time after Pentecost

Isaac Watts, hymnwriter, died 1748

Matthew 12:46-50

The true kindred of Jesus

While [Jesus] was still speaking to the crowds, his mother and his brothers were standing outside, wanting to speak to him. Someone told him, "Look, your mother and your brothers are standing outside, wanting to speak to you." But to the one who had told him this, Jesus replied, "Who is my mother, and who are my brothers?" And pointing to his disciples, he said, "Here are my mother and my brothers! For whoever does the will of my Father in heaven is my brother and sister and mother." (Matt. 12:46-50)

Psalm
Psalm 95:1-7a
We are the people of God's pasture

Additional Reading
Isaiah 44:21-28
Cyrus, a shepherd for the Lord

Hymn: O God, Who Gives Us Life, ACS 1086

Blessed Lord, inspire us with your love, challenge us with your truth, and empower us with your strength, that we might live as people for whom nothing matters but the doing of your will, in your way, for your world.

Sunday, November 26, 2023
Christ the King

Matthew 25:31-46

The separation of sheep and goats

[Jesus concluded the parable:] "Then [the king] will say to those at his left hand, 'You that are accursed, depart from me into the eternal fire prepared for the devil and his angels; for I was hungry and you gave me no food, I was thirsty and you gave me nothing to drink, I was a stranger and you did not welcome me, naked and you did not give me clothing, sick and in prison and you did not visit me.' Then they also will answer, 'Lord, when was it that we saw you hungry or thirsty or a stranger or naked or sick or in prison, and did not take care of you?' Then he will answer them, 'Truly I tell you, just as you did not do it to one of the least of these, you did not do it to me.'" (Matt. 25:41-45)

Psalm

Psalm 95:1-7a
We are the people of God's pasture

Additional Readings

Ezekiel 34:11-16, 20-24
God will shepherd Israel

Ephesians 1:15-23
The reign of Christ

Hymn: Come Now, You Blessed, ACS 1059

O God of power and might, your Son shows us the way of service, and in him we inherit the riches of your grace. Give us the wisdom to know what is right and the strength to serve the world you have made, through Jesus Christ, our Savior and Lord, who lives and reigns with you and the Holy Spirit, one God, now and forever.

Monday, November 27, 2023
Time after Pentecost

Psalm 7
God the righteous judge

O let the evil of the wicked come to an end,
    but establish the righteous,
you who test the minds and hearts,
    O righteous God.
God is my shield,
    who saves the upright in heart.
God is a righteous judge,
    and a God who has indignation every day. (Ps. 7:9-11)

Additional Readings
Esther 2:1-18
Lowly Esther becomes queen

2 Timothy 2:8-13
Those who endure with Christ reign with him

Hymn: Jesus Shall Reign, ELW 434

Enough is enough, God! Make us strong to encourage those in need of support. Show us where love and faith and hope are needed and enable us this day to do some work of peace for you.

Tuesday, November 28, 2023
Time after Pentecost

Esther 8:3-17
Queen Esther saves her people

Then Esther spoke again to the king; she fell at his feet, weeping and pleading with him to avert the evil design of Haman the Agagite and the plot that he had devised against the Jews. The king held out the golden scepter to Esther, and Esther rose and stood before the king. She said, "If it pleases the king, and if I have won his favor, and if the thing seems right before the king, and I have his approval, let an order be written to revoke the letters devised by Haman son of Hammedatha the Agagite, which he wrote giving orders to destroy the Jews who are in all the provinces of the king. For how can I bear to see the calamity that is coming on my people? Or how can I bear to see the destruction of my kindred?" (Esther 8:3-6)

Psalm
Psalm 7
God the righteous judge

Additional Reading
Revelation 19:1-9
Praise of God's judgments

Hymn: The Trumpets Sound, the Angels Sing, ELW 531

O God of justice, for such a time as this we come before you with our quest for peace on earth and good will among all people. Hear our cries and strengthen us to change those things that contradict your love.

Wednesday, November 29, 2023
Time after Pentecost

John 5:19-40
The judgment of the Son

[Jesus said,] "Very truly, I tell you, the hour is coming, and is now here, when the dead will hear the voice of the Son of God, and those who hear will live. For just as the Father has life in himself, so he has granted the Son also to have life in himself; and he has given him authority to execute judgment, because he is the Son of Man. Do not be astonished at this; for the hour is coming when all who are in their graves will hear his voice and will come out—those who have done good, to the resurrection of life, and those who have done evil, to the resurrection of condemnation." (John 5:25-29)

Psalm
Psalm 7
God the righteous judge

Additional Reading
Ezekiel 33:7-20
The righteous will live

Hymn: For All the Saints, ELW 422

O Lord of life who triumphs over death, open our eyes that we may see the needs of others; open our ears that we may hear their cries; and help us to be ambassadors of your resurrection power.

Thursday, November 30, 2023
Andrew, Apostle

John 1:35-42
Jesus calls Andrew

One of the two who heard John speak and followed him was Andrew, Simon Peter's brother. He first found his brother Simon and said to him, "We have found the Messiah" (which is translated Anointed). He brought Simon to Jesus, who looked at him and said, "You are Simon son of John. You are to be called Cephas" (which is translated Peter). (John 1:40-42)

Psalm
Psalm 19:1-6
The heavens declare God's glory

Additional Readings
Ezekiel 3:16-21
A sentinel for the house of Israel

Romans 10:10-18
Faith comes from the word of Christ

Hymn: Jesus Calls Us; o'er the Tumult, ELW 696

Almighty God, you gave your apostle Andrew the grace to obey the call of your Son and to bring his brother to Jesus. Give us also, who are called by your holy word, grace to follow Jesus without delay and to bring into his presence those who are near to us, for he lives and reigns with you and the Holy Spirit, one God, now and forever.

Prayer List for December

_____

_____

_____

_____

_____

_____

_____

_____

_____

Friday, December 1, 2023
Time after Pentecost

1 Thessalonians 4:1-18
A life pleasing God to the end

But we do not want you to be uninformed, brothers and sisters, about those who have died, so that you may not grieve as others do who have no hope. For since we believe that Jesus died and rose again, even so, through Jesus, God will bring with him those who have died. For this we declare to you by the word of the Lord, that we who are alive, who are left until the coming of the Lord, will by no means precede those who have died. For the Lord himself, with a cry of command, with the archangel's call and with the sound of God's trumpet, will descend from heaven, and the dead in Christ will rise first. Then we who are alive, who are left, will be caught up in the clouds together with them to meet the Lord in the air; and so we will be with the Lord forever. (1 Thess. 4:13-17)

Psalm
Psalm 80:1-7, 17-19
We shall be saved

Additional Reading
Zechariah 14:1-9
God will come to rule

Hymn: Lo! He Comes with Clouds Descending, ELW 435

Your trumpet announces the promise that in life and death we belong to you, O God. There is nothing that can separate us from your loving embrace. Engrave upon our hearts that you accompany us always.

Saturday, December 2, 2023

Time after Pentecost

Micah 2:1-13

God will gather all

I will surely gather all of you, O Jacob,
    I will gather the survivors of Israel;
I will set them together
    like sheep in a fold,
like a flock in its pasture;
    it will resound with people.
The one who breaks out will go up before them;
    they will break through and pass the gate,
    going out by it.
Their king will pass on before them,
    the LORD at their head. (Micah 2:12-13)

Psalm

Psalm 80:1-7, 17-19
We shall be saved

Additional Reading

Matthew 24:15-31
Be ready for that day

Hymn: The King of Love My Shepherd Is, ELW 502

Good Shepherd, throughout the ages you have gathered your people into one. You have sought the lost and carried home the weary. Encourage us to welcome and care for all. Open the gate for all to enter.

Advent

In the days of Advent, Christians prepare to celebrate the presence of God's Word among us in our own day. During these four weeks, we pray that the reign of God, which Jesus preached and lived, would come among us. We pray that God's justice would flourish in our land, that the people of the earth would live in peace, that the weak and the sick and the hungry would be strengthened, healed, and fed with God's merciful presence.

During the last days of Advent, Christians welcome Christ with names inspired by the prophets: wisdom, liberator of slaves, mighty power, radiant dawn and sun of justice, the keystone of the arch of humanity, and Emmanuel—God with us.

The Advent Wreath

One of the best-known customs for the season is the Advent wreath. The wreath and winter candle-lighting in the midst of growing darkness strengthen some of the Advent images found in the Bible. The unbroken circle of greens is clearly an image of everlasting life, a victory wreath, the crown of Christ, or the wheel of time itself. Christians use the wreath as a sign that Christ reaches into our time to lead us to the light of everlasting life. The four candles mark the progress of the four weeks of Advent and the growth of light. Sometimes the wreath is embellished with natural dried flowers or fruit. Its evergreen branches lead the household and the congregation to the evergreen Christmas tree. In many homes, the family gathers for prayer around the wreath.

An Evening Service of Light for Advent

This brief order may be used on any evening during the season of Advent. If the household has an Advent wreath (one candle for each of the four weeks of Advent), it may be lighted during this service. Alternatively, one simple candle (perhaps a votive candle) may be lighted instead.

Lighting the Advent Wreath

May this candle/these candles be a sign of the coming light of Christ.

One or more candles may be lighted. Use this blessing when lighting the first candle.

Blessed are you, God of Jacob, for you promise to transform weapons of war into implements of planting and harvest and to teach us your way of peace; you promise that our night of sin is far gone and that your day of salvation is dawning.

As we light the first candle on this wreath, wake us from our sleep, wrap us in your light, empower us to live honorably, and guide us along your path of peace.

O house of Jacob, come,
let us walk in the light of the Lord. Amen.

Blessings for the second, third, and fourth weeks of Advent are provided on pages 380, 388, and 396, respectively.

Reading

Read one or more of the scripture passages appointed for the day in the dated pages that follow.

Hymn

One of the following, or the hymn suggested for the day, may be sung. The hymn might be accompanied by small finger cymbals.

Light One Candle to Watch for Messiah, ELW 240
People, Look East, ELW 248
Savior of the Nations, Come, ELW 263

During the final seven days of the Advent season (beginning on December 17), the hymn "O Come, O Come, Emmanuel" (ELW 257) is particularly appropriate. The stanzas of that hymn are also referred to as the "O Antiphons." The first stanza of the hymn could be sung each day during the final days before Christmas in addition to the stanza that is specifically appointed for the day.

First stanza

O come, O come, Emmanuel,
and ransom captive Israel,
that mourns in lonely exile here
until the Son of God appear.
Refrain   Rejoice! Rejoice! Emmanuel shall come to you, O Israel.

December 17

O come, O Wisdom from on high,
embracing all things far and nigh:
in strength and beauty come and stay;
teach us your will and guide our way.   *Refrain*

December 18

O come, O come, O Lord of might,
as to your tribes on Sinai's height
in ancient times you gave the law
in cloud, and majesty, and awe.   *Refrain*

December 19

O come, O Branch of Jesse, free
your own from Satan's tyranny;
from depths of hell your people save,
and give them vict'ry o'er the grave.   *Refrain*

December 20

O come, O Key of David, come,
and open wide our heav'nly home;
make safe the way that leads on high,
and close the path to misery.   *Refrain*

December 21

O come, O Dayspring, come and cheer;
O Sun of justice, now draw near.
Disperse the gloomy clouds of night,
and death's dark shadow put to flight.   *Refrain*

December 22

O come, O King of nations, come,
O Cornerstone that binds in one:
refresh the hearts that long for you;
restore the broken, make us new.   *Refrain*

December 23

O come, O come, Emmanuel,
and ransom captive Israel,
that mourns in lonely exile here
until the Son of God appear.   *Refrain*

Text: *Psalteriolum Cantionum Catholicarum*, Köln, 1710; tr. composite
Text sts. 2, 6, 7 © 1997 Augsburg Fortress

Table Prayer for Advent

For use when a meal follows.

Blessed are you, O Lord our God,
the one who is, who was, and who is to come.
At this table you fill us with good things.
May these gifts strengthen us
to share with the hungry and all those in need,
as we wait and watch for your coming among us
in Jesus Christ our Lord. Amen.

Candles may be extinguished now or after the meal, if one is to follow.

Sunday, December 3, 2023
First Sunday of Advent

Francis Xavier, missionary to Asia, died 1552

Mark 13:24-37
The coming of the Son of Man

[Jesus said,] "But about that day or hour no one knows, neither the angels in heaven, nor the Son, but only the Father. Beware, keep alert; for you do not know when the time will come. It is like a man going on a journey, when he leaves home and puts his slaves in charge, each with his work, and commands the doorkeeper to be on the watch. Therefore, keep awake—for you do not know when the master of the house will come, in the evening, or at midnight, or at cockcrow, or at dawn, or else he may find you asleep when he comes suddenly. And what I say to you I say to all: Keep awake." (Mark 13:32-37)

Psalm
Psalm 80:1-7, 17-19
We shall be saved

Additional Readings
Isaiah 64:1-9
God will come with power and compassion

1 Corinthians 1:3-9
Gifts of grace sustain us

Hymn: Wake, Awake, for Night Is Flying, ELW 436

Stir up your power, Lord Christ, and come. By your merciful protection awaken us to the threatening dangers of our sins, and keep us blameless until the coming of your new day, for you live and reign with the Father and the Holy Spirit, one God, now and forever.

Monday, December 4, 2023
Week of Advent 1

John of Damascus, theologian and hymnwriter, died around 749

Psalm 79
Prayer for deliverance

Do not remember against us the iniquities of our ancestors;
>   let your compassion come speedily to meet us,
>   for we are brought very low.
Help us, O God of our salvation,
>   for the glory of your name;
deliver us, and forgive our sins,
>   for your name's sake.
Why should the nations say,
>   "Where is their God?"
Let the avenging of the outpoured blood of your servants
>   be known among the nations before our eyes. (Ps. 79:8-10)

Additional Readings
Micah 4:1-5   **Revelation 15:1-8**
A promise of peace   *A liturgy of glory*

Hymn: Lord of Our Life, ELW 766

O merciful One, your heart is full of compassion. From generation to generation you shower us with love and grace. Send us forth renewed and open to receive and share your abundant love with all.

Tuesday, December 5, 2023
Week of Advent 1

Revelation 18:1-10
Judgment upon human pride

After this I saw another angel coming down from heaven, having great authority; and the earth was made bright with his splendor. He called out with a mighty voice,

"Fallen, fallen is Babylon the great!
It has become a dwelling place of demons,
a haunt of every foul spirit,
a haunt of every foul bird,
a haunt of every foul and hateful beast.
For all the nations have drunk
of the wine of the wrath of her fornication,
and the kings of the earth have committed fornication with her,
and the merchants of the earth have grown rich
from the power of her luxury." (Rev. 18:1-3)

Psalm
Psalm 79
Prayer for deliverance

Additional Reading
Micah 4:6-13
A promise of restoration after exile

Hymn: Come, Thou Long-Expected Jesus, ELW 254

God of hope, you have walked with your people in times of deep misery. You know the pain and struggle of your people and all creation. Inspire us with hope in your promises, that we carry on each day knowing that you are at work to make all things new.

Wednesday, December 6, 2023
Week of Advent 1

Nicholas, Bishop of Myra, died around 342

Micah 5:1-5a

A promise of a shepherd

But you, O Bethlehem of Ephrathah,
    who are one of the little clans of Judah,
from you shall come forth for me
    one who is to rule in Israel,
whose origin is from of old,
    from ancient days.
Therefore he shall give them up until the time
    when she who is in labor has brought forth;
then the rest of his kindred shall return
    to the people of Israel.
And he shall stand and feed his flock in the strength of the LORD,
    in the majesty of the name of the LORD his God.
And they shall live secure, for now he shall be great
    to the ends of the earth;
and he shall be the one of peace. (Micah 5:2-5a)

Psalm

Psalm 79
Prayer for deliverance

Additional Reading

Luke 21:34-38
Be alert for that day

Hymn: Now the Heavens Start to Whisper, ACS 901

Giver of peace and joy, from the town of Bethlehem a new kind of ruler was born. You promised that your people would live securely. You proclaimed peace to the ends of the earth. Fill us with holy peace.

Thursday, December 7, 2023
Week of Advent 1

Ambrose, Bishop of Milan, died 397

Psalm 85:1-2, 8-13
Righteousness and peace

Let me hear what God the LORD will speak,
  for he will speak peace to his people,
  to his faithful, to those who turn to him in their hearts.
Surely his salvation is at hand for those who fear him,
  that his glory may dwell in our land.

Steadfast love and faithfulness will meet;
  righteousness and peace will kiss each other.
Faithfulness will spring up from the ground,
  and righteousness will look down from the sky.
The LORD will give what is good,
  and our land will yield its increase. (Ps. 85:8-12)

Additional Readings

Hosea 6:1-6
Return to the God of life and love

1 Thessalonians 1:2-10
Paul thanks God for the Thessalonians

Hymn: People, Look East, ELW 248

Eternal wellspring of peace, your steadfast love and faithfulness shape human community. We are anchored in your abundant love for us. Help us to live each day basking in the knowledge of your love for all creation.

Friday, December 8, 2023
Week of Advent 1

Jeremiah 1:4-10
God appoints a prophet

Now the word of the LORD came to me saying,

"Before I formed you in the womb I knew you,
and before you were born I consecrated you;
I appointed you a prophet to the nations."

Then I said, "Ah, Lord GOD! Truly I do not know how to speak, for I am only a boy." But the LORD said to me,

"Do not say, 'I am only a boy';
for you shall go to all to whom I send you,
and you shall speak whatever I command you,
Do not be afraid of them,
for I am with you to deliver you,

says the LORD." (Jer. 1:4-8)

Psalm
Psalm 85:1-2, 8-13
Righteousness and peace

Additional Reading
Acts 11:19-26
The new community called "Christian"

Hymn: Here I Am, Lord, ELW 574

Spirit of the living God, your word has been boldly proclaimed throughout history. You have called your people to follow you. You continue to call and invite us into community. Give us courage and strength to follow.

Saturday, December 9, 2023
Week of Advent 1

Ezekiel 36:24-28
A new heart and a new spirit

I will take you from the nations, and gather you from all the countries, and bring you into your own land. I will sprinkle clean water upon you, and you shall be clean from all your uncleannesses, and from all your idols I will cleanse you. A new heart I will give you, and a new spirit I will put within you; and I will remove from your body the heart of stone and give you a heart of flesh. I will put my spirit within you, and make you follow my statutes and be careful to observe my ordinances. Then you shall live in the land that I gave to your ancestors; and you shall be my people, and I will be your God. (Ezek. 36:24-28)

Psalm
Psalm 85:1-2, 8-13
Righteousness and peace

Additional Reading
Mark 11:27-33
Jesus a prophet like John the Baptist

Hymn: God, My Lord, My Strength, ELW 795

God of endless possibilities, you desire for your people to be united as one. You give us a new heart. You put your spirit within us. Help us live confidently, knowing we are your people and you are our God.

Lighting the Advent Wreath

Use this blessing when lighting the first two candles.

Blessed are you, God of hope, for you promise to bring forth a shoot from the stump of Jesse who will bring justice to the poor, who will deliver the needy and crush the oppressor, who will stand as a signal of hope for all people.

As we light these candles, turn our wills to bear the fruit of repentance, transform our hearts to live in justice and harmony with one another, and fix our eyes on the root of Jesse, Jesus Christ, the hope of all nations.

O people of hope, come,
let us rejoice in the faithfulness of the Lord. Amen.

Sunday, December 10, 2023
Second Sunday of Advent

Mark 1:1-8

John appears from the wilderness

John the baptizer appeared in the wilderness, proclaiming a baptism of repentance for the forgiveness of sins. And people from the whole Judean countryside and all the people of Jerusalem were going out to him, and were baptized by him in the river Jordan, confessing their sins. Now John was clothed with camel's hair, with a leather belt around his waist, and he ate locusts and wild honey. He proclaimed, "The one who is more powerful than I is coming after me; I am not worthy to stoop down and untie the thong of his sandals. I have baptized you with water; but he will baptize you with the Holy Spirit." (Mark 1:4-8)

Psalm

Psalm 85:1-2, 8-13
Righteousness and peace

Additional Readings

Isaiah 40:1-11
God's coming to the exiles

2 Peter 3:8-15a
Waiting for the day of God

Hymn: Hark! A Thrilling Voice Is Sounding! ELW 246

Stir up our hearts, Lord God, to prepare the way of your only Son. By his coming strengthen us to serve you with purified lives; through Jesus Christ, our Savior and Lord, who lives and reigns with you and the Holy Spirit, one God, now and forever.

Monday, December 11, 2023
Week of Advent 2

Psalm 27
God's level path

Teach me your way, O LORD,
> and lead me on a level path
> because of my enemies.
Do not give me up to the will of my adversaries,
> for false witnesses have risen against me,
> and they are breathing out violence.

I believe that I shall see the goodness of the LORD
> in the land of the living.
Wait for the LORD;
> be strong, and let your heart take courage;
> wait for the LORD! (Ps. 27:11-14)

Additional Readings
Isaiah 26:7-15
The way of the righteous is level

Acts 2:37-42
Baptism in the name of Jesus

Hymn: Lead Me, Guide Me, ELW 768

Teach us your way, O Lord. Fill us with the promise and hope that your goodness is within and around us. Give us strength and courage to be the people you have created us to be.

Tuesday, December 12, 2023
Week of Advent 2

Isaiah 4:2-6
God will wash Israel clean

On that day the branch of the LORD shall be beautiful and glorious, and the fruit of the land shall be the pride and glory of the survivors of Israel. Whoever is left in Zion and remains in Jerusalem will be called holy, everyone who has been recorded for life in Jerusalem, once the LORD has washed away the filth of the daughters of Zion and cleansed the bloodstains of Jerusalem from its midst by a spirit of judgment and by a spirit of burning. Then the LORD will create over the whole site of Mount Zion and over its places of assembly a cloud by day and smoke and the shining of a flaming fire by night. Indeed over all the glory there will be a canopy. It will serve as a pavilion, a shade by day from the heat, and a refuge and a shelter from the storm and rain. (Isa. 4:2-6)

Psalm
Psalm 27
God's level path

Additional Reading
Acts 11:1-18
John and Peter baptize

Hymn: Lost in the Night, ELW 243

Comforting God, you promise to walk with us in our life together. You are present in the darkness and in the light of each day. You provide a canopy of love and peace that protects us always.

Wednesday, December 13, 2023
Week of Advent 2

Lucy, martyr, died 304

Luke 1:5-17

The messenger in the temple

The angel said to [Zechariah], "Do not be afraid, Zechariah, for your prayer has been heard. Your wife Elizabeth will bear you a son, and you will name him John. You will have joy and gladness, and many will rejoice at his birth, for he will be great in the sight of the Lord. He must never drink wine or strong drink; even before his birth he will be filled with the Holy Spirit. He will turn many of the people of Israel to the Lord their God. With the spirit and power of Elijah he will go before him, to turn the hearts of parents to their children, and the disobedient to the wisdom of the righteous, to make ready a people prepared for the Lord." (Luke 1:13-17)

Psalm
Psalm 27
God's level path

Additional Reading
Malachi 2:10—3:1
The coming messenger

Hymn: Comfort, Comfort Now My People, ELW 256

God of joy, you listen to the prayers of your people. You celebrated with Elizabeth and Zechariah as the angel brought them joyous news. Give us confidence to lift our prayers to you.

Thursday, December 14, 2023
Week of Advent 2

John of the Cross, renewer of the church, died 1591

Psalm 126
God does great things for us

When the LORD restored the fortunes of Zion,
 we were like those who dream.
Then our mouth was filled with laughter,
 and our tongue with shouts of joy;
then it was said among the nations,
 "The LORD has done great things for them."
The LORD has done great things for us,
 and we rejoiced. (Ps. 126:1-3)

Additional Readings
Habakkuk 2:1-5
A vision concerning the end

Philippians 3:7-11
The righteousness that comes through faith

Hymn: Hark, the Glad Sound! ELW 239

Creative God, you restore what is broken. You have filled people with child-like laughter and shouts of joy. Help us to recognize and celebrate all the great things you have done.

Friday, December 15, 2023

Week of Advent 2

Philippians 3:12-16

The prize of God's call in Christ

Not that I have already obtained this or have already reached the goal; but I press on to make it my own, because Christ Jesus has made me his own. Beloved, I do not consider that I have made it my own; but this one thing I do: forgetting what lies behind and straining forward to what lies ahead, I press on toward the goal for the prize of the heavenly call of God in Christ Jesus. Let those of us then who are mature be of the same mind; and if you think differently about anything, this too God will reveal to you. Only let us hold fast to what we have attained. (Phil. 3:12-16)

Psalm

Psalm 126
God does great things for us

Additional Reading

Habakkuk 3:2-6
A prayer for God's glory and mercy

Hymn: My Faith Looks Up to Thee, ELW 759

God of all that has been, all that is, and all that is to come, you claim us as your own. You promise to walk beside us. Sustain us on the journey. Open our ears to hear your voice.

Saturday, December 16, 2023
Week of Advent 2

Habakkuk 3:13-19
God's devastation, God's deliverance

Though the fig tree does not blossom,
 and no fruit is on the vines;
though the produce of the olive fails
 and the fields yield no food;
though the flock is cut off from the fold
 and there is no herd in the stalls,
yet I will rejoice in the LORD;
 I will exult in the God of my salvation.
God, the LORD, is my strength;
 he makes my feet like the feet of a deer,
 and makes me tread upon the heights. (Hab. 3:17-19)

Psalm
Psalm 126
God does great things for us

Additional Reading
Matthew 21:28-32
Resistance to God in the present generation

Hymn: Fling Wide the Door, ELW 259

God of eternal hope, you never give up on all that you have made. You create new life out of that which appears barren and near death. Give us eyes of hope to see your hands at work in the world.

Lighting the Advent Wreath

Use this blessing when lighting three candles.

Blessed are you, God of might and majesty, for you promise to make the desert rejoice and blossom, to watch over the strangers, and to set the prisoners free.

As we light these candles, satisfy our hunger with your good gifts, open our eyes to the great things you have done for us, and fill us with patience until the coming of the Lord Jesus.

O ransomed people of the Lord, come,
**let us travel on God's holy way
and enter into Zion with singing. Amen.**

Sunday, December 17, 2023
Third Sunday of Advent

John 1:6-8, 19-28
A witness to the light

This is the testimony given by John when the Jews sent priests and Levites from Jerusalem to ask him, "Who are you?" He confessed and did not deny it, but confessed, "I am not the Messiah." And they asked him, "What then? Are you Elijah?" He said, "I am not." "Are you the prophet?" He answered, "No." Then they said to him, "Who are you? Let us have an answer for those who sent us. What do you say about yourself?" He said,

"I am the voice of one crying out in the wilderness,
'Make straight the way of the Lord,'"
as the prophet Isaiah said. (John 1:19-23)

Psalm
Psalm 126
God does great things for us

Additional Readings
Isaiah 61:1-4, 8-11
Righteousness and praise flourish like a garden

1 Thessalonians 5:16-24
Kept in faith until the coming of Christ

Hymn: There's a Voice in the Wilderness, ELW 255

Stir up the wills of your faithful people, Lord God, and open our ears to the words of your prophets, that, anointed by your Spirit, we may testify to your light; through Jesus Christ, our Savior and Lord, who lives and reigns with you and the Holy Spirit, one God, now and forever.

Monday, December 18, 2023
Week of Advent 3

Psalm 125
Prayer for blessing

Those who trust in the LORD are like Mount Zion,
    which cannot be moved, but abides forever.
As the mountains surround Jerusalem,
    so the LORD surrounds his people,
    from this time on and forevermore.
For the scepter of wickedness shall not rest
    on the land allotted to the righteous,
    so that the righteous might not stretch out
    their hands to do wrong.
Do good, O LORD, to those who are good,
    and to those who are upright in their hearts.
But those who turn aside to their own crooked ways
    the LORD will lead away with evildoers.
    Peace be upon Israel! (Ps. 125:1-5)

Additional Readings
1 Kings 18:1-18
Elijah condemns King Ahab

Ephesians 6:10-17
The armor of God against the powers

Hymn: Light One Candle to Watch for Messiah, ELW 240

*O Lord, your goodness surrounds us. Your loving embrace supports us.
Encourage us to put our trust and faith in you. Open our hearts to share
your abundant grace and compassion with everyone.*

Tuesday, December 19, 2023
Week of Advent 3

Acts 3:17—4:4
Peter preaches about the prophets

While Peter and John were speaking to the people, the priests, the captain of the temple, and the Sadducees came to them, much annoyed because they were teaching the people and proclaiming that in Jesus there is the resurrection of the dead. So they arrested them and put them in custody until the next day, for it was already evening. But many of those who heard the word believed; and they numbered about five thousand. (Acts 4:1-4)

Psalm
Psalm 125
Prayer for blessing

Additional Reading
2 Kings 2:9-22
Elisha receives Elijah's spirit

Hymn: Gracious Spirit, Heed Our Pleading, ELW 401

Spirit of the living God, your holy voice speaks to us in ever new ways. You call us to proclaim the news of your unconditional love. May your living spirit and your holy breath blow upon us.

Wednesday, December 20, 2023
Week of Advent 3

Katharina von Bora Luther, renewer of the church, died 1552

Mark 9:9-13
Questions about Elijah

As [Jesus, Peter, James, and John] were coming down the mountain, [Jesus] ordered them to tell no one about what they had seen, until after the Son of Man had risen from the dead. So they kept the matter to themselves, questioning what this rising from the dead could mean. Then they asked him, "Why do the scribes say that Elijah must come first?" He said to them, "Elijah is indeed coming first to restore all things. How then is it written about the Son of Man, that he is to go through many sufferings and be treated with contempt? But I tell you that Elijah has come, and they did to him whatever they pleased, as it is written about him." (Mark 9:9-13)

Psalm
Psalm 125
Prayer for blessing

Additional Reading
Malachi 3:16—4:6
Elijah and the coming one

Hymn: Oh, Wondrous Image, Vision Fair, ELW 316

Living God, you speak to us from the mountain and the seashore. Your voice calls us to hear and proclaim the story of your deep love. Encourage us to listen to your voice calling us into new ways of being community.

Thursday, December 21, 2023
Week of Advent 3

Psalm 89:1-4, 19-26
I sing of your love

I will sing of your steadfast love, O LORD, forever;
>   with my mouth I will proclaim your faithfulness to all generations.
I declare that your steadfast love is established forever;
>   your faithfulness is as firm as the heavens.

You said, "I have made a covenant with my chosen one,
>   I have sworn to my servant David:
'I will establish your descendants forever,
>   and build your throne for all generations.'" (Ps. 89:1-4)

Additional Readings
2 Samuel 6:1-11
The advent of the ark of the Lord

Hebrews 1:1-4
In the last days God speaks by a Son

Hymn: Great Is Thy Faithfulness, ELW 733

Living God, your people have spoken of your steadfast love and faithfulness from generation to generation. Help us to sing with ancestors of every time and place about your unfailing love and hope.

Friday, December 22, 2023
Week of Advent 3

Hebrews 1:5-14

The advent of one higher than angels

For to which of the angels did God ever say,
>"You are my Son;
>>today I have begotten you"? . . .

And again, when he brings the firstborn into the world, he says,
>"Let all God's angels worship him."

Of the angels he says,
>"He makes his angels winds,
>>and his servants flames of fire."

But of the Son he says,
>"Your throne, O God, is forever and ever,
>>and the righteous scepter is the scepter of your kingdom.
>You have loved righteousness and hated wickedness;
>therefore God, your God, has anointed you
>>with the oil of gladness beyond your companions."

(Heb. 1:5a, 6-9)

Psalm
Psalm 89:1-4, 19-26
I sing of your love

Additional Reading
2 Samuel 6:12-19
The ark of God enters Jerusalem

Hymn: As the Dark Awaits the Dawn, ELW 261

Holy One, you make winds for the angels and flames of fire for your servants. You bring hope where there is despair. You bring righteousness where there is wickedness. Anoint us with the oil of gladness.

Saturday, December 23, 2023
Week of Advent 3

John 7:40-52

The Messiah, David, and Bethlehem

When they heard [Jesus'] words, some in the crowd said, "This is really the prophet." Others said, "This is the Messiah." But some asked, "Surely the Messiah does not come from Galilee, does he? Has not the scripture said that the Messiah is descended from David and comes from Bethlehem, the village where David lived?" So there was a division in the crowd because of him. Some of them wanted to arrest him, but no one laid hands on him. (John 7:40-44)

Psalm

Psalm 89:1-4, 19-26
I sing of your love

Additional Reading

Judges 13:2-24
The birth of Samson

Hymn: O Come, O Come, Emmanuel, ELW 257

God of hope, your people have listened for your voice throughout human history. We have yearned to see you and hear you speak. Open our hearts to receive the message you bring today with joy, hope, wonder, and peace.

Lighting the Advent Wreath

Use this blessing when lighting all four candles.

Blessed are you, God of hosts, for you promised to send a Son, Emmanuel, who brought your presence among us; and you promise through your Son Jesus to save us from our sin.

As we light these candles, turn again to us in mercy; strengthen our faith in the word spoken by your prophets; restore us and give us life that we may be saved.

O house of David, come,
**let us rejoice, for the Son of God, Emmanuel,
comes to be with us. Amen.**

Sunday, December 24, 2023

Fourth Sunday of Advent
Nativity of Our Lord
Christmas Eve

Luke 1:26-38

The angel appears to Mary

In the sixth month the angel Gabriel was sent by God to a town in Galilee called Nazareth, to a virgin engaged to a man whose name was Joseph, of the house of David. The virgin's name was Mary. And he came to her and said, "Greetings, favored one! The Lord is with you." But she was much perplexed by his words and pondered what sort of greeting this might be. The angel said to her, "Do not be afraid, Mary, for you have found favor with God. And now, you will conceive in your womb and bear a son, and you will name him Jesus." (Luke 1:26-31)

Psalm

Luke 1:46b-55
The Mighty One raises the lowly

Additional Readings

2 Samuel 7:1-11, 16
God's promise to David

Romans 16:25-27
The mystery revealed in Jesus Christ

Hymn: No Wind at the Window, ACS 906

Stir up your power, Lord Christ, and come. With your abundant grace and might, free us from the sin that would obstruct your mercy, that willingly we may bear your redeeming love to all the world, for you live and reign with the Father and the Holy Spirit, one God, now and forever.

Christmas

Over the centuries, various customs have developed which focus the household on welcoming the light of Christ: the daily or weekly lighting of the Advent wreath, the blessing of the lighted Christmas tree, the candlelit procession of Las Posadas, the flickering lights of the luminaria, the Christ candle at Christmas.

The Christian household not only welcomes the light of Christ at Christmas, but celebrates the presence of that light throughout the Twelve Days, from Christmas until the Epiphany, January 6. In the Christmas season, Christians welcome the light of Christ that is already with us through faith. In word and gesture, prayer and song, in the many customs of diverse cultures, Christians celebrate this life-giving Word and ask that it dwell more deeply in the rhythm of daily life.

Table Prayer for the Twelve Days of Christmas

With joy and gladness we feast upon your love, O God.
You have come among us in Jesus, your Son,
and your presence now graces this table.
May Christ dwell in us that we might bear his love to all the world,
for he is Lord forever and ever. Amen.

Lighting the Christmas Tree

Use this prayer when you first illumine the tree or when you gather at the tree.

Holy God,
we praise you as we light this tree.
It gives light to this place
as you shine light into darkness through Jesus,
the light of the world.

God of all,
we thank you for your love,
the love that has come to us in Jesus.
Be with us now as we remember that gift of love
and help us to share that love with a yearning world.

Creator God,
you made the stars in the heavens.
Thank you for the light that shines on us in Jesus,
the bright morning star.
Amen.

Blessing of the Nativity Scene

This blessing may be used when figures are added to the nativity scene and throughout the days of Christmas.

Bless us, O God, as we remember a humble birth. With each angel and shepherd we place here before you, show us the wonder found in a stable. In song and prayer, silence and awe, we adore your gift of love, Christ Jesus our Savior.
Amen.

Monday, December 25, 2023

Nativity of Our Lord
Christmas Day

John 1:1-14

The Word became flesh

In the beginning was the Word, and the Word was with God, and the Word was God. He was in the beginning with God. All things came into being through him, and without him not one thing came into being. What has come into being in him was life, and the life was the light of all people. The light shines in the darkness, and the darkness did not overcome it. (John 1:1-5)

Psalm

Psalm 98
The victory of our God

Additional Readings

Isaiah 52:7-10
Heralds announce God's salvation

Hebrews 1:1-4 [5-12]
God has spoken by a Son

Hymn: O Come, All Ye Faithful, ELW 283

Almighty God, you gave us your only Son to take on our human nature and to illumine the world with your light. By your grace adopt us as your children and enlighten us with your Spirit, through Jesus Christ, our Redeemer and Lord, who lives and reigns with you and the Holy Spirit, one God, now and forever.

Tuesday, December 26, 2023
Stephen, Deacon and Martyr

Acts 6:8—7:2a, 51-60
Stephen is stoned to death

Filled with the Holy Spirit, [Stephen] gazed into heaven and saw the glory of God and Jesus standing at the right hand of God. "Look," he said, "I see the heavens opened and the Son of Man standing at the right hand of God!" But they covered their ears, and with a loud shout all rushed together against him. Then they dragged him out of the city and began to stone him; and the witnesses laid their coats at the feet of a young man named Saul. While they were stoning Stephen, he prayed, "Lord Jesus, receive my spirit." Then he knelt down and cried out in a loud voice, "Lord, do not hold this sin against them." When he had said this, he died. (Acts 7:55-60)

Psalm
Psalm 17:1-9, 15
I call upon you, O God

Additional Readings
2 Chronicles 24:17-22
Zechariah is stoned to death

Matthew 23:34-39
Jesus laments that Jerusalem kills her prophets

Hymn: What Child Is This, ELW 296

We give you thanks, O Lord of glory, for the example of Stephen the first martyr, who looked to heaven and prayed for his persecutors. Grant that we also may pray for our enemies and seek forgiveness for those who hurt us, through Jesus Christ, our Savior and Lord, who lives and reigns with you and the Holy Spirit, one God, now and forever.

Wednesday, December 27, 2023
John, Apostle and Evangelist

John 21:20-25
The beloved disciple remains with Jesus

Peter turned and saw the disciple whom Jesus loved following them; he was the one who had reclined next to Jesus at the supper and had said, "Lord, who is it that is going to betray you?" When Peter saw him, he said to Jesus, "Lord, what about him?" Jesus said to him, "If it is my will that he remain until I come, what is that to you? Follow me!" . . .

This is the disciple who is testifying to these things and has written them, and we know that his testimony is true. But there are also many other things that Jesus did; if every one of them were written down, I suppose that the world itself could not contain the books that would be written. (John 21:20-22, 24-25)

Psalm
Psalm 116:12-19
The death of faithful servants

Additional Readings
Genesis 1:1-5, 26-31
Humankind is created by God

1 John 1:1—2:2
Jesus, the word of life

Hymn: The Bells of Christmas, ELW 298

Merciful God, through John the apostle and evangelist you have revealed the mysteries of your Word made flesh. Let the brightness of your light shine on your church, so that all your people, instructed in the holy gospel, may walk in the light of your truth and attain eternal life, through Jesus Christ, our Savior and Lord, who lives and reigns with you and the Holy Spirit, one God, now and forever.

Thursday, December 28, 2023
The Holy Innocents, Martyrs

Matthew 2:13-18
Herod kills innocent children

Now after [the magi] had left [Bethlehem], an angel of the Lord appeared to Joseph in a dream and said, "Get up, take the child and his mother, and flee to Egypt, and remain there until I tell you; for Herod is about to search for the child, to destroy him." Then Joseph got up, took the child and his mother by night, and went to Egypt, and remained there until the death of Herod. This was to fulfill what had been spoken by the Lord through the prophet, "Out of Egypt I have called my son."

When Herod saw that he had been tricked by the wise men, he was infuriated, and he sent and killed all the children in and around Bethlehem who were two years old or under, according to the time that he had learned from the wise men. (Matt. 2:13-16)

Psalm
Psalm 124
We have escaped like a bird

Additional Readings
Jeremiah 31:15-17
Rachel weeps for her children

1 Peter 4:12-19
Continue to do good while suffering

Hymn: How Long, O God, ELW 698

We remember today, O God, the slaughter of the innocent children of Bethlehem by order of King Herod. Receive into the arms of your mercy all innocent victims. By your great might frustrate the designs of evil tyrants and establish your rule of justice, love, and peace, through Jesus Christ, our Savior and Lord, who lives and reigns with you and the Holy Spirit, one God, now and forever.

Friday, December 29, 2023
Fifth Day of Christmas

Psalm 148

God's splendor is over earth and heaven

Praise the LORD!
Praise the LORD from the heavens;
>   praise him in the heights!
Praise him, all his angels;
>   praise him, all his host!

Praise him, sun and moon;
>   praise him, all you shining stars!
Praise him, you highest heavens,
>   and you waters above the heavens! (Ps. 148:1-4)

Additional Readings

Isaiah 49:5-15
God like a nursing mother

Matthew 12:46-50
Jesus' true family

Hymn: Joy to the World, ELW 267

Creator of the heavens and the earth, you created us to live our days with thanksgiving and praise. You created us to marvel at the sun, moon, and shining stars. Lift our voices in praise for all you have made.

Saturday, December 30, 2023
Sixth Day of Christmas

2 Peter 3:8-13

A thousand years as one day

But do not ignore this one fact, beloved, that with the Lord one day is like a thousand years, and a thousand years are like one day. The Lord is not slow about his promise, as some think of slowness, but is patient with you, not wanting any to perish, but all to come to repentance. But the day of the Lord will come like a thief, and then the heavens will pass away with a loud noise, and the elements will be dissolved with fire, and the earth and everything that is done on it will be disclosed. (2 Peter 3:8-10)

Psalm

Psalm 148
God's splendor is over earth and heaven

Additional Reading

Proverbs 9:1-12
Your days will be multiplied

Hymn: When Long before Time, ELW 861

Creator God, each day we wake to explore and enjoy all that you have made. Each new day is filled with hope and promise. Open our hearts to receive the countless gifts of this day.

Luke 2:22-40
The presentation of the child

Now there was a man in Jerusalem whose name was Simeon; this man was righteous and devout, looking forward to the consolation of Israel, and the Holy Spirit rested on him. It had been revealed to him by the Holy Spirit that he would not see death before he had seen the Lord's Messiah. Guided by the Spirit, Simeon came into the temple; and when the parents brought in the child Jesus, to do for him what was customary under the law, Simeon took him in his arms and praised God. (Luke 2:25-28a)

Psalm

Psalm 148
God's splendor is over earth and heaven

Additional Readings

Isaiah 61:10—62:3
Clothed in garments of salvation

Galatians 4:4-7
Children and heirs of God

Hymn: O Lord, Now Let Your Servant, ELW 313

Almighty God, you wonderfully created the dignity of human nature and yet more wonderfully restored it. In your mercy, let us share the divine life of the one who came to share our humanity, Jesus Christ, your Son, our Lord, who lives and reigns with you and the Holy Spirit, one God, now and forever.

Lesser Festivals and Commemorations

Interested in enriching your prayer life further and in learning more about the people included among the festivals and commemorations? See Gail Ramshaw's *More Days for Praise: Festivals* and *Commemorations in Evangelical Lutheran Worship* (Augsburg Fortress, 2016; 320 pages; ISBN 9781451496215). Each day's entry includes a brief chronology of the person's life; a summary of why the person is remembered by the church; an image of, or related to, the commemoration; a quote from the person, where possible; and devotional hymn and prayer suggestions for the day.

January 1—Name of Jesus Every Jewish boy was circumcised and formally named on the eighth day of his life. Already in his infancy, Jesus bore the mark of a covenant that he made new through the shedding of his blood on the cross.

January 2—Johann Konrad Wilhelm Loehe Wilhelm Loehe was a pastor in nineteenth-century Germany. From the small town of Neuendettelsau he sent pastors to North America, Australia, New Guinea, Brazil, and the Ukraine.

January 15—Martin Luther King Jr. Martin Luther King Jr. is remembered as an American prophet of justice among races and nations. Many churches hold commemorations near Dr. King's birth date of January 15, in conjunction with the American civil holiday honoring him.

January 17—Antony of Egypt Antony was one of the earliest Egyptian desert fathers. He became the head of a group of monks who lived in a cluster of huts and devoted themselves to communal prayer, worship, and manual labor.

January 17—Pachomius Another of the desert fathers, Pachomius was born in Egypt about 290. He organized hermits into a religious community in which the members prayed together and held their goods in common.

January 18—Confession of Peter; *Week of Prayer for Christian Unity begins* The Week of Prayer for Christian Unity is framed by two commemorations, the Confession of Peter and the Conversion of Paul. On this day the church remembers that Peter was led by God's grace to acknowledge Jesus as "the Christ, the Son of the living God" (Matt. 16:16).

January 19—Henry When Erik, king of Sweden, determined to invade Finland for the purpose of converting the people there to Christianity, Henry went with him. Henry is recognized as the patron saint of Finland.

January 21—Agnes Agnes was a girl of about thirteen living in Rome, who had chosen a life of service to Christ as a virgin, despite the Roman emperor Diocletian's ruling that had outlawed all Christian activity. She gave witness to her faith and was put to death as a result.

January 25—Conversion of Paul; *Week of Prayer for Christian Unity ends* As the Week of Prayer for Christian Unity comes to an end, the church remembers how a man of Tarsus named Saul, a former persecutor of the early Christian church, was led to become one of its chief preachers.

January 26—Timothy, Titus, Silas On the two days following the celebration of the Conversion of Paul, his companions are remembered. Timothy, Titus, and Silas were missionary coworkers with Paul.

January 27—Lydia, Dorcas, Phoebe On this day the church remembers three women who were companions in Paul's ministry.

January 28—Thomas Aquinas Thomas Aquinas was a brilliant and creative theologian who immersed himself in the thought of Aristotle and worked to explain Christian beliefs amid the philosophical culture of the day.

February 2—Presentation of Our Lord Forty days after the birth of Christ, the church marks the day Mary and Joseph presented him in the temple in accordance with Jewish law. Simeon greeted Mary and Joseph, responding with a canticle that begins "Now, Lord, you let your servant go in peace" (see ELW S113).

February 3—Ansgar Ansgar was a monk who led a mission to Denmark and later to Sweden. His work ran into difficulties with the rulers of the day, and he was forced to withdraw into Germany, where he served as a bishop in Hamburg.

February 5—The Martyrs of Japan In the sixteenth century, Jesuit missionaries, followed by Franciscans, introduced the Christian faith in Japan. By 1630, Christianity was driven underground. This day commemorates the first martyrs of Japan, twenty-six missionaries and converts, who were killed by crucifixion.

February 14—Cyril, Methodius These brothers from a noble family in Thessalonika in northeastern Greece were priests who are regarded as the founders of Slavic literature. Their work in preaching and worshiping in the language of the people is honored by Christians in both East and West.

February 18—Martin Luther On this day Luther died at the age of sixty-two. For a time, he was an Augustinian monk, but it is primarily for his work as a biblical scholar, translator of the Bible, reformer of the liturgy, theologian, educator, and father of German vernacular literature that he is remembered.

February 23—Polycarp Polycarp was bishop of Smyrna and a link between the apostolic age and the church at the end of the second century. At the age of eighty-six he was martyred for his faith.

February 25—Elizabeth Fedde Fedde was born in Norway and trained as a deaconess. Among her notable achievements is the establishment of the Deaconess House in Brooklyn and the Deaconess House and Hospital of the Lutheran Free Church in Minneapolis.

March 1—George Herbert Herbert was ordained a priest in 1630 and served the little parish of St. Andrew Bremerton until his death. He is best remembered, however, as a writer of poems and hymns, such as "Come, My Way, My Truth, My Life" and "The King of Love My Shepherd Is."

March 2—John Wesley, Charles Wesley The Wesleys were leaders of a revival in the Church of England. Their spiritual methods of frequent communion, fasting, and advocacy for the poor earned them the name "Methodists."

March 7—Perpetua, Felicity In the year 202 the emperor Septimius Severus forbade conversions to Christianity. Perpetua, a noblewoman; Felicity, a slave; and other companions were all catechumens at Carthage in North Africa, where they were imprisoned and sentenced to death.

March 10—Harriet Tubman, Sojourner Truth Harriet Tubman helped about three hundred slaves to escape via the Underground Railroad until slavery was abolished in the United States. After slavery was abolished in New York in 1827, Sojourner Truth became deeply involved in Christianity, and in later life she was a popular speaker against slavery and for women's rights.

March 12—Gregory the Great Gregory held political office and at another time lived as a monk, all before he was elected to the papacy. He also established a school to train church musicians; thus Gregorian chant is named in his honor.

March 17—Patrick Patrick went to Ireland from Britain to serve as a bishop and missionary. He made his base in the north of Ireland and from there made many missionary journeys, with much success.

March 19—Joseph The Gospel of Luke shows Joseph acting in accordance with both civil and religious law by returning to Bethlehem for the census and by presenting the child Jesus in the temple on the fortieth day after his birth.

March 21—Thomas Cranmer Cranmer's lasting achievement is contributing to and overseeing the creation of the *Book of Common Prayer*, which remains (in revised form) the worship book of the Anglican Communion. He was burned at the stake under Queen Mary for his support of the Protestant Reformation.

March 22—Jonathan Edwards Edwards was a minister in Connecticut and has been described as the greatest of the New England Puritan preachers. Edwards carried out mission work among the Housatonic Indians of Massachusetts and became president of the College of New Jersey, later to be known as Princeton University.

March 24—Oscar Arnulfo Romero Romero is remembered for his advocacy on behalf of the poor in El Salvador, though it was not a characteristic of his early priesthood. After several years of threats to his life, Romero was assassinated while presiding at the eucharist.

March 25—Annunciation of Our Lord Nine months before Christmas, the church celebrates the annunciation. In Luke the angel Gabriel announces to Mary that she will give birth to the Son of God, and she responds, "Here am I, the servant of the Lord" (Luke 1:38).

March 29—Hans Nielsen Hauge Hans Nielsen Hauge was a layperson who began preaching in Norway and Denmark after a mystical experience that he believed called him to share the assurance of salvation with others. At the time, itinerant preaching and religious gatherings held without the supervision of a pastor were illegal, and Hauge was arrested several times.

March 31—John Donne This priest of the Church of England is commemorated for his poetry and spiritual writing. Most of his poetry was written before his ordination and is sacred and secular, intellectual and sensuous.

April 4—Benedict the African Benedict's fame as a confessor brought many visitors to him, and he was eventually named superior of a Franciscan community.

April 6—Albrecht Dürer, Matthias Grünewald, Lucas Cranach These great artists revealed through their work the mystery of salvation and the wonder of creation. Though Dürer remained a Roman Catholic, at his death Martin Luther wrote to a friend, "Affection bids us mourn for one who was the best." Several religious works are included in Grünewald's small surviving corpus, the most famous being the Isenheim Altarpiece. Cranach was widely known for his woodcuts, some of which illustrated the first German printing of the New Testament.

April 9—Dietrich Bonhoeffer In 1933, and with Hitler's rise to power, Bonhoeffer became a leading spokesman for the Confessing Church, a resistance movement against the Nazis. After leading a worship service on April 8, 1945, at Schönberg prison, he was taken away to be hanged the next day.

April 10—Mikael Agricola Agricola began a reform of the Finnish church along Lutheran lines. He translated the New Testament, the prayer book, hymns, and the mass into Finnish and through this work set the rules of orthography that are the basis of modern Finnish spelling.

April 19—Olavus Petri, Laurentius Petri These two brothers are commemorated for their introduction of the Lutheran movement to the Church of Sweden after studying at the University of Wittenberg. Together the brothers published a complete Bible in Swedish and a revised liturgy in 1541.

April 21—Anselm This eleventh-century Benedictine monk stands out as one of the greatest theologians between Augustine and Thomas Aquinas. He is perhaps best known for his "satisfaction" theory of atonement, in which God takes on human nature in Jesus Christ in order to make the perfect payment for sin.

April 23—Toyohiko Kagawa Toyohiko Kagawa's vocation to help the poor led him to live among them. He was arrested for his efforts to reconcile Japan and China after the Japanese attack of 1940.

April 25—Mark Though Mark himself was not an apostle, it is likely that he was a member of one of the early Christian communities. The gospel attributed to him is brief and direct and is considered by many to be the earliest gospel.

April 29—Catherine of Siena Catherine was a member of the Order of Preachers (Dominicans), and among Roman Catholics she was the first woman to receive the title Doctor of the Church. She also advised popes and any uncertain persons who told her their problems.

May 1—Philip, James Philip and James are commemorated together because the remains of these two saints were placed in the Church of the Apostles in Rome on this day in 561.

May 2—Athanasius At the Council of Nicea in 325 and when he himself served as bishop of Alexandria, Athanasius defended the full divinity of Christ against the Arian position held by emperors, magistrates, and theologians.

May 4—Monica Almost everything known about Monica comes from Augustine's *Confessions*, his autobiography. Her dying wish was that her son remember her at the altar of the Lord, wherever he was.

May 8—Julian of Norwich Julian was most likely a Benedictine nun living in an isolated cell attached to the Carrow Priory in Norwich, England. When she was about thirty years old, she reported visions that she later compiled into a book, *Sixteen Revelations of Divine Love*, which is a classic of medieval mysticism.

May 9—Nicolaus Ludwig von Zinzendorf Drawn from an overly intellectual Lutheran faith to Pietism, at the age of twenty-two Count Zinzendorf permitted a group of Moravians to live on his lands. Zinzendorf participated in worldwide missions emanating from this community and is also remembered for writing hymns characteristic of his Pietistic faith.

May 14—Matthias After Christ's ascension, the apostles met in Jerusalem to choose a replacement for Judas. Though little is known about him, Matthias had traveled among the disciples from the time of Jesus' baptism until his ascension.

May 18—Erik Erik, long considered the patron saint of Sweden, ruled there from 1150 to 1160. He is honored for efforts to bring peace to the nearby pagan kingdoms and for his crusades to spread the Christian faith in Scandinavia.

May 21—Helena Helena was the mother of Constantine, a man who later became the Roman emperor. Helena is remembered for traveling through Palestine and building churches on the sites she believed to be where Jesus was born, where he was buried, and from which he ascended.

May 24—Nicolaus Copernicus, Leonhard Euler Copernicus formally studied astronomy, mathematics, Greek, Plato, law, medicine, and canon law and is chiefly remembered for his work as an astronomer and his idea that the sun, not the earth, is the center of the solar system. Euler is regarded as one of the founders of the science of pure mathematics and made important contributions to mechanics, hydrodynamics, astronomy, optics, and acoustics.

May 27—John Calvin Having embraced the views of the Reformation by his mid-twenties, John Calvin was a preacher in Geneva, was banished once, and later returned to reform the city with a rigid, theocratic discipline. Calvin is considered the father of the Reformed churches.

May 29—Jiří Tranovský Jiří Tranovský is considered the "Luther of the Slavs" and the father of Slovak hymnody. He produced a translation of the Augsburg Confession and published his hymn collection *Cithara Sanctorum* (Lyre of the Saints), also known as the Tranoscius, which is the foundation of Slovak Lutheran hymnody.

May 31—Visit of Mary to Elizabeth Sometime after the annunciation, Mary visited her cousin Elizabeth, who greeted Mary with the words "Blessed are you among women" (Luke 1:42), and Mary responded with her famous song, the Magnificat.

June 1—Justin Justin was a teacher of philosophy and engaged in debates about the truth of the Christian faith. Having been arrested and jailed for practicing an unauthorized religion, he refused to renounce his faith, and he and six of his students were beheaded.

June 3—The Martyrs of Uganda King Mwanga of Uganda was angered by Christian members of the court whose first allegiance was not to him but to Christ. On this date in 1886, thirty-two young men were burned to death for refusing to renounce Christianity. Their persecution led to a much stronger Christian presence in the country.

June 3—John XXIII Despite the expectation upon his election that the seventy-seven-year-old John XXIII would be a transitional pope, he had great energy and spirit. He convened the Second Vatican Council in order to "open the windows" of the church. The council brought about great changes in Roman Catholic worship and ecumenical relationships.

June 5—Boniface Boniface led large numbers of Benedictine monks and nuns in establishing churches, schools, and seminaries. Boniface was preparing a group for confirmation on the eve of Pentecost when he and others were killed by a band of pagans.

June 7—Seattle The city of Seattle was named after Noah Seattle against his wishes. After Chief Seattle became a Roman Catholic, he began the practice of morning and evening prayer in the tribe, a practice that continued after his death.

June 9—Columba, Aidan, Bede These three monks from the British Isles were pillars among those who kept alive the light of learning and devotion during the Middle Ages. Columba founded three monasteries, including one on the island of Iona, off the coast of Scotland. Aidan, who helped bring Christianity to the Northumbria area of England, was known for his pastoral style and ability to stir people to charity and good works. Bede was a Bible translator and scripture scholar who wrote a history of the English church and was the first historian to date events "anno Domini" (AD), the "year of our Lord."

June 11—Barnabas Though Barnabas was not among the Twelve mentioned in the gospels, the book of Acts gives him the title of apostle. When Paul came to Jerusalem after his conversion, Barnabas took him in over the fears of the other apostles who doubted Paul's discipleship.

June 14—Basil the Great, Gregory of Nyssa, Gregory of Nazianzus, Macrina The three men in this group are known as the Cappadocian fathers; all three explored the mystery of the Holy Trinity. Basil's Longer Rule and Shorter Rule for monastic life are the basis for Eastern monasticism to this day, and express a preference for communal monastic life over that of hermits. Gregory of Nazianzus defended Orthodox trinitarian and christological doctrines, and his preaching won over the city of Constantinople. Gregory of Nyssa is remembered as a writer on spiritual life and the contemplation of God in worship and sacraments. Macrina was the older sister of Basil and Gregory of Nyssa, and her teaching was influential within the early church.

June 17—Emanuel Nine On June 17, 2015, Clementa C. Pinckney, Cynthia Marie Graham Hurd, Susie Jackson, Ethel Lee Lance, DePayne Middleton-Doctor, Tywanza Sanders, Daniel Lee Simmons, Sharonda Coleman-Singleton, and Myra Thompson were murdered by a self-professed white supremacist while they were gathered for Bible study and prayer at the Emanuel African Methodist Episcopal Church (often referred to as Mother Emanuel) in Charleston, South Carolina. A resolution to commemorate June 17 as a day of repentance for the martyrdom of the Emanuel Nine was adopted by the Churchwide Assembly of the Evangelical Lutheran Church in America on August 8, 2019.

June 21—Onesimos Nesib Nesib, an Ethiopian, was captured by slave traders and taken from his homeland to Eritrea, where he was bought, freed, and educated by Swedish missionaries. He translated the Bible into Oromo and returned to his homeland to preach the gospel there.

June 24—John the Baptist The birth of John the Baptist is celebrated exactly six months before Christmas Eve. For Christians in the Northern Hemisphere, these two dates are deeply symbolic, since John said that he must decrease as Jesus increased. John was born as the days are longest and then steadily decrease, while Jesus was born as the days are shortest and then steadily increase.

June 25—Presentation of the Augsburg Confession On this day in 1530 the German and Latin editions of the Augsburg Confession were presented to Emperor Charles of the Holy Roman Empire. The Augsburg Confession was written by Philipp Melanchthon and endorsed by Martin Luther and consists of a brief summary of points in which the reformers saw their teaching as either agreeing with or differing from that of the Roman Catholic Church of the time.

June 25—Philipp Melanchthon Though he died on April 19, Philipp Melanchthon is commemorated today because of his connection with the Augsburg Confession. Colleague and co-reformer with Martin Luther, Melanchthon was a brilliant scholar, known as "the teacher of Germany."

June 27—Cyril Remembered as an outstanding theologian, Cyril defended the Orthodox teachings about the person of Christ against Nestorius, who was at that time bishop of Constantinople. Eventually it was decided that Cyril's interpretation that Christ's person included both divine and human natures was correct.

June 28—Irenaeus Irenaeus believed that only Matthew, Mark, Luke, and John were trustworthy gospels. As a result of his battles with the Gnostics, he was one of the first to speak of the church as "catholic," meaning that congregations did not exist by themselves but were linked to one another throughout the whole church.

June 29—Peter, Paul One of the things that unites Peter and Paul is the tradition that says they were martyred together on this date in 67 or 68 CE. What unites them even more closely is their common confession of Jesus Christ.

July 1—Catherine Winkworth, John Mason Neale Many of the most beloved hymns in the English language are the work of these gifted poets. Catherine Winkworth devoted herself to the translation of German hymns into English, while John Mason Neale specialized in translating many ancient Latin and Greek hymns.

July 3—Thomas Alongside the doubt for which Thomas is famous, the Gospel according to John shows Thomas moving from doubt to deep faith. Thomas makes one of the strongest confessions of faith in the New Testament, "My Lord and my God!" (John 20:28).

July 6—Jan Hus Jan Hus was a Bohemian priest who spoke against abuses in the church of his day in many of the same ways Luther would a century later. The followers of Hus became known as the Czech Brethren and later became the Moravian Church.

July 11—Benedict of Nursia Benedict is known as the father of Western monasticism. Benedict encouraged a generous spirit of hospitality. Visitors to Benedictine communities are to be welcomed as Christ himself.

July 12—Nathan Söderblom In 1930 this Swedish theologian, ecumenist, and social activist received the Nobel Prize for peace. Söderblom organized the Universal Christian Council on Life and Work, which was one of the organizations that in 1948 came together to form the World Council of Churches.

July 17—Bartolomé de Las Casas Bartolomé de Las Casas was a Spanish priest and a missionary in the Western Hemisphere. Throughout the Caribbean and Central America, he worked to stop the enslavement of native people, to halt the brutal treatment of women by military forces, and to promote laws that humanized the process of colonization.

July 22—Mary Magdalene The gospels report that Mary Magdalene was one of the women of Galilee who followed Jesus. As the first person to whom the risen Lord appeared, she returned to the disciples with the news and has been called "the apostle to the apostles" for her proclamation of the resurrection.

July 23—Birgitta of Sweden Birgitta's devotional commitments led her to give to the poor and needy all that she owned while she began to live a more ascetic life. She founded an order of monks and nuns, the Order of the Holy Savior (Birgittines), whose superior was a woman.

July 25—James James was one of the sons of Zebedee and is counted as one of the twelve disciples. James was the first of the Twelve to suffer martyrdom and is the only apostle whose martyrdom is recorded in scripture.

July 28—Johann Sebastian Bach, Heinrich Schütz, George Frederick Handel These three composers did much to enrich the worship life of the church. Johann Sebastian Bach drew on the Lutheran tradition of hymnody and wrote about two hundred cantatas, including at least two for each Sunday and festival day in the Lutheran calendar of his day. George Frederick Handel was not primarily a church musician, but his great work *Messiah* is a musical proclamation of the scriptures. Heinrich Schütz wrote choral settings of biblical texts and paid special attention to ways his composition would underscore the meaning of the words.

July 29—Mary, Martha, Lazarus of Bethany Mary and Martha are remembered for the hospitality and refreshment they offered Jesus in their home. Following the characterization drawn by Luke, Martha represents the active life, and Mary, the contemplative.

July 29—Olaf Olaf is considered the patron saint of Norway. While at war in the Baltic and in Normandy, he became a Christian; then he returned to Norway and declared himself king, and from then on Christianity was the dominant religion of the realm.

August 8—Dominic Dominic believed that a stumbling block to restoring heretics to the church was the wealth of clergy, so he formed an itinerant religious order, the Order of Preachers (Dominicans), who lived in poverty, studied philosophy and theology, and preached against heresy.

August 10—Lawrence Lawrence was one of seven deacons of the congregation at Rome and, like the deacons appointed in Acts, was responsible for financial matters in the church and for the care of the poor.

August 11—Clare At age eighteen, Clare of Assisi heard Francis preach a sermon. With Francis's help she and a growing number of companions established a women's Franciscan community called the Order of Poor Ladies, or Poor Clares.

August 13—Florence Nightingale, Clara Maass Nightingale led a group of thirty-eight nurses to serve in the Crimean War, where they worked in appalling conditions. She returned to London as a hero and there resumed her work for hospital reform. Clara Maass was born in New Jersey and served as a nurse in the Spanish-American War, where she encountered the horrors of yellow fever. Later responding to a call for subjects in research on yellow fever, Maass contracted the disease and died.

August 14—Maximilian Kolbe, Kaj Munk Confined in Auschwitz, Father Kolbe was a Franciscan priest who gave generously of his meager resources and finally volunteered to be starved to death in place of another man who was a husband and father. Kaj Munk, a Danish Lutheran pastor and playwright, was an outspoken critic of the Nazis. His plays frequently highlighted the eventual victory of the Christian faith despite the church's weak and ineffective witness.

August 15—Mary, Mother of Our Lord The honor paid to Mary as mother of our Lord goes back to biblical times, when Mary herself sang, "From now on all generations will call me blessed" (Luke 1:48). Mary's song speaks of reversals in the reign of God: the mighty are cast down, the lowly are lifted up, the hungry are fed, and the rich are sent away empty-handed.

August 20—Bernard of Clairvaux Bernard was a Cistercian monk who became an abbot of great spiritual depth. Through translation his several devotional writings and hymns are still read and sung today.

August 24—Bartholomew Bartholomew is mentioned as one of Jesus' disciples in Matthew, Mark, and Luke. Except for his name on these lists of the Twelve, little is known about him.

August 28—Augustine As an adult, Augustine came to see Christianity as a religion appropriate for a philosopher. Augustine was baptized by Ambrose at the Easter Vigil in 387, was made bishop of Hippo in 396, and was one of the greatest theologians of the Western church.

August 28—Moses the Black A man of great strength and rough character, Moses the Black was converted to Christian faith toward the close of the fourth century. The change in his heart and life had a profound impact on his native Ethiopia.

September 2—Nikolai Frederik Severin Grundtvig Grundtvig was a prominent Danish theologian of the nineteenth century. From his university days, he was convinced that poetry spoke to the human spirit better than prose, and he wrote more than a thousand hymns.

September 9—Peter Claver Peter Claver was born into Spanish nobility and was persuaded to become a Jesuit missionary. He served in Cartagena (in what is now Colombia) by teaching and caring for the slaves.

September 13—John Chrysostom John was a priest in Antioch and an outstanding preacher. His eloquence earned him the nickname Chrysostom ("golden mouth"), but he also preached against corruption among the royal court, whereupon the empress sent him into exile.

September 14—Holy Cross Day The celebration of Holy Cross Day commemorates the dedication of the Church of the Resurrection in 335 CE on the location believed to be where Christ was buried.

September 16—Cyprian During Cyprian's time as bishop, many people had denied the faith under duress. In contrast to some who held the belief that the church should not receive these people back, Cyprian believed they ought to be welcomed into full communion after a period of penance.

September 17—Hildegard, Abbess of Bingen Hildegard lived virtually her entire life in convents yet was widely influential. She advised and reproved kings and popes, wrote poems and hymns, and produced treatises in medicine, theology, and natural history.

September 18—Dag Hammarskjöld Dag Hammarskjöld was a Swedish diplomat and humanitarian who served as secretary general of the United Nations. The depth of Hammarskjöld's Christian faith was unknown until his private journal, *Markings*, was published following his death.

September 21—Matthew Matthew was a tax collector, an occupation that was distrusted, because tax collectors were frequently dishonest and worked as agents for the occupying Roman government; yet it was these outcasts to whom Jesus showed his love. Since the second century, tradition has attributed the first gospel to him.

September 29—Michael and All Angels The scriptures speak of angels who worship God in heaven, and in both testaments angels are God's messengers on earth. Michael is an angel whose name appears in Daniel as the heavenly being who leads the faithful dead to God's throne on the day of resurrection, while in the book of Revelation, Michael fights in a cosmic battle against Satan.

September 30—Jerome Jerome translated the scriptures into the Latin that was spoken and written by the majority of people in his day. His translation is known as the Vulgate, which comes from the Latin word for "common."

October 4—Francis of Assisi Francis renounced wealth and future inheritance and devoted himself to serving the poor. Since Francis had a spirit of gratitude for all of God's creation, this commemoration has been a traditional time to bless pets and animals, creatures Francis called his brothers and sisters.

October 4—Theodor Fliedner Fliedner's work was instrumental in the revival of the ministry of deaconesses among Lutherans. Fliedner's deaconess motherhouse in Kaiserswerth, Germany, inspired Lutherans all over the world to commission deaconesses to serve in parishes, schools, prisons, and hospitals.

October 6—William Tyndale Tyndale's plan to translate the scriptures into English met opposition from Henry VIII. Though Tyndale completed work on the New Testament in 1525 and worked on a portion of the Old Testament, he was tried for heresy and burned at the stake.

October 7—Henry Melchior Muhlenberg Muhlenberg was prominent in setting the course for Lutheranism in the United States by helping Lutheran churches make the transition from the state churches of Europe to independent churches of America. Among other things, he established the first Lutheran synod in America and developed an American Lutheran liturgy.

October 15—Teresa of Avila Teresa of Avila (also known as Teresa de Jesús) chose the life of a Carmelite nun after reading the letters of Jerome. Teresa's writings on devotional life are widely read by members of various denominations.

October 17—Ignatius Ignatius was the second bishop of Antioch in Syria. When his own martyrdom approached, he wrote in one of his letters, "I prefer death in Christ Jesus to power over the farthest limits of the earth.... Do not stand in the way of my birth to real life."

October 18—Luke Luke, as author of both Luke and Acts, was careful to place the events of Jesus' life in both their social and religious contexts. Some of the most loved parables and canticles are found only in this gospel.

October 23—James of Jerusalem James is described in the New Testament as the brother of Jesus, and the secular historian Josephus called him "the brother of Jesus, the so-called Christ." Little is known about James, but Josephus reported that the Pharisees respected him for his piety and observance of the law.

October 26—Philipp Nicolai, Johann Heermann, Paul Gerhardt These three outstanding hymnwriters all worked in Germany in the seventeenth century during times of war and plague. Philipp Nicolai's hymns "Wake, Awake, for Night Is Flying" and "O Morning Star, How Fair and Bright!" were included in a series of meditations he wrote to comfort his parishioners during the plague. The style of Johann Heermann's hymns (including "Ah, Holy Jesus") moved away from the more objective style of Reformation hymnody toward expressing the emotions of faith. Paul Gerhardt, whom some have called the greatest of Lutheran hymnwriters, lost a preaching position at St. Nicholas's Church in Berlin because he refused to sign a document stating he would not make theological arguments in his sermons.

October 28—Simon, Jude Little is known about Simon and Jude. In New Testament lists of the apostles, Simon the Zealot is mentioned, but he is never mentioned apart from these lists. Jude, sometimes called Thaddaeus, is also mentioned in lists of the Twelve.

October 31—Reformation Day By the end of the seventeenth century, many Lutheran churches celebrated a festival commemorating Martin Luther's posting of the 95 Theses, a summary of abuses in the church of his time. At the heart of the reform movement was the gospel, the good news that it is by grace through faith that we are justified and set free.

November 1—All Saints Day The custom of commemorating all of the saints of the church on a single day goes back at least to the third century. All Saints Day celebrates the baptized people of God, living and dead, who make up the body of Christ.

November 3—Martín de Porres Martín was a lay brother in the Order of Preachers (Dominicans) and engaged in many charitable works. He is recognized as an advocate for Christian charity and interracial justice.

November 7—John Christian Frederick Heyer, Bartholomaeus Ziegenbalg, Ludwig Nommensen Heyer was the first missionary sent out by American Lutherans, and he became a missionary in the Andhra region of India. Ziegenbalg was a missionary to the Tamils of Tranquebar on the southeast coast of India. Nommensen worked among the Batak people, who had previously not seen Christian missionaries.

November 11—Martin of Tours In 371 Martin was elected bishop of Tours. As bishop he developed a reputation for intervening on behalf of prisoners and heretics who had been sentenced to death.

November 11—Søren Aabye Kierkegaard Kierkegaard, a nineteenth-century Danish theologian whose writings reflect his Lutheran heritage, was the founder of modern existentialism. Kierkegaard's work attacked the established church of his day—its complacency, its tendency to intellectualize faith, and its desire to be accepted by polite society.

November 17—Elizabeth of Hungary This Hungarian princess gave away large sums of money, including her dowry, for relief of the poor and sick. She founded hospitals, cared for 392 orphans, and used the royal food supplies to feed the hungry.

November 23—Clement Clement is best remembered for a letter he wrote to the Corinthian congregation still having difficulty with divisions in spite of Paul's canonical letters. Clement's letter is also a witness to early understandings of church government and the way each office in the church works for the good of the whole.

November 23—Miguel Agustín Pro Miguel Agustín Pro grew up amid oppression in Mexico and worked on behalf of the poor and homeless. Miguel and his two brothers were arrested, falsely accused of throwing a bomb at the car of a government official, and executed by a firing squad.

November 24—Justus Falckner, Jehu Jones, William Passavant Not only was Falckner the first Lutheran pastor to be ordained in North America, but he published a catechism that was the first Lutheran book published on the continent. Jones was the Lutheran Church's first African American pastor and carried out missionary work in Philadelphia, which led to the formation there of the first African American Lutheran congregation (St. Paul's). William Passavant helped to establish hospitals and orphanages in a number of cities and was the first to introduce deaconesses to the work of hospitals in the United States.

November 25—Isaac Watts Watts wrote about six hundred hymns, many of them in a two-year period beginning when he was twenty years old. When criticized for writing hymns not taken from scripture, he responded that if we can pray prayers that are not from scripture but written by us, then surely we can sing hymns that we have made up ourselves.

November 30—Andrew Andrew was the first of the Twelve. As a part of his calling, he brought other people, including Simon Peter, to meet Jesus.

December 3—Francis Xavier Francis Xavier became a missionary to India, Southeast Asia, Japan, and the Philippines. Together with Ignatius Loyola and five others, Francis formed the Society of Jesus (Jesuits).

December 4—John of Damascus John left a career in finance and government to become a monk in an abbey near Jerusalem. He wrote many hymns as well as theological works, including *The Fount of Wisdom,* a work that touches on philosophy, heresy, and the orthodox faith.

December 6—Nicholas Nicholas was a bishop in what is now Turkey. Legends that surround Nicholas tell of his love for God and neighbor, especially the poor.

December 7—Ambrose Ambrose was baptized, ordained, and consecrated a bishop all on the same day. While bishop, he gave away his wealth and lived in simplicity.

December 13—Lucy Lucy was a young Christian of Sicily who was martyred during the persecutions under Emperor Diocletian. Her celebration became particularly important in Sweden and Norway, perhaps because the feast of Lucia (whose name means "light") originally fell on the shortest day of the year.

December 14—John of the Cross John was a monk of the Carmelite religious order who met Teresa of Avila when she was working to reform the Carmelite Order and return it to a stricter observance of its rules. His writings, like Teresa's, reflect a deep interest in mystical thought and meditation.

December 20—Katharina von Bora Luther Katharina took vows as a nun, but around age twenty-four she and several other nuns who were influenced by the writings of Martin Luther left the convent. When she later became Luther's wife, she proved herself a gifted household manager and became a trusted partner.

December 26—Stephen Stephen, a deacon and the first martyr of the church, was one of those seven upon whom the apostles laid hands after they had been chosen to serve widows and others in need. Later, Stephen's preaching angered the temple authorities, and they ordered him to be put to death by stoning.

December 27—John John, a son of Zebedee, was a fisherman and one of the Twelve. Tradition has attributed authorship of the gospel and the three epistles bearing his name to the apostle John.

December 28—The Holy Innocents The infant martyrs commemorated on this day were the children of Bethlehem, two years old and younger, who were killed by Herod, who worried that his reign was threatened by the birth of a new king named Jesus.

Anniversary of Baptism (abbreviated)

This order is intended for use in the home. It may be adapted for use in another context, such as a Christian education setting. When used in the home, a parent or sponsor may be the leader. A more expanded version of this order appears in *Evangelical Lutheran Worship Pastoral Care* (pp. 128–135).

A bowl of water may be placed in the midst of those who are present.

Gathering

A baptismal hymn or acclamation (see Evangelical Lutheran Worship #209–217, 442–459) may be sung.

The sign of the cross may be made by all in remembrance of their baptism as the leader begins.

In the name of the Father, and of the + Son, and of the Holy Spirit.
Amen.

The candle received at baptism or another candle may be used. As it is lighted, the leader may say:

Jesus said, I am the light of the world.
Whoever follows me will have the light of life.

Reading

One or more scripture readings follow. Those present may share in reading.

A reading from Mark: People were bringing little children to Jesus in order that he might touch them; and the disciples spoke sternly to them. But when Jesus saw this, he was indignant and said, "Let the little children come to me; do not stop them; for it is to such as these that the kingdom of God belongs.". . . And he took them up in his arms, laid his hands on them, and blessed them. *(Mark 10:13-14, 16)*

A reading from Second Corinthians: If anyone is in Christ, there is a new creation: everything old has passed away; see, everything has become new! *(2 Corinthians 5:17)*

A reading from First John: Beloved, let us love one another, because love is from God; everyone who loves is born of God and knows God. *(1 John 4:7)*

Those present may share experiences related to baptism and their lives as baptized children of God. A portion of the Small Catechism (Evangelical Lutheran Worship, pp. 1160–1167) may be read as part of this conversation.

A baptismal hymn or acclamation may be sung.

Baptismal Remembrance

A parent or sponsor may trace a cross on the forehead of the person celebrating a baptismal anniversary. Water from a bowl placed in the midst of those present may be used. These or similar words may be said.

Name, when you were baptized, you were marked with the cross of Christ forever.
Remember your baptism with thanksgiving and joy.

Prayers

Prayers may include the following or other appropriate prayers. Others who are present may place a hand on the head or shoulder of the one who is celebrating the anniversary.

Let us pray.
Gracious God, we thank you for the new life you give us through holy baptism. Especially, we ask you to bless *name* on the anniversary of *her/his* baptism. Continue to strengthen *name* with the Holy Spirit, and increase in *her/him* your gifts of grace: the spirit of wisdom and understanding, the spirit of counsel and might, the spirit of knowledge and the fear of the Lord, the spirit of joy in your presence; through Jesus Christ, our Savior and Lord.
Amen.

Other prayers may be added. Those present may offer petitions and thanksgivings.

The prayers may conclude with the Lord's Prayer.

Our Father in heaven,
> **hallowed be your name, your kingdom come,**
> **your will be done, on earth as in heaven.**

Give us today our daily bread.
Forgive us our sins
> **as we forgive those who sin against us.**

Save us from the time of trial and deliver us from evil.
For the kingdom, the power, and the glory are yours,
> **now and forever. Amen.**

Blessing

The order may conclude with this or another suitable blessing.

Almighty God, who gives us a new birth by water and the Holy Spirit and forgives us all our sins, strengthen us in all goodness and by the power of the Holy Spirit keep us in eternal life through Jesus Christ our Lord.
Amen.

The greeting of peace may be shared by all.

Other suggested readings for this service:
John 3:1-8: *Born again from above*
Romans 6:3-11: *Raised with Christ in baptism*
Galatians 3:26-28: *All are one in Christ*
Ephesians 4:1-6: *There is one body and one Spirit*
Colossians 1:11-13: *Claimed by Christ, heirs of light*
1 Peter 2:2-3: *Long for spiritual food*
1 Peter 2:9: *Chosen in baptism to tell about God*
Revelation 22:1-2: *The river of the water of life*

Prayers for Various Situations

A prayer to begin the work day

May the graciousness of the Lord our God be upon us;
prosper the work of our hands. (Ps. 90:17, *ELW*)
Generous God, you call us to lives of service.
In my words and actions this day, move me to serve in Christ's name.
When I lack energy, inspire me. When I lack courage, strengthen me.
When I lack compassion, be merciful to me.
You may make the sign of the cross.

In all things, O God, you are our way, our truth, and our life. Reveal through me your life-giving work, that I love my neighbors as myself. I ask this in Jesus' name. Amen.

A prayer to begin the school day

Show me your ways, O Lord, and teach me your paths. (Ps. 25:4, *ELW*)
Christ be with me: in you I am never alone.
Christ within me: your Spirit is at work in me.
Christ behind me: reassure me when I struggle.
Christ before me: lead me when I am uncertain.
Christ beneath me: support me when I am weak.
Christ above me: encourage me to do my best.
Christ in quiet: I listen for the sound of your voice.
Christ in danger: I will not fear, for you are with me.
You may make the sign of the cross.

In all things, O God, you are our way, our truth, and our life.
Teach me to love you and my neighbors as myself.
I ask this in Jesus' name. Amen.
(Based on the Prayer of St. Patrick)

Blessing for pets and animals

Use this prayer on St. Francis Day, October 4, or whenever it is appropriate.

Gracious God,
in your love you created us in your image
and made us stewards of the animals
that live in the skies, the earth, and the sea.
Bless us in our care for our *pet/s* (*animal/s*) (names may be added here).
Help us recognize your power and wisdom
in the variety of creatures that live in our world,
and hear our prayer for all that suffer overwork, hunger, and ill-treatment.
Protect your creatures and guard them from all evil, now and forever. Amen.

Time of conflict, crisis, disaster

O God, where hearts are fearful and constricted, grant courage and hope. Where anxiety is infectious and widening, grant peace and reassurance. Where impossibilities close every door and window, grant imagination and resistance. Where distrust twists our thinking, grant healing and illumination. Where spirits are daunted and weakened, grant soaring wings and strengthened dreams. All these things we ask in the name of Jesus Christ, our Savior and Lord. Amen.

Health of body and soul

By your power, great God, our Lord Jesus healed the sick and gave new hope to the hopeless. Though we cannot command or possess your power, we pray for those who want to be healed. Mend their wounds, soothe fevered brows, and make broken people whole again. Help us to welcome every healing as a sign that, though death is against us, you are for us, and have promised renewed and risen life in Jesus Christ the Lord. Amen.

Those in affliction

Lord Christ, you came into the world as one of us, and suffered as we do. As we go through the trials of life, help us to realize that you are with us at all times and in all things; that we have no secrets from you; and that your loving grace enfolds us for eternity. In the security of your embrace we pray. Amen.

Those in trouble or bereavement

Almighty God, your love never fails, and you can turn the shadow of death into daybreak. Help us to receive your word with believing hearts, so that, confident in your promises, we may have hope and be lifted out of sorrow into the joy and peace of your presence; through Jesus Christ our Savior and Lord. Amen.

Those suffering from addiction

O blessed Jesus, you ministered to all who came to you. Look with compassion upon all who through addiction have lost their health and freedom. Restore to them the assurance of your unfailing mercy; remove the fears that attack them; strengthen those who are engaged in the work of recovery; and to those who care for them, give honesty, understanding, and persevering love; for your mercy's sake. Amen.

The chronically ill and those who support them

Loving God, your heart overflows with compassion for your whole creation. Pour out your Spirit on all people living with illness for which there is no cure, as well as their families and loved ones. Help them to know that you claim them as your own and deliver them from fear and pain; for the sake of Jesus Christ, our healer and Lord. Amen.

Caregivers and others who support the sick

God, our refuge and strength, our present help in time of trouble, care for those who tend the needs of *name*. Strengthen them in body and spirit. Refresh them when weary; console them when anxious; comfort them in grief; and hearten them in discouragement. Be with us all, and give us peace at all times and in every way; through Christ our peace. Amen.

Recovery from sickness

Almighty and merciful God, you are the only source of health and healing; you alone can bring calmness and peace. Grant to us, your children, an awareness of your presence and a strong confidence in you. In our pain, our weariness, and our anxiety, surround us with your care, protect us by your loving might, and permit us once more to enjoy health and strength and peace; through Jesus Christ, our Savior and Lord. Amen.

A prayer attributed to Francis of Assisi

Lord, make us instruments of your peace. Where there is hatred, let us sow love; where there is injury, pardon; where there is discord, union; where there is doubt, faith; where there is despair, hope; where there is darkness, light; where there is sadness, joy. Grant that we may not so much seek to be consoled as to console; to be understood as to understand; to be loved as to love. For it is in giving that we receive; it is in pardoning that we are pardoned; and it is in dying that we are born to eternal life. Amen.

A prayer of Catherine of Siena

Power of the eternal Father, help me. Wisdom of the Son, enlighten the eye of my understanding. Tender mercy of the Holy Spirit, unite my heart to yourself. Eternal God, restore health to the sick and life to the dead. Give us a voice, your own voice, to cry out to you for mercy for the world. You, light, give us light. You, wisdom, give us wisdom. You, supreme strength, strengthen us. Amen.

A prayer of Julian of Norwich

In you, Father all-mighty, we have our preservation and our bliss. In you, Christ, we have our restoring and our saving. You are our mother, brother, and savior. In you, our Lord the Holy Spirit, is marvelous and plenteous grace. You are our clothing; for love you wrap us and embrace us. You are our maker, our lover, our keeper. Teach us to believe that by your grace all shall be well, and all shall be well, and all manner of things shall be well. Amen.

A prayer of Martin Luther

Behold, Lord, an empty vessel that needs to be filled. My Lord, fill it. I am weak in the faith; strengthen me. I am cold in love; warm me and make me fervent, that my love may go out to my neighbor. I do not have a strong and firm faith; at times I doubt and am unable to trust you altogether. O Lord, help me. Strengthen my faith and trust in you. In you I have sealed the treasure of all I have. I am poor; you are rich and came to be merciful to the poor. I am a sinner; you are upright. With me, there is an abundance of sin; in you is the fullness of righteousness. Therefore I will remain with you, of whom I can receive, but to whom I may not give. Amen.

Prayers on pages 420–423 from *Evangelical Lutheran Worship* and *Sundays and Seasons 2022*.

Morning Blessing

You may make the sign of the cross.

I am a beloved child of God, marked with the cross of Christ forever.

Your mercies are new every morning. *(Based on Lam. 3:23)*

Thank you, gracious God, for the gift of this new day.
Awaken me to your abiding presence;
open my eyes to your creation;
open my ears to your promises;
open my heart to the needs of others.
Fill me with your Spirit and guide me this day
in works of kindness, justice, and mercy.
I ask this in the name of Jesus, the light and life of the world.
Amen.

A Simplified Form for Morning Prayer

Opening

O Lord, open my lips,
and my mouth shall proclaim your praise.
Glory to the Father, and to the Son,
and to the Holy Spirit:
as it was in the beginning, is now,
and will be forever. Amen.

The alleluia is omitted during Lent.

[Alleluia.]

Psalmody

The psalmody may begin with Psalm 63, Psalm 67, Psalm 95, Psalm 100, or another psalm appropriate for morning. Psalms provided in this book for each day may be used instead of or in addition to the psalms mentioned.

A time of silence follows.

A hymn may follow (see the suggested hymn for each day).

Readings

One or more readings for each day may be selected from those provided in this book. The reading of scripture may be followed by silence for reflection.

The reflection may conclude with these or similar words.

Long ago God spoke to our ancestors
in many and various ways by the prophets,
but in these last days God has spoken to us by the Son.

Gospel Canticle

The song of Zechariah may be sung or said.

Blessed are you, Lord, the God of Israel,
you have come to your people and set them free.
You have raised up for us a mighty Savior,
born of the house of your servant David.
Through your holy prophets, you promised of old
to save us from our enemies,
from the hands of all who hate us,
to show mercy to our forebears,
and to remember your holy covenant.
This was the oath you swore to our father Abraham:
to set us free from the hands of our enemies,
free to worship you without fear,
holy and righteous before you, all the days of our life.
And you, child, shall be called the prophet of the Most High,
for you will go before the Lord to prepare the way,
to give God's people knowledge of salvation
by the forgiveness of their sins.
In the tender compassion of our God
the dawn from on high shall break upon us,
to shine on those who dwell in darkness and the shadow of death,
and to guide our feet into the way of peace.

Prayers

Various intercessions may be spoken at this time. The prayer provided in this book for each day may also be used.

The following prayer is especially appropriate for morning.

Almighty and everlasting God,
you have brought us in safety to this new day.
Preserve us with your mighty power,
that we may not fall into sin

nor be overcome in adversity.
In all we do, direct us to the fulfilling of your purpose;
through Jesus Christ our Lord.
Amen.

The Lord's Prayer

Our Father in heaven,
   hallowed be your name,
   your kingdom come,
   your will be done, on earth as in heaven.
Give us today our daily bread.
Forgive us our sins
   as we forgive those who sin against us.
Save us from the time of trial
   and deliver us from evil.
For the kingdom, the power, and the glory are yours,
   now and forever. Amen.

Blessing

Let us bless the Lord.
Thanks be to God.

Almighty God,
the Father, + the Son, and the Holy Spirit,
bless and preserve us.
Amen.

Additional materials for daily prayer are available in Evangelical Lutheran Worship
(pp. 295–331) and may supplement this simple order.

A Simplified Form for Evening Prayer

Opening
Jesus Christ is the light of the world,
the light no darkness can overcome.
Stay with us, Lord, for it is evening,
and the day is almost over.
Let your light scatter the darkness
and illumine your church.

Psalmody
The psalmody may begin with Psalm 141, Psalm 121, or another psalm appropriate for evening. Psalms provided in this book for each day may be used instead of or in addition to the psalms mentioned.

A time of silence follows.

A hymn may follow (see the suggested hymn for each day).

Readings
One or more readings for each day may be selected from those provided in this book. The reading of scripture may be followed by silence for reflection.

The reflection may conclude with these or similar words.

Jesus said, I am the light of the world.
Whoever follows me will never walk in darkness.

Gospel Canticle

The song of Mary may be sung or said.

My soul proclaims the greatness of the Lord,
my spirit rejoices in God my Savior,
for you, Lord, have looked with favor on your lowly servant.
From this day all generations will call me blessed:
you, the Almighty, have done great things for me,
and holy is your name.
You have mercy on those who fear you,
from generation to generation.
You have shown strength with your arm
and scattered the proud in their conceit,
casting down the mighty from their thrones
and lifting up the lowly.
You have filled the hungry with good things
and sent the rich away empty.
You have come to the aid of your servant Israel,
to remember the promise of mercy,
the promise made to our forebears,
to Abraham and his children forever.

Prayers

Various intercessions may be spoken at this time. The prayer provided in this book for each day may also be used.

The following prayer is especially appropriate for evening.

We give thanks to you, heavenly Father,
through Jesus Christ your dear Son,
that you have graciously protected us today.
We ask you to forgive us all our sins, where we have done wrong,
and graciously to protect us tonight.
For into your hands we commend ourselves:
our bodies, our souls, and all that is ours.

Let your holy angels be with us,
so that the wicked foe may have no power over us.
Amen.

The Lord's Prayer

Our Father in heaven,
 hallowed be your name,
 your kingdom come,
 your will be done, on earth as in heaven.
Give us today our daily bread.
Forgive us our sins
 as we forgive those who sin against us.
Save us from the time of trial
 and deliver us from evil.
For the kingdom, the power, and the glory are yours,
 now and forever. Amen.

Blessing

Let us bless the Lord.
Thanks be to God.

The peace of God,
which surpasses all understanding,
keep our hearts and our minds in Christ Jesus.
Amen.

Additional materials for daily prayer are available in Evangelical Lutheran Worship
(pp. 295–331) and may supplement this simple order.

Evening Blessing

You may make the sign of the cross.

I am a beloved child of God, marked with the cross of Christ forever.
Come to me, all you that are weary . . . and I will give you rest.
(Matt. 11:28)

Thank you, gracious God, for the gift of this coming night.
Restore me with your right spirit. Calm my mind. Quiet my heart.
Enfold me with your bountiful mercy.
Protect me from all harm,
that I sleep assured of the peace found in you alone.
I ask this in the name of Jesus, who gives us rest. Amen.

Night Prayers with Children

Dear Jesus, as a hen covers her chicks with her wings to keep them safe,
protect us this night under your golden wings; for your mercy's sake.
Amen.

We bless you, God, for the day just spent,
for laughter, tears, and all you've sent.
Grant us, Good Shepherd, through this night,
a peaceful sleep till morning light.

A parent or caregiver may trace the cross on the child's forehead or heart and say one of
these blessings:

God the Father, Son, and Holy Spirit watch over you.
May God protect you through the night.
May the Lord Jesus keep you in his love.

Suggestions for Daily Reflection

God's word for me this day is:

God's word will shape my day by:

I will share God's word with others through:

My prayers today will include:

- The church universal, its ministry, and the mission of the gospel

- The well-being of creation

- Peace and justice in the world, the nations and those in authority, the community

- The poor, oppressed, sick, bereaved, lonely

- All who suffer in body, mind, or spirit

- Special concerns